CW00376046

The P

CENTE

COOKI

1904–2004

The PWMU
CENTENARY
~ COOKBOOK ~

1904 – 2004

Revised by Mairi Harman and
Susan Stenning

Lothian
BOOKS

Thomas C. Lothian
132 Albert Road, South Melbourne, Victoria 3205
www.lothian.com.au

National Library of Australia
Cataloguing-in-Publication data:

The PWMU centenary cookbook, 1904–2004

ISBN 0 7344 0647 9

1. Cookery. I. Harman, Mairi, 1937– . II. Stenning, Susan.
III. Presbyterian Women's Missionary Union.
614.5

Cover design by Ranya Langenfelds
Text design by John van Loon
Index by Russell Brooks
Printed in Singapore by Craft Print International Ltd

CONTENTS

FOREWORD

The letters PWMU stand for the Presbyterian Women's Missionary Union of Victoria, which first produced its *Cookery Book* in 1904. During the past century it has gone through three major revisions and over 30 reprints, and its popularity has continued to the present day. To celebrate its centenary a combined PWMU (Presbyterian Women's Missionary Union) and UCAF (Uniting Church Adult Fellowship) commitee has prepared this special enlarged edition. The members of the present commitee are Peter Barr (Convenor), Christine Closter, Mairi Harman, Dawn Kelly, Sylvia Schultz, Margaret McKinnon and Margaret Watson. All profits from sales are now divided equally between the PWMU and the UCAF for the continued support of out-reach projects, details of which are given at the end of the book.

Many of the alterations made in this fourth revision reflect changes in Australian cuisine stemming from the multicul-tural population represented in our churches. New additions have come from congregational members and we thank all who participated in the revision process. We are very sorry we were only able to use a selection of the recipes received.

To maintain a link with the original edition of 1904, some of its recipes have been inserted throughout this book. These can be recognised by the box format in which they appear.

Mairi Harman

STARTING OUT

∽ HINTS ∾

EQUIPMENT

Before you begin cooking, make sure that your kitchen contains the best equipment possible.

1. A reliable cooktop and oven.
2. A refrigerator/freezer.
3. An accurate set of scales.
4. A set of Australian standard measuring spoons, ranging from $1/4$ teaspoon (1.25 ml) to 1 tablespoon (20 ml). These can be used for measuring liquids and dry ingredients.
5. A graduated measuring jug — for larger amounts of liquid.
6. A set of Australian standard measuring cups for measuring dry ingredients, ranging in size from $1/4$ cup to 1 cup.
7. A set of heavy-based saucepans and a frying pan.
8. A variety of cake tins, slice tins and biscuit trays.
9. A food processor, if possible.
10. Sharp knives, a wooden spoon and a variety of kitchen utensils.
11. Storage space for utensils close to the food preparation area. A well-ventilated pantry and airtight storage containers.
12. A spray can of vegetable oil for greasing trays and pans.
13. Cooling rack for cakes and muffins.
14. Oven mitts and potholders for handling saucepans and hot items.

Efficient cooking

1. Before you start, collect all ingredients and utensils.
2. Read through the recipe carefully.
3. Prepare any baking tins.
4. Preheat the oven to the required temperature.
5. Keep your work area tidy and clean up as you go.
6. Measure ingredients accurately. Spoon and cup measures should be level, not heaped, unless indicated.
7. Prepare any ingredients before beginning to mix; e.g. sift flour, beat eggs.

Buying food

When purchasing food and groceries consider the following hints:

1. Plan a weekly budget for purchasing food and groceries and stay within it.
2. Fruit and vegetables are tastiest and cheapest if purchased when in season.
3. Buy fruit and vegetables that are unblemished. Spoilage will begin where blemishes occur.
4. Shop personally where possible or, if using the Internet to purchase fruit and vegetables or groceries, make sure that the quality is good.
5. The protein content of cheaper cuts of meat is the same as the more expensive varieties, but watch for the amount of fat.

Storing fresh food

Vegetables Store salad vegetables and greens in plastic bags or an appropriate container low in the refrigerator. Potatoes need to be stored in a dry, dark cupboard to avoid greening. Ensure adequate ventilation. Onions need to be stored in a dry, well-ventilated cupboard.

Fruit Store berries and stone fruit in the refrigerator and use promptly. Do not wash berries before storing. Berries can be frozen by packing into plastic bags, sealing and freezing. Stone fruit can be cut into pieces, sprinkled with sugar and packed into a container before freezing. Apples, pears and citrus fruit can be stored in a well-ventilated place or refrigerated to store for longer periods. Bananas should be purchased slightly green and stored in a well-ventilated space; storing them in the refrigerator will blacken skins.

Meat, fish and eggs Meat that is not to be used immediately should be sealed in plastic, labelled with the date and name of the cut and frozen. Meat that is to be refrigerated should be removed from its sealed plastic meat tray, placed on a plate and covered lightly with a piece of paper towel then stored in the refrigerator away from any cooked food.

Fish should be cooked and served as soon as possible. Any fish that does not smell fresh and pleasant should be discarded. Freeze any fish that is not to be used straightaway but check that the fish has not previously been frozen and thawed at the supermarket. Do not refreeze any fish that has been defrosted.

Eggs should be stored low in the refrigerator. Store in their carton with the pointed end of the egg down.

Milk and cheese Store milk in its original container in the refrigerator below 4°C. UHT milk can be stored in the pantry until the carton is opened. Milk cannot be frozen.

Cheese should be stored in the refrigerator at 4°C. Store the cheese in its original wrapper and check the use-by date. Fresh cheeses such as cottage and ricotta should be used within a week of purchase. Mozzarella, cheddar and other yellow cheeses keep for several weeks, and hard cheeses such as Parmesan keep for longer.

TIME-SAVING HINTS

1. When buying meat, or chicken in bulk quantities for the freezer, package in meal-sized quantities with freezer paper between cuts to prevent sticking. Label and date.
2. When cooking casseroles, make a large quantity and freeze extra with sufficient serves to make a meal in each package.

3. Adding undiluted canned soups to browned meat and vegetables saves time when making stews and casseroles.
4. Quick sauces can be made from undiluted, canned soups. A little cream or evaporated milk may be added to enrich the flavour.
5. Packet soups and sauces save time and stretch meals when extra serves are needed.
6. Garlic bread may be made ahead of time and frozen in foil. Heat to serve.
7. Large quantities of parsley can be chopped in the food processor with a little water and frozen in ice-cube trays. Cubes can be stored in plastic bags and used directly in soups and stews.
8. Stale bread and crusts can be processed in the food processor to make crumbs and stored in plastic bags in the freezer.
9. A spoonful of vegetable oil added to boiling water when cooking pasta or rice will prevent boiling over.
10. Keep grated cheese in the freezer for toppings, savouries, and sandwiches.
11. When boiling chicken or meat, strain stock and store in covered containers in the freezer. (Margarine and ice-cream containers are perfect for this purpose.)
12. Buy minced meat in a large quantity and make into hamburgers. Place burgers on polythene trays with freezer paper between layers and freeze. Label and date.
13. Meatballs for casseroles can be made the same way as burgers. Use quantity required and return rest to freezer immediately.
14. Hard-boiled eggs stored in the refrigerator will keep for several days and are useful for salads, sandwiches, etc. Use a felt-tipped pen to label the cooked egg with the date.
15. Nuts chopped in the processor and frozen in tightly sealed containers are useful for sweets, garnishes, etc.
16. Packaged cake mixes are useful for cakes and desserts when time is limited.
17. Quick meals can be made from pita breads or uncooked mini pizzas.

✺ Terms Used in ✺ Cooking

Bake blind Line a pie plate with pastry, cover with baking paper weighed down with baking weights, rice or dried beans and partly cook.

Blanch Plunge food into boiling water for a short time then cool quickly by plunging into cold water.

Blend To mix a dry ingredient and a liquid to a smooth paste.

Boiling point To bring water to 100°C. The surface of the liquid should bubble rapidly.

Braise To cook meat on a bed of diced vegetables in a small amount of liquid.

Chop To cut food into small, irregularly shaped pieces.

Cream Beat together sugar and butter or margarine until the mixture resembles whipped cream.

Croûton A small piece of dry or fried bread used as a garnish for soups, salads or stews.

Dice To cut into even-sized cubes.

Dredge To dust food thickly with a dry ingredient.

Garnish To decorate food prior to serving.

Glaze A liquid brushed over a baked food to improve the appearance.

Julienne To cut vegetables into matchstick-sized strips.

Marinate To soak meat in a mixture of aromatic and acid liquids (a marinade); to develop flavour and tenderness.

Mask To cover food with a sauce.

Parboil To partly cook food in boiling liquid.

Poach To cook gently in liquid just below boiling point — cooler than simmering.

Purée To process or sieve cooked food, reducing it to a fine mash.

Ramekin An individual-sized heatproof bowl.

Sauté To cook food quickly in a small amount of butter or oil.

Shortening Butter, margarine or oil used in baking.

Sift   To shake flour and dry ingredients through a sifter or sieve to remove lumps and to aerate.

Simmer   To cook food in liquid at a temperature just below boiling point.

Stew   To cook food in liquid at a simmer for a period of time.

Toss   To lightly lift and mix ingredients.

Whip   To beat rapidly in order to incorporate air and increase volume.

ᨣ GUIDELINES ᨣ
FOR HEALTHY EATING

1. Eat a variety of foods.
2. Eat less fat.
3. Eat less sugar.
4. Eat less salt.
5. Drink less alcohol.
6. Eat more foods rich in fibre — wholegrain cereals, vegetables and fruit.

Choose foods from each of the following five food groups every day:

1. Cereals and bread, preferably wholemeal: at least five serves a day.
2. Vegetables and fruit: at least seven serves a day.
3. Meat, fish, poultry or nuts, lentils or eggs: 1–2 serves daily.
4. Milk, cheese or yoghurt: 300 ml milk for an adult, 600 ml for a child.
5. Fats: 30 g of butter, margarine or oil.

ᨣ SUBSTITUTIONS ᨣ
FOR COMMON INGREDIENTS

It is sometimes possible to substitute popular ingredients to reduce dietary fat intake or to suit the ingredients that are in the pantry.

1. Margarine can be substituted for butter but do not cook with 'light' margarine as it has a lower fat content and more water.
2. Natural yoghurt can be substituted for cream in savoury dishes but should be added at the last moment, when cooking is complete. Warm gently without boiling.
3. Evaporated milk can be substituted for cream. When chilled for several hours, evaporated milk can be whipped.
4. Evaporated milk with a few drops of coconut essence can be a low-fat substitute for coconut milk.
5. 1 cup milk with 1 teaspoon lemon juice added can be substituted for 1 cup buttermilk.
6. Sweetener containing sucralose can be used instead of sugar in baked foods.
7. One cup plain flour sifted with 2 teaspoons baking powder can be used instead of 1 cup self-raising flour.

∾ Hints on Quantities ∾

- A chicken weighing about 1 kg yields approximately 500 g of meat including skin. A cup of chopped cooked chicken weighs 120 g.
- 500 g of steak or veal yields four portions.
- A turkey weighing 9 kg yields approximately 3 kg meat. For each person, allow 90 g cooked meat.
- Ham: 6 kg of thinly sliced ham serves 50.
- Crayfish: 1 kg crayfish will serve 4 as a salad; 2 kg crayfish will serve 10 cooked as a curry or similar.
- A 200 g can of fish with 1 cup of thick white sauce should fill 3–3$^{1}/_{2}$ dozen pastry cases.
- A large loaf of bread (650 g) yields 20 slices.
- 250–375 g butter will spread a large loaf of bread.
- One litre of milk is sufficient for 40 cups of tea.
- Ice-cream: 1 litre serves 8–10.
- Fruit salad: $^{1}/_{2}$ cup is sufficient for 1 serve.
- Cheese (with biscuits): 1–1$^{1}/_{2}$ kg will serve 50.
- Potatoes: 500 g mashed yields 7 small serves; there are about 6 new potatoes per 500 g.

- Rice: 1 cup uncooked rice yields 3 cups cooked; 500 g uncooked rice will serve 16.
- Soup: $3/4$ cup per serve; 9–10 litres serves 50.
- Tomatoes (sliced and quartered): 500 g serves 8.

∼ Metric Conversion ∼

It is recommended that users of this book purchase sets of standard metric measuring cups and spoons for measuring dry ingredients. Standard metric measure jugs — with 1 cup (250 ml) graduations — are available for measuring liquids. Remember all measures are level.

The tables below are approximate and serve as a guide to metric measurement.

Conversion of weighed ingredients from imperial to metric

Imperial measure	Metric measure
1 oz	30 g
4 oz ($1/4$ lb)	125 g
8 oz ($1/2$ lb)	250 g
12 oz ($3/4$ lb)	375 g
16 oz (1 lb)	500 g (0.5 kg)
24 oz ($1^1/2$ lb)	750 g
32 oz (2 lb)	1000 g (1 kg)

Conversion of liquid and dry ingredient cup measures to metric equivalent

Imperial liquid measure	Cup measure	Metric liquid measure
2 fluid ounces	1/4 cup	
2 1/2 fluid ounces	1/3 cup	
4 fluid ounces	1/2 cup	125 ml
6 fluid ounces	3/4 cup	
8 fluid ounces	1 cup	250 ml
10 fluid ounces	1 1/4 cup	
16 fluid ounces	2 cups	500 ml
20 fluid ounces	2 1/2 cups	
	4 cups	1 litre

∿ Measuring ∿ Ingredients

The following table gives the approximate mass in grams of the standard metric cup or tablespoon measures.

Butter, margarine, copha	1 cup = 250 g
Desiccated coconut	1 cup = 90 g
Dried breadcrumbs	1 cup = 100 g
Dried fruit	1 cup = 160 g
Fresh breadcrumbs	1 cup = 60 g
Flours — plain, self-raising, wholemeal, corn, rice, arrowroot	1 cup = 150 g
Grated cheese	1 cup = 125 g
Jam, honey, treacle	1 tablespoon = 30 g
Nuts	1 cup = 125 g
Rice	1 cup = 200 g
Rolled oats	1 cup = 90 g
Sugar — white, caster	1 cup = 250 g
— icing	1 cup = 150 g
— soft brown	1 cup = 150 g

∾ Description of ∾ Oven Temperatures

Description	Thermostat setting (°C)
Plate warming	60
Keep warm	80
Cool	100
Very slow	120
Slow	150
Moderately slow	160
Moderate	180
Moderately hot	190
Hot	200
Very hot	220

If you have a fan-forced oven, set it at a temperature 10°C lower than the temperatures recommended in the recipes or check your owner's manual.

∾ Abbreviations Used ∾ in Cooking

g	=	gram
kg	=	kilogram
ml	=	millilitre
L	=	litre

∽ Herbs ∾

Herbs are plants that are commonly used for cooking and medicinal purposes. Herbs complement and bring out the flavour of food, especially in low-kilojoule and salt-reduced meals. The more commonly used herbs are easily grown in the garden or in pots and ensure a supply of fresh herbs for the kitchen. Fresh herbs are widely available in greengrocers and supermarkets. Some are grown hydroponically and come complete with roots. These can be stood in a container with a little water and will keep quite well. Herbs may be preserved by chopping and freezing in ice cubes or they can be dried by hanging up in bunches or on racks. Dried herbs are stored in jars.

The most commonly used herbs are:
Basil Excellent for flavouring tomato dishes but also good with egg dishes, pasta and meat dishes. Gives an Italian flavour.
Bay leaf Used for stocks, soups, fish, lamb and beef dishes. Also good for placing in lids of storage jars to keep weevils out.
Chervil Delicately flavoured, resembles parsley and is used for soups, salads, egg and fish dishes.
Chives Have a mild onion flavour and can be used as a garnish for soups, savouries, salads and sandwiches.
Coriander Resembles parsley but has a pungent flavour. The fresh and dried leaves, the seed and the ground root are used widely in Asian cooking, curries and salads.
Dill Seeds are used to flavour pickles, especially cucumber for bread and butter pickles. Fresh dill leaves are also used in fish dishes and salads such as potato and coleslaw.
Fennel Used mainly in seasonings and with fish. Used widely in Mediterranean cooking.
Garlic Has a strong odour and flavour. It is used in meat dishes, chutneys, sauces, salads and dips. If a cut clove of garlic is rubbed round a salad bowl, enough flavour is imparted, especially in a lettuce salad.

Lemongrass   Used in Asian cooking to give an aromatic lemon flavour. The leaves are also used for making a tea.

Marjoram   Used in mixed herbs with thyme and sage for flavouring seasonings and savoury dishes.

Mint   Leaves and sprigs from the spearmint family are used in mint sauce for roast lamb and also to flavour new potatoes, green peas, fruit drinks, pea and lentil soups, and salads.

Oregano   Used in Italian cookery, omelettes, pilafs and meat dishes.

Parsley   Leaves are used to flavour and garnish most savoury dishes, eggs, soups, and sauces. It is easily grown in the garden and is much better if fresh.

Rosemary   A small evergreen bush easily grown in the garden. It can be used fresh or dried with lamb, fish and poultry and Mediterranean-style dishes. Use as sprigs or chopped.

Sage   Used with onion to flavour seasoning for roast pork and duck.

Savoury   Similar to mint and used for meat, chicken and egg dishes and to flavour sauces and salads.

Tarragon   Used to flavour vinegar and some seafood recipes.

Thyme   Used in bouquet garni, savoury dishes and seasonings.

Vietnamese mint   A narrow-leaved pungent herb used in Asian cookery.

HERB BLENDS

Bouquet garni   A bunch of herbs tied together or tied securely in a small muslin bag. It consists of 3 sprigs of parsley, 2 sprigs of thyme, 1 sprig of marjoram and 1 bay leaf. It is used to flavour stocks, stews, soups and casseroles.

Fines herbes   This is a mixture of equal quantities of chopped parsley, chives, tarragon, and chervil. It is used for sauces, soups, egg dishes, cheese dishes, and salads. May be used to flavour or garnish food.

∽ SPICES ∾

Spices are used to give flavour and variety to both sweet and savoury recipes. They should only be bought in small quantities as they deteriorate rapidly. Many can be purchased whole. Some commonly used spices are:

Allspice The pimento berry, ground and used for meat dishes.

Caraway Used to flavour breads, cakes, biscuits, cheeses and gravies.

Cayenne A very hot red pepper made from dried ground chillies. It is used in savoury dishes, sauces, casseroles, and cheese recipes.

Chillies The fiery tasting fruit of the chilli plant, ranging in heat from the mild green chilli to the extremely hot jalapeno chilli. Use the finely chopped flesh and seeds in Mexican, Asian and Indian cooking. The seeds and the inner membranes are the hottest part of the chilli so discard for a slightly milder flavour. Take care when preparing, as chilli is very irritating to the eye.

Curry powder Used extensively in Asian countries and can vary according to the ingredients in the curry blend. Used to flavour meat, vegetable, chicken, egg and fish dishes.

Five spice powder A blend of cinnamon, cloves, star anise, fennel seeds and Sichuan pepper. Use in stir-fries and Chinese cooking.

Galangal A member of the ginger family; a rhizome with a strong ginger flavour.

Garam masala A blend of spices used in Indian cooking. It often includes cardamom, cinnamon, cloves, coriander, cumin and nutmeg.

Ginger May be bought fresh in the green form and used for casseroles, stir-fries and other meat dishes. It may be crystallised or preserved in syrup, or ground as a spice. It is used for pickles, sauces, cakes, biscuits, puddings and meat dishes.

Horseradish Used mainly to make a sauce to serve with roast beef. May be purchased as a sauce or dried.

Kaffir lime leaves The aromatic leaves of a small citrus tree. Used in Asian cookery.

Mace Similar in flavour to nutmeg. It is used for cakes, sauces and savoury dishes.

Mixed spice A mixture of ground sweet spices. It is used for cakes, buns and savoury dishes.

Mustard Used as a condiment with meats, especially corned meats. Also used for cheese and savoury recipes, pickles, sauces, relishes and chutneys. It is available as seeds, ground as a powder and ready-made as a paste.

Nutmeg May be purchased whole or ground. It is used to flavour cakes, biscuits, milk and other puddings.

Palm sugar Sold as a disc or cylinder and must be pared or grated. It is a sugar with a mild caramel flavour and is used in Asian cooking.

Paprika Looks similar to cayenne but is not as pungent in flavour. Used in savouries.

Pepper White pepper is used as a table condiment. Black pepper is stronger and used in pickles, sauces and chutneys. Lemon pepper can be purchased and gives a good flavour to chicken, fish, seafood, and salads. Peppercorns are the whole berries and are used for soups, stews and pickles.

Pimento A berry used for stocks, meat dishes and pickles.

Poppy seeds Small, nutritious black seeds used to sprinkle on bread, bread rolls and biscuits before baking.

Saffron The bright orange-gold stamen of a crocus variety. Used in tiny quantities to flavour rice, soups and jellies.

Sambal oelek A salty paste made of minced chillies and vinegar. It is used in Indonesian recipes.

Sesame seeds Used mainly to sprinkle on breads, buns, biscuits and confectionery.

Star anise A star-shaped pod containing aniseed-flavoured seeds. Used in Asian recipes.

Turmeric A fragrant yellow spice used to colour pickles, rice dishes and dressings for salads.

Wasabi A fiery green paste made from an Asian horse-radish, usually served with Japanese food.

Spice blend

Ras el hanout   A classical blend used in Moroccan cooking containing about 23 spices including paprika, cumin, cardamom, allspice and saffron. It can be used with fish, chicken and to flavour couscous.

Some Simple Recipes

↜ Eggs ↝

Bacon and Egg

1 bacon rasher   1 egg

Utensils

frying pan   *egg lifter*

Remove rind from bacon. Place in a cold frying pan without any oil and fry very slowly until the bacon fat is clear. Remove the bacon from the pan. If there is insufficient bacon fat in the pan, add a little butter or vegetable oil then gently break the egg into the frying pan. Cook the egg over gentle heat until set. If desired, turn the egg over and cook a little longer to set the yolk. Remove from the pan, drain well and serve on hot toast with the bacon.

Note Thick slices of tomato fried in the pan for 2–3 minutes on each side add to the meal!

Soft-Boiled Eggs

Utensils

saucepan   *soup spoon*

There are two methods of soft-boiling eggs:

1. Bring water to the boil in a saucepan, gently lower eggs into the boiling water with a soup spoon and cook for 3 minutes.
2. Place eggs in cold water, bring to the boil and boil for 1 minute.

Serve with fingers of buttered toast.

HARD-BOILED EGGS

UTENSILS

saucepan   soup spoon

Bring water to the boil in a saucepan, gently lower eggs into the boiling water with a soup spoon and cook for 8–10 minutes.

POACHED EGG ON TOAST

1 slice hot buttered toast   1 egg
6 drops vinegar

UTENSILS

frying pan   egg lifter

Make buttered toast and keep hot. Half fill a small frying pan with water and bring to boil. Add vinegar. Break the egg carefully into a saucer, stir water around quickly and, while it is still moving, slip the egg gently into the middle of it. Turn heat down and cook for 3–5 minutes until egg white sets. Lift egg out carefully with an egg lifter, place on toast and serve at once.

Microwave instructions Break egg into a saucer or a microwave-safe ramekin and pierce yolk. Place in the microwave and cook on HIGH for 45 seconds. Serve on buttered toast.

SCRAMBLED EGG ON TOAST

1 slice hot buttered toast   shake of pepper
1 teaspoon butter   2 tablespoons milk
1 egg   1/4 teaspoon chopped parsley
pinch of salt

UTENSILS

saucepan   wooden spoon
measuring spoons   fork

Make toast and keep it warm. Melt butter in a saucepan, lightly beat egg with a fork and add milk, salt and pepper, then put mixture into saucepan. Gently cook over low heat, stirring often until it becomes slightly thickened. Remove from heat and continue stirring until the egg finishes cooking — about a minute after taking off the heat. Add parsley, pile on to the toast and serve.

৩ Other Simple Recipes ৩

Basic Pasta

150 g spaghetti or noodles	pinch of salt
1 L water	1 teaspoon olive or vegetable oil

Utensils

large saucepan	colander or strainer

Place water and salt in a large saucepan and bring to the boil. Add pasta and oil and stir until the water returns to the boil. Reduce heat and simmer for 10–15 minutes. Strain using a colander and use as required: top with a commercial pasta sauce, or simply serve with a little butter and grated cheese.

Cheese on Toast

1 slice bread	cheddar cheese, sliced
butter or margarine	

Preheat grill and lightly toast bread on both sides. Remove toast from the grill and spread with a little butter or margarine. Place slices of cheddar cheese on top of the toasted bread and return to grill. Cook until the cheese melts and is bubbly and golden.

Variation A slice of ham or slices of tomato can be placed on the toast before adding cheese.

Pizza Muffins

1 English muffin
1 tablespoon tomato paste
2 slices salami
2 slices green capsicum

2 pineapple rings
2 spring onions, chopped
$^1/_2$ cup (60 g) grated cheese

Preheat grill on high. Split muffin and toast until brown on both sides. Spread thinly with tomato paste and top with salami. Heat under the grill until salami is warm. Remove from the grill and top with green capsicum. Heat under the grill again. Repeat with the pineapple and spring onion. Top with grated cheese and grill until golden.

Porridge

$^1/_2$ cup (50 g) rolled oats
$^1/_4$ teaspoon salt

1$^1/_2$ cups (375 ml) water

Utensils

small saucepan
measuring cup

wooden spoon

Place rolled oats, salt and water in a saucepan. Heat until boiling, stirring continuously. Lower heat and cook gently for 10–15 minutes, stirring frequently. Serve with milk and sugar or golden syrup.

Note Cooking time may be reduced by:
• Soaking oatmeal overnight;
• Using 1-minute oats in place of rolled oats.

Steamed Vegetables

Choose from any of these vegetables that are suitable for steaming: potatoes, pumpkin, carrot, zucchini, cabbage, green beans, peas, turnip, sweet potato, cauliflower and broccoli.

Wash and scrub vegetables. Peel any vegetable with a thick skin such as sweet potato, pumpkin and turnip. Cut the vegetable into serving-size pieces. Place the vegetable in a saucepan and add 1–2 cm of water. Cover saucepan with a close-fitting lid and bring to the boil. Cook until the vegetable is just tender but still slightly crisp; however, cook potatoes, sweet potatoes, turnip and pumpkin until completely tender. To serve, drain water from vegetables, toss with a little butter or pepper and lemon juice and serve.

Microwave instructions Arrange prepared vegetables in a microwave-proof casserole with the larger pieces at the outer edge of the bowl and smaller pieces towards the centre. Add about 2 tablespoons water. Cover with a lid. Microwave on HIGH for about 5–8 minutes.

STEWED DRIED APRICOTS

250 g dried apricots   *¹/₂ cup (125 g) sugar*
water   *ice-cream or yoghurt*

UTENSILS
medium saucepan   *bowl*
measuring cups

Wash apricots, drain and place in a bowl. Cover with water and stand for 2–3 hours. Remove apricots from water and set aside, add more water to make up to 2 cups and put in a saucepan with the sugar. Bring to the boil and cook for 3 minutes. Add apricots and simmer gently for 5 minutes. Serve hot or cold with ice-cream or yoghurt.

STEWED FRUIT

500 g apples, peaches, pears, plums, apricots or rhubarb
2 tablespoons sugar   *¹/₂ cup (125 ml) water*

UTENSILS
medium saucepan   *measuring spoons*
sharp knife   *measuring cups*
vegetable peeler

Peel the fruit and cut into suitable pieces. Put sugar and water in a saucepan and bring to the boil. Add fruit, reduce heat and cook gently until tender. The sweetness of the stewed fruit can be adjusted if necessary by adding a little more sugar.

Variations

If stewing apples, 2 cloves added to the pan will enhance the flavour, or a little lemon rind may be used instead.
Cloves or cinnamon stick improve the flavour of pears.
A pinch of ground ginger added to rhubarb will improve the flavour.

Notes Stewed rhubarb requires extra sugar.
Rhubarb does not require peeling but stems should be washed, trimmed and cut into 3 cm lengths.

Microwave instructions Reduce the quantity of water to 1 tablespoon. Cut fruit into even-sized pieces. Place water, sugar and fruit in a microwave-safe dish and cover. Microwave on HIGH for 5–6 minutes or until tender.

DIPS AND FINGER FOODS

✌ DIPS ✌

CUCUMBER AND YOGHURT DIP

2 Lebanese cucumbers
1 teaspoon salt
1 teaspoon lemon juice

1 x 200 g carton natural yoghurt
1 clove garlic, crushed
ground black pepper to taste

Peel and finely chop the cucumber and place in a medium bowl, sprinkle with salt and stir to combine. Stand for a few minutes, then drain off any excess liquid and discard. Add lemon juice, yoghurt, garlic and pepper to the cucumber and blend well. Serve with pita bread and raw vegetable sticks.

CURRIED EGG DIP

3 eggs, hard-boiled
1 teaspoon curry powder

1 cup (250 ml) Mayonnaise
(see p. 51)

Finely chop eggs. Combine all ingredients and chill.

GUACAMOLE

flesh of 2 ripe avocados
1 clove garlic
3 spring onions

$^1/_2$ small red chilli
1 ripe tomato
1 tablespoon lemon juice

Halve the avocadoes and scrape the flesh into a bowl. Mash with a fork until smooth. Crush garlic, finely chop spring onions and deseed and chop chilli. Dice tomato. Add the garlic, spring onions, chilli, tomato and lemon juice to the avocado and mix well. Chill. Serve with corn chips.

HUMMUS — CHICKPEA DIP

2 cloves garlic
1 x 440 g can chickpeas, drained
juice of 1 lemon
black pepper

1/4–1/3 cup (60–80 ml) tahini paste
pinch of paprika

Put garlic and chickpeas in the food processor and process, then add lemon juice, pepper and tahini, processing well. Garnish with paprika on top and serve with Lebanese bread.

Hint For a slightly thinner consistency, add a little of the chickpea liquid.

RAW VEGETABLE DIP

1 cup (250 ml) thick Mayonnaise (see p. 51)
3/4 teaspoon curry powder

1 tablespoon lemon juice
2 tablespoons (40 g) chutney
1 tablespoon finely chopped onion

Combine all ingredients and refrigerate. Serve with vegetables — carrot sticks, green capsicum, cauliflower, celery and cherry tomatoes.

SALSA DI RUCCOLA

250 g fresh rocket (ruccola)
2 tablespoons (50 g) pine nuts

1 cup (250 g) Parmesan cheese
1/2 cup (125 ml) olive oil

Wash rocket, dry well, tear each leaf into 3 or 4 pieces and put into food processor. Add pine nuts and process until it forms a paste. Add cheese and drizzle in oil. Serve with tomatoes and use over pasta, gnocchi, jacket potatoes, and cooked beans such as borlotti or lima beans, or as a dip.

Note   Salsa is a chunky, uncooked sauce-cum-dip made from chopped ingredients such as tomatoes, vinegar, chillies, apples, beans, oil, garlic and fresh herbs, such as coriander and basil.

SUN-DRIED TOMATO AND BASIL DIP

1 clove garlic, crushed
2 spring onions, chopped
1/4 cup fresh basil
1/2 cup (90 g) semi-sun-dried
*   tomatoes*

1 tablespoon tomato paste
200 g cream cheese
1/2 cup (125 ml) light sour cream

Place garlic, spring onion, basil and tomatoes in a food processor and process until finely chopped. Add the remaining ingredients and mix well. Serve with pita triangles (see below) or vegetable sticks.

PITA TRIANGLES

1 packet small wholemeal
*   pita breads*

50 g butter
lemon pepper to taste

Split each of the pita breads completely in half. Melt butter and brush over one side of the pita bread circles, sprinkle with lemon pepper and cut each circle into triangles. Heat the oven to moderate (180°C). Place the pita bread triangles on an oven tray and bake for 10 minutes or until golden brown and crisp. Remove from the oven and cool. Store in an airtight container.

ᦠ FINGER FOODS ᦡ

ANGELS ON HORSEBACK

oysters
lemon juice
salt

black pepper
1/2 bacon rasher per oyster
toothpicks

Sprinkle oysters with lemon juice, salt and pepper. Wrap each oyster in bacon and secure with toothpick. Place under hot griller, in frying pan or in hot oven, cook quickly until bacon is lightly brown. Serve immediately.

ASPARAGUS ROLLS

8 slices fresh bread
butter or margarine
8 canned asparagus tips

toothpicks
parsley for garnish

Remove crusts of bread and spread with a little butter or margarine. Place an asparagus tip diagonally on each slice. Roll up cornerwise and secure each with a toothpick. Garnish with parsley sprigs, cover with foil and refrigerate before serving.

CHEESE AND BACON PUFFS

3 bacon rashers
2 medium onions
1/2 cup (125 ml) milk
1 egg, lightly beaten

2 cups (240 g) coarsely grated
  cheddar cheese
1 cup (150 g) self-raising flour
1 teaspoon French mustard

Dice bacon and finely chop onions. Combine milk and egg in a large bowl. Add remaining ingredients and mix well. Drop rounded teaspoons of mixture on to greased oven trays. Bake in a hot oven (200°C) for about 20 minutes or until golden brown. Serve hot.

CHEESE AND SPINACH TRIANGLES
Makes approximately 40 triangles

2 spring onions
1/2 cup (125 g) fetta cheese
250 g frozen spinach, thawed
1/2 cup (125 g) ricotta cheese

pinch of nutmeg
1/2 cup polyunsaturated
  vegetable oil
1 x 250 g packet of fillo pastry

Finely chop the spring onions and crumble the fetta cheese. In a bowl mix well together the spinach, ricotta, fetta, spring onion and nutmeg. Brush 3 sheets of fillo lightly with oil and stack them on top of each other. Cut into 6 strips across the widest side of the pastry. Use one strip for each triangle. Place a teaspoonful of the spinach and cheese mixture in the right-hand corner of the strip and fold the corner over to form a triangle. Continue folding to the end of the strip, keeping the triangle shape with each fold. Place on a lightly greased oven tray with the seam side down. Brush the tops lightly with oil. Repeat for the remaining pastry sheets and filling. Bake in a hot oven (200°C) for 15–20 minutes or until golden brown.

DEVILS ON HORSEBACK

prunes   squares of bread   strips of bacon

Remove stones from prunes and roll each prune in a small strip of bacon. Place on squares of bread and bake for 20 minutes in moderate oven (180°C).

DOLMADES

1 bunch flat-leaf parsley
1 tomato, finely chopped
1 onion, finely chopped
salt to taste
1/4 cup chopped mint
150 g long-grain rice, cooked

1/2 cup (125 ml) lemon juice
1/2 cup (125 ml) oil
pinch of allspice
40 vine leaves, blanched
extra 4 ripe tomatoes

Wash the parsley, trim off stalks and chop. In a bowl mix all ingredients except the vine leaves and ripe tomatoes. Allow to soak for an hour, drain, reserving liquid. Unroll the vine leaves, wash them under running water, then place a small amount of rice mixture in each leaf, fold in corners with care and roll up. Each roll should be finger width.

Slice the ripe tomatoes into 6 mm rounds and place in a medium-sized saucepan with a few extra leaves. Place the rolls on top of tomatoes, packing the rolls close together. Pour reserved liquid on top. Put a plate over the rolls to prevent them from unrolling. Simmer over a low heat for 30 minutes. Turn off heat and leave in pan to cool. Cover rolls with plastic wrap and store in refrigerator.

Note Silverbeet or cabbage leaves may be used instead of vine leaves, but may have to be cut into 2 or 4 pieces, depending on size.

HAM AND CHEESE TRIANGLES

1 cup (250 g) creamed cottage cheese
2 hard-boiled eggs, finely chopped

6 slices ham
parsley for garnish

Mix cheese and eggs together. Spread over ham slices and sandwich together. Chill then cut each sandwich into triangles. Garnish with parsley.

NORI ROLLS

600 ml water
425 g koshihikari rice, washed
  and drained
5 tablespoons (100 ml) rice
  vinegar
2 tablespoons (40 g) caster sugar
2 teaspoons sea salt
5 cm knob of fresh ginger,
  peeled and grated

2 cloves garlic, crushed
1/4 red capsicum
1 Lebanese cucumber
100 g smoked salmon
4 spring onions
4 nori sheets
50 ml soy sauce
wasabi paste, to taste

Boil water in a saucepan, add the koshihikari rice and simmer, covered, for 12 minutes. Drain and allow to stand for 5 minutes. Mix vinegar, sugar, salt, ginger and garlic and stir into the rice. Slice red capsicum lengthways into 0.5 cm wide strips. Cut the cucumber lengthways into fine strips. Slice the smoked salmon into strips 2 cm wide. Trim the spring onions and halve lengthways. Place 1 sheet of nori on a sheet of plastic wrap. Put a thin layer of rice on the nori square, leaving a 2 cm margin at the right-hand side. On the left-hand side of the nori and rice, arrange strips of smoked salmon down the side. Top with a strip of red pepper, spring onion and cucumber. Roll the nori from the left to the right, pulling away the plastic as you go. Wrap the finished roll in plastic wrap and secure with a twist at each end. Refrigerate for 2 hours. Make dipping sauce: mix soy sauce with 1/2 teaspoon of wasabi paste. To serve, remove rolls from the plastic wrap and cut into 2 cm long slices, arrange on a platter with the dipping sauce in a small bowl.

Notes
Wasabi paste is extremely hot and should be used with caution. A smear of wasabi can be spread down the left-hand side of the nori and rice under the smoked salmon before rolling if desired.

Koshihikari rice is a short-grained Japanese rice which will cling, allowing rolling and slicing of the nori rolls.

SALMON MUFFINS

1 x 180 g can salmon
1/3 cup (80 ml) sour cream
1/4 cup (40 g) finely chopped celery
1/4 cup (40 g) chopped spring onion
1 tablespoon chopped dill
pepper to taste
11/2 cups (225 g) flour
1/4 cup (30 g) grated cheddar cheese
1 tablespoon sugar
2 teaspoons baking powder
1/2 teaspoon salt
1 egg
3/4 cup (90 ml) milk
1/3 cup (80 ml) vegetable oil

Drain salmon, discard bones, and place flesh in a bowl. Stir in sour cream, celery, onion, dill and pepper. In a large bowl combine flour, cheese, sugar, baking powder and salt. Whisk egg, milk and oil together and pour over dry ingredients. Pour salmon mixture over top and stir until just mixed. Spoon into greased muffin pans. Bake in preheated oven at 180°C for 20–25 minutes.

Note This recipe makes 10 large muffins. For bite-sized savouries bake in mini muffin trays instead.

SATAY STICKS

250 g sliced beef
1 tablespoon honey
1 teaspoon soy sauce
salt and pepper
1/4 teaspoon ground cumin

1/4 teaspoon ground coriander
1 teaspoon lemon juice
1/4 teaspoon oil
12 skewers

Combine honey, soy, salt, pepper, cumin, coriander, lemon juice and oil and marinate meat in this mixture for at least 30 minutes. Place on skewers. Grill for 4–5 minutes, turning once. Serve with satay sauce.

SATAY SAUCE

1 tablespoon smooth peanut
* butter*
1 clove garlic
1 tablespoon lemon or lime
* juice*

1 teaspoon sesame or vegetable
* oil*
1 tablespoon soy sauce
1 spring onion, chopped
2 teaspoons brown sugar

Put all the sauce ingredients into a blender and blend. If sauce is too thick, add a small amount of water and blend again. Pour into a small bowl.

SCOTCH EGGS

4 eggs, hard-boiled
flour

1 cup (250 g) sausage meat
dry breadcrumbs or cornflake
* crumbs*

Shell eggs, roll in flour and cover with sausage meat. Roll in crumbs. Cook in preheated hot oven (200°C) for 30 minutes, or deep fry until golden brown. Serve whole or sliced in half, either hot or cold.

TUNA SLICE

125 g cornflakes
125 g grated cheese
1 onion, finely chopped
1 x 425 g can tuna

salt and pepper
3 eggs, lightly beaten
1 cup (250 ml) milk

In a bowl combine the cornflakes, cheese, onion and drained, flaked tuna. Add seasoning to taste, and stir in eggs and milk. Place in a greased 28 x 18 cm lamington tin and bake in a preheated moderate oven (180°C) for 45 minutes until mixture is set. Serve hot or cold in slices.

Hint Savoury biscuits may be substituted for cornflakes.

WONTONS

2 dried Chinese mushrooms
90 g lean minced pork
60 g prawn meat, minced
2 water chestnuts, finely chopped
4 spring onions, finely chopped

1 tablespoon soy sauce
16 wonton wrappers
1 egg, lightly beaten
vegetable oil for frying

Soak Chinese mushrooms in warm water for 20 minutes, remove and squeeze dry. Remove the stalks from the mushrooms and finely chop the caps. Combine mushrooms, pork, prawn, water chestnuts, spring onions and soy sauce and stand for 30 minutes. Place 1 teaspoon of the filling slightly off the centre of each wonton wrapper. Fold the wrapper in half diagonally and press the edges together to seal them. Bring the corners at the base of the triangle to the centre and overlap them. Seal the overlap with a little beaten egg. Heat oil in a fry pan or deep fryer and fry gently until golden brown and crisp. Drain on absorbent paper and serve with plum sauce.

ZUCCHINI SLICE

2 cups (250 g) grated zucchini
1 large onion, finely chopped
1/2 cup (125 ml) oil
1 cup (120 g) grated cheese

5 eggs, lightly beaten
salt and pepper
2 tablespoons chopped parsley
1 cup (150 g) self-raising flour

Mix all ingredients except flour together, then stir in the flour. Pour into a lightly greased flan tin and bake for about 30 minutes in a preheated oven at 180°C. May be served hot or cold.

STOCKS AND SOUPS

✄ STOCKS ✄

BASIC STOCK

2 kg meat bones
12 cups (3 L) cold water
1 medium carrot
1 medium turnip

1 medium onion
12 peppercorns
2 teaspoons salt

Wash bones (cooked or uncooked) and put in large pot with water and salt. Wash and cut all vegetables roughly, leaving skin on carrot and onion but peeling turnip. Add vegetables and seasonings to pot. Simmer for at least 2 hours. Strain stock and if fatty, allow to cool and skim off fat.

Note Other spices and herbs (such as parsley, bay leaf or a pinch of nutmeg) may be added if desired.

Variations
For *White Stock* use veal or rabbit bones instead of beef or lamb.
For *Chicken Stock* use chicken carcasses.
For *Vegetable Stock* use a variety of vegetables (doubling the amount of vegetables) and omit the bones.

Hint Ready-made stock, stock cubes, stock powder and stock powder concentrates are all available in supermarkets with directions on how to use.

FISH STOCK

500 g fish bones
4¹/₂ cups (1.25 L) water

1 medium onion
2 stalks celery

few stalks parsley
6 peppercorns
pinch of nutmeg

salt and pepper
$1/2$ lemon

Wash bones, put in a large pot then add water and bring slowly to the boil. Add all the other ingredients. Simmer for 20 minutes, and then pour through a fine strainer.

✄ SOUPS ∾

Soups may be prepared when vegetables are plentiful, then frozen for use during the year. If freezing a soup in which milk, cream or coconut milk are ingredients, these should be added after thawing if the soup is to be served cold and before reheating if it is to be served hot.

BOUILLABAISSE
Serves 4

4 tomatoes
1 red capsicum
2 tablespoons (40 ml) oil
$1/4$ cup (40 g) finely chopped
  onion
2 tablespoons chopped parsley
2 tablespoons (40 ml) tomato
  paste

$1^1/2$ kg fish (scallops, prawns
  and any fleshy fish)
2 bay leaves
$1/2$ teaspoon grated orange rind
2 teaspoons salt
$2^1/2$ cups (625 ml) water
1 stick French bread
pepper

Remove skin from tomatoes and chop roughly, and chop capsicum. Heat oil, add onion, tomatoes, capsicum, parsley (keep some for garnish) and tomato paste. Cook, stirring, until onion is transparent. Add fish, cut into 4 cm pieces, crushed bay leaves, orange rind, salt and pepper. DO NOT STIR once fish is added. Cover with water and cook rapidly for 15 minutes. To serve, cut slices of French stick and toast them. Place slices of toast in bowl and pour soup on top. Sprinkle with reserved chopped parsley.

CHILLED CHERRY SOUP
Serves 4

1 x 425 g can black cherries
2 cups (500 ml) water
1 stick cinnamon
4 cloves

3–4 chicken stock cubes
1 lemon
2 tablespoons cornflour

GARNISH
fresh whipped or sour cream and mint sprigs

Remove pips from cherries, reserving liquid from can. Place cherries and their liquid in pan with water, spices and stock cubes. Squeeze lemon, add juice and a slice of lemon peel. Bring to the boil and simmer for a few minutes. Blend cornflour with a little cold water and add to the soup. Cook for 2 minutes. Remove cinnamon stick, cloves and lemon peel. Chill thoroughly. To serve, top with a spoonful of cream and a sprig of mint. If desired serve also with fingers of dry toast.

CHICKEN BROTH
Serves 4

1¹/2 cups (190 g) diced carrot
1¹/2 cups (225 g) chopped onion
1 tablespoon chopped shallots
1¹/4 cups (330 g) rice
4 cups (1 L) chicken stock

1 cup finely chopped cooked
   chicken
salt and pepper to taste
pinch of nutmeg or mace
1 tablespoon chopped chives

GARNISH
whipped cream and parsley sprigs

Place vegetables, rice, stock, salt, pepper and spice in a soup pot. Bring slowly to boil and simmer for 40 minutes. Add chopped chicken, reheat gently, adjust seasoning, add nutmeg and chives. Serve with a spoonful of cream on top and garnished with parsley.

CORN AND BACON CHOWDER
Serves 4

3 rashers bacon	2¹/₂ cups (625ml) milk
1 small onion, finely sliced	¹/₂ cup (50 g) diced celery
1 potato, peeled and diced	1 x 420 g can sweet corn kernels
1 cup (250 ml) hot water	pinch of cayenne pepper
1 tablespoon butter	salt to taste
1 tablespoon flour	1 tablespoon chopped parsley

Chop bacon and sauté it in a large, heavy-based pan. Remove from pan. Add onion and cook until soft, not brown. Add diced potato and hot water and simmer for 10 minutes. In another pan make white sauce from butter, flour and milk (see p. 48). Add white sauce, celery and sweet corn to potato mixture and simmer for 15 minutes — as this is a very thick soup it should be stirred frequently to prevent sticking. Add cayenne and salt to taste. To serve, sprinkle bacon and parsley on top.

CREAM OF ASPARAGUS SOUP
Serves 4–6

1 bunch asparagus	1 cup (250 ml) water
or 1 x 420 g can asparagus	1 cup (250 ml) milk
2 cups (500 ml) stock	pepper
1 medium onion, finely chopped	onion salt (if using canned
1¹/₂ tablespoons (30 g) butter	asparagus)
1 tablespoon flour	whipped cream

If using fresh asparagus, cut off hard ends and cook spears in stock with finely chopped onion till soft. Drain vegetables, setting stock aside. Reserve a few tips for garnishing and purée rest of vegetables in processor. If using tinned asparagus just reserve a few tips and purée remainder of asparagus. Melt butter, blend in flour and cook for 1 minute. Add reserved stock gradually, stirring well to avoid lumps. Blend in puréed vegetables, water and milk. Bring to boil, stirring constantly then reduce heat and simmer for a few minutes. Season to taste, using onion salt if necessary. Serve hot with a spoonful of whipped cream and garnished with asparagus tips.

CREAM OF CELERY SOUP

Serves 6

1 head celery	pinch of nutmeg
1 medium onion	2 cups (500 ml) stock
1 white turnip	2 cups (500 ml) milk
2 cups (500 ml) boiling water	1 tablespoon cornflour
salt and pepper	1/2 cup (125 ml) cream (optional)

Shred celery finely or process in processor, peel and chop onion and turnip finely. Put all vegetables in pot, add boiling water and cook till soft, then add seasoning, nutmeg and stock, and simmer for 30 minutes. Use about 2 tablespoons of milk to blend with cornflour. Mix cornflour paste with rest of milk, add to pot and bring to the boil. Cook for 1 minute. Add cream. Serve hot with dice of toast. For a variation a spoonful of cream sprinkled with chopped chives or parsley may be added to each bowl.

EGG DROP SOUP

Serves 4–6

1/2 cup (80 g) fresh green peas	salt and pepper
5 cups (1.25 L) chicken stock	3 eggs, well beaten
2 teaspoons soy sauce	

Boil peas for 10 minutes in a small amount of boiling water. Drain peas and spoon into soup bowls. Boil stock with soy sauce, add seasoning to taste. Pour beaten egg in a thin stream into swirling stock. Stir in one direction until egg threads are cooked. Pour soup over peas in bowls.

FISH SOUP

Serves 3–4

1 tablespoon butter	juice of 1/2 lemon
1 tablespoon flour	1 cup (250 ml) milk
2 cups (500 ml) fish stock	salt and pepper
1 cup chopped or flaked white fish	2 teaspoons chopped parsley

Melt butter in saucepan, blend in flour and cook for 1 minute. Add stock gradually and stir until boiling. Simmer for 2 minutes. Add fish, lemon juice, then simmer for 3–4 minutes. Add milk but do not allow to boil. Adjust seasoning and if too thick add a little more milk. Serve sprinkled with parsley.

Variations
Instead of the white fish, for:
Crab Soup add 1 can crabmeat;
Crayfish Soup add 1 cup chopped crayfish;
Oyster Soup add 1 dozen oysters plus 1 teaspoon anchovy sauce.

GAZPACHO
Serves 4

2 cloves garlic, crushed	1 teaspoon salt
2 tablespoons (40 ml) olive oil	1 x 440 g can tomatoes
2 teaspoons sugar	1¹/₂ cups (375 ml) chicken
1 tablespoon vinegar	stock
1 teaspoon paprika	1 small green cucumber
pinch of cayenne pepper	6 spring onions
	1 small green capsicum

Place garlic, oil, sugar, vinegar and seasoning in a blender, process until thick then add tomatoes and process again. Put blended ingredients in a large bowl and add stock. Finely chop cucumber, spring onions and deseeded capsicum and add to bowl. Cover and chill well before serving. Extra chopped spring onion may be scattered on top to garnish.

Hint This soup may be served hot or cold.

GREEN PEA SOUP
Serves 6

2 stalks celery	³/4 cup (90 g) bacon pieces
1 small onion	6 cups (1.5 L) stock
1 carrot	1 teaspoon cornflour
1 cup (200 g) split green peas	pepper to taste

Chop vegetables and put in pan with peas, bacon pieces and stock. Bring to boil and simmer for 2 hours. Process in blender. Reheat in saucepan, and add cornflour blended with 2 teaspoons cold water. Bring to the boil, adjust seasoning and serve garnished with croûtons.

Hint To make the South Australian specialty Pie Floater, place a hot meat pie upside-down in a bowl of Green Pea Soup and add tomato sauce.

ICED CUCUMBER SOUP
Serves 2–3

2 continental cucumbers	2 cups (500 ml) chicken stock
1 medium onion	salt and pepper
3 tablespoons (60 g) butter	2–3 mint leaves
2 tablespoons (20 g) flour	1/2 cup (125 ml) cream

GARNISH
1 tablespoon chopped chives

Peel and slice cucumbers and peel and chop onion. Melt butter and sauté vegetables for 10 minutes but do not brown. Stir in flour and cook 1 minute, gradually add stock, stir until boiling. Add seasoning and chopped mint then cook until vegetables are soft. Blend in processor when cool. Chill and add cream. Serve with chopped chives sprinkled on top.

KHAO TOM GAI – THAI RICE SOUP WITH CHICKEN, PORK OR SEAFOOD
Serves 4–6

1/2 cup (100 g) uncooked rice	1 teaspoon pepper
8 cups (2 L) water	3 tablespoons (60 ml) fish sauce
1 tablespoon vegetable oil	2 tablespoons (40 g) sliced onion
1 tablespoon chopped garlic	1 tablespoon chopped coriander
1 tablespoon sliced ginger root	1 tablespoon chopped shallots
200 g chicken, cut in small pieces, or pork or seafood	

GARNISH

crispy fried noodles	*sliced chillies or capsicum*
fresh herb leaves	*chopped shallots*

Place rice in soup pot with water and bring to the boil. Simmer slowly until rice is quite soft and liquid reduces to about 1.5 litres. In another large pot, heat oil and stir fry garlic and ginger, then add chicken (pork or fish), pepper and fish sauce. Stir fry until cooked, then add onion, rice and rice stock, stirring well and cook for a further few minutes. Just before serving, stir in coriander and shallots and add garnish as desired.

LENTIL SOUP

Serves 6

1 cup (200 g) red lentils	*6 cups (1.5 L) water*
1 medium onion	*1 teaspoon curry powder*
1 medium carrot	*3–4 (500 g) bacon bones*
2 stalks celery	

Put all ingredients in a large pot. Bring to the boil and simmer for 2 hours. Remove bones. Purée when cool using a sieve or blender. Reheat in saucepan and adjust seasoning. Serve with croûtons.

Variation Lentil soup may also be flavoured with tomatoes: use 1 x 140 g can tomato paste.

MINESTRONE

Serves 6

1 tablespoon olive oil	*3 stalks celery, chopped*
2 bacon rashers, diced	*2 medium carrots, sliced*
1/2 clove garlic	*2 medium potatoes, diced*
1 small onion, diced	*2 cups (500 g) cooked brown beans*
1 tablespoon chopped sage	*1/4 small cabbage, shredded*
1 teaspoon salt	*1 cup shelled peas*
1/2 teaspoon pepper	*5 cups (1.25 L) water or stock*
1 tablespoon tomato paste	*1 cup (100 g) macaroni*
1 cup (200 g) diced pumpkin	*Parmesan cheese*

Heat oil in large soup pot, add bacon, garlic, onion, sage, salt and pepper, and brown gently. Stir in tomato paste, add remaining vegetables, water or stock, and simmer for 45 minutes. Add macaroni and cook for 10 minutes. To serve ladle into bowls and sprinkle with Parmesan cheese.

Note If preferred, a 420 g can of Four Bean Mix can be used in place of brown beans.

MJADARA – GREEN LENTIL SOUP
Serves 6–8

1 medium onion, chopped
1 tablespoon olive oil
1 cup (200 g) whole green lentils
6 cups (1.5 L) water

1 teaspoon salt
1 teaspoon pepper
¼ cup (50 g) rice

Fry onion in oil until very brown. Add lentils, stir and add water. Bring to the boil, add salt and pepper, lower heat and simmer for 45 minutes. Purée when cool using a sieve or blender, then return to boil. Add rice, stir until boiling, then simmer 15–20 minutes until rice is cooked.

MULLIGATAWNY SOUP
Serves 4

1 tomato or 1 tablespoon
  tomato sauce or paste
1 medium apple, diced
2 medium onions
1 tablespoon (20 g) flour

2 teaspoons curry powder
salt and pepper
1 tablespoon oil
4 cups (1 L) stock
1–2 teaspoons lemon juice

Wash tomato and apple, skin onion and cut all into small pieces. Mix flour, curry powder, salt and pepper together. Heat oil in saucepan, add vegetables and sauté until they begin to brown. Add flour mixture and stir well. Add stock and lemon juice, and stir until boiling. Simmer 1 hour.

OXTAIL SOUP
Serves 4–6

1 kg oxtail pieces
2 stalks celery
1 medium carrot
1 medium onion
1 medium white turnip

5 cups (1.25 L) stock
2 cloves
pinch of nutmeg
salt and pepper

GARNISH
chopped parsley

Wash oxtail, remove excess fat. Place in soup pot with chopped vegetables, stock and seasoning. Bring slowly to boil and simmer for 4 hours. Strain and allow to cool. Remove fat when set. Cut the meat from the bones, chop finely and discard bones. Bring soup to boil, add the meat and serve garnished with parsley.

PUMPKIN SOUP
Serves 4

750 g pumpkin
1 medium onion
2 stalks celery
1 medium potato
2 tablespoons (60 g) butter
3 cups (750 ml) chicken stock

1 cup (250 ml) milk
pinch of cayenne pepper
salt and pepper
squeeze of lemon juice
$^3/4$ cup (200 ml) cream
1 tablespoon chopped parsley
    or chives or nutmeg

Prepare and chop vegetables. Melt butter in saucepan, sauté vegetables lightly, add stock and simmer till vegetables are soft. Blend in processor, add milk, heat gently, then add pinch of cayenne and adjust seasoning. Before serving add squeeze of lemon juice. To serve, add a spoon of cream to each bowl and sprinkle with chopped parsley, chopped chives or nutmeg.

Hints Butternut pumpkin makes the nicest soup.
The pumpkin may be cut in pieces and cooked in the microwave for 4–6 minutes before scraping out the flesh and using in the soup.

To get a more caramelised flavour, the pieces of pumpkin may be baked in the oven for 1 hour and then used.

Ginger can be added to Pumpkin Soup at the time of sautéing the vegetables.

Pumpkin Soup freezes well.

SCOTCH BROTH
Serves 6

1/2 cup (100 g) pearl barley	2 stalks celery
1 kg mutton necks or soup bones	1 large onion
6 cups (1.5 L) water	1 small parsnip
3 medium carrots	salt and pepper
2 medium turnips	1/4 cup chopped parsley

Wash barley, cut meat into pieces. Place both in saucepan with water. Prepare and dice vegetables finely and add to pan. Boil for 2½–3 hours. Add salt and pepper to taste and some of the parsley. Remove bones and skim any fat from top. Serve hot with remaining parsley sprinkled on top.

Note Soup mix may be used instead of pearl barley, and soup bones or shanks may be substituted for mutton necks.

SHANK BROTH
Serves 4

3 mutton shanks (about 1 kg)	1 medium turnip
4 cups (1 L) water	1 medium onion
1/4 cup (50 g) pearl barley	2 stalks celery
salt and pepper to taste	2 tablespoons chopped parsley
1 medium carrot	

Wash meat and place shanks in saucepan with water, pearl barley, salt and pepper. Bring slowly to boil and skim carefully. Prepare vegetables and cut into small dice. Add to boiling soup and simmer for 2½–3 hours. Remove shanks, skim fat from top, adjust seasoning and add chopped parsley. Serve hot garnished with croûtons.

Hint After removing the shanks, the meat can be cut off, added to parsley sauce and served on toast as a quick meal.

TOMATO SOUP

Serves 3–4

6 medium tomatoes
1 medium onion
1 teaspoon butter
3 cups (500 ml) stock

1 bacon bone (about 125 g)
$1/2$ tablespoon sago
salt and pepper

GARNISH

yoghurt

chopped chives

Scald and peel tomatoes then cut up roughly. Peel and chop onion. Heat butter and sauté vegetables without browning for a few minutes. Add stock and bacon bone, stir until boiling and cook for 30 minutes. Rub through sieve, return to saucepan, add sago and cook carefully until clear. Skim if necessary, adjust seasoning and serve. Serve in bowls with dollop of yoghurt and sprinkled with chives.

VEGETABLE SOUP (SUCH AS ZUCCHINI, CELERY OR CARROT)

Serves 4

2 medium onions, chopped
3 tablespoons (60 g) butter
750 g vegetable of choice

4 cups (1 L) stock or chicken stock
cubes dissolved in 1 L water

Lightly fry onions in butter, add chopped vegetable and stock or chicken cubes and water. Bring to the boil and simmer until vegetables are tender. When cooled slightly, purée the mixture in a food processor. If freezing, place mixture in a container with a label indicating the contents, the date prepared and the quantity of milk to be added. Place the container in the freezer. When required for use, thaw; add $1/2$–1 cup milk or cream. Serve hot (do not boil) or cold.

Note Peppercorns or 1–2 bay leaves can be added to many soups before cooking. They should be placed in a muslin bag, which is then removed prior to processing in the blender.

VICHYSSOISE
Serves 4

1 large leek
2 stalks celery
2 medium potatoes
1 tablespoon butter

2 cups (500 ml) chicken stock
salt and pepper
3/4 cup (190 ml) milk
1/4 cup (60 ml) cream

GARNISH
chopped chives

Wash vegetables and prepare. Discard green part of leeks, peel potatoes and chop all vegetables finely then sauté in butter until soft — do not brown. Add stock and bring to boil. Season to taste. Simmer for 15–20 minutes, then purée in blender. Add milk and cream to purée in saucepan. Reheat gently then serve with chopped chives sprinkled on top.

Notes For a richer soup add 1/2 cup milk plus 1/4 cup cream.

This soup can be served cold.

✷ ACCOMPANIMENTS ✷ TO SERVE WITH SOUP (HOT OR COLD)

CROÛTONS

Cut 1–2 slices of bread into cubes. Heat a small amount of oil in a frying pan, add bread and fry until golden brown. Drain on absorbent kitchen paper towel and serve in a small dish.

Hint For people concerned about using oil, the bread cubes may be placed on a baking tray and allowed to become golden brown in a preheated moderate (180°C) oven.

DICE OF TOAST

A simple accompaniment to soups is made by cutting a toasted slice of bread into 1 cm dice. It is particularly suitable for serving with creamed soups.

GINGER TOAST

¹/₂ cup (125 g) butter
4 tablespoons (80 ml) oil

2 teaspoons ground ginger
6 slices bread

Melt butter and oil and stir in ginger. Coat both sides of bread with this mixture. Place on baking tray covered with baking paper or similar. Bake in oven at 150°C for almost 1 hour or until the bread is crisp. Cut into quarters, cool. These may be stored in an airtight container for several days.

MARINADES, SAUCES AND GRAVIES

∿ MARINADES ∿

A marinade can be used to tenderise and flavour cuts of meat, particularly chops, steak and chicken pieces. A marinade consists of an acid ingredient such as lemon juice to tenderise the meat, an oil to add moistness, and flavouring to give each marinade its distinct character. Marinate meat for several hours to get maximum benefits from your marinade. Brush meat as it is cooking with remaining marinade to keep it moist. The marinade recipes here are suitable to marinate 500 g–1 kg of chicken or meat.

GARLIC MARINADE

3 spring onions, chopped
1/2 cup (125 ml) olive oil
1 clove garlic, crushed
1/2 teaspoon ground coriander
rind and juice of 1/2 a lemon

Combine all ingredients, add steak, cover and stand for several hours or overnight, turning meat occasionally. Drain the steak and grill or barbecue as usual.

HONEY SOY MARINADE

3 tablespoons (60 ml) soy sauce
2 tablespoons (40 ml) vinegar
1 tablespoon honey
1 tablespoon oil
1 clove garlic, crushed
1 teaspoon grated fresh ginger
1/2 teaspoon mixed spice

Combine all ingredients well in a bowl, add pork and marinate for several hours or overnight. Grill or barbecue over gentle heat.

Note Marinades which contain sugar or honey burn easily and need to be cooked over gentle heat to avoid burning.

Pineapple Marinade

1 cup (250 ml) pineapple juice
2 tablespoons (40 ml) soy sauce
2 tablespoons (40 ml)
  vegetable oil
2 teaspoons grated fresh ginger

2 teaspoons French mustard
2^1/2 teaspoons curry powder
1 clove garlic, crushed

Combine all ingredients, add meat and stand several hours. Drain meat then grill or barbecue over a medium heat, brushing meat occasionally with the marinade as it cooks.

Red Pepper Marinade

1 large onion
1 clove garlic
1 small red capsicum
2 tablespoons (40 ml) oil

1 tablespoon vinegar
1 tablespoon soy sauce
1 teaspoon curry powder
1 teaspoon ground ginger

Chop onion, crush garlic, and deseed and finely chop or process red capsicum. Mix all ingredients together well. Pour marinade over diced meat or steaks and stand for several hours.

∽ Sauces for Meat, Fish ∾ and Vegetables

Anchovy Sauce

1 tablespoon butter
1 tablespoon flour
1 cup (250 ml) water

1 tablespoon anchovy essence or
  1 tablespoon mashed anchovies
pepper

Melt butter in a saucepan, stir in flour and cook 2–3 minutes. Add water and stir constantly until it boils. Simmer a few minutes, add anchovy essence and pepper.

APPLE SAUCE

4 apples
juice of 1/2 lemon
1 tablespoon sugar

1 tablespoon water
2 tablespoons (40 g) butter

Peel and core apples and cut into slices. Cook with other ingredients over low heat in a small pan, covered, until tender. Process or pass through a sieve, reheat and serve with roast pork or poultry.

BARBECUE SAUCE

2 medium onions, sliced
2 cloves garlic, crushed
2 tablespoons (40 ml)
    vegetable oil
1 x 440 g can tomatoes

1/4 cup (60 ml) vinegar
1/4 cup (45 g) brown sugar
1 tablespoon Worcester sauce
2 teaspoons mustard powder
salt and pepper

Sauté onions and garlic in oil until tender. Add the remaining ingredients and bring to the boil, stirring well. Reduce the heat and simmer for 30 minutes. Purée or process sauce in food processor.

BASIC WHITE SAUCE

2 tablespoons flour
1 tablespoon butter

1 cup (250 ml) milk or stock
salt and pepper

Melt butter in a saucepan and remove from heat. Add flour and stir until smooth. Return to gentle heat and cook for 1 minute, stirring well. Blend milk or stock with flour and butter mixture until smooth. Return to heat, stir until boiling. Boil for 2–3 minutes, stirring constantly until thick and smooth. Stir in salt and pepper.

Variations
Cheese Sauce Add 3 tablespoons grated cheese.
Egg Sauce Add 2–3 diced hard-boiled eggs and a little cayenne pepper.

Mushroom Sauce Sauté 90 g sliced mushrooms in butter and add to white sauce.

Mustard Sauce When adding flour to the butter in the white sauce, add 2 teaspoons mustard powder. When sauce is cooked, add 1 tablespoon vinegar.

Onion Sauce Slice and sauté a small onion in butter until translucent. Add to the white sauce.

Parsley Sauce Add 1 tablespoon chopped parsley.

BREAD SAUCE

1 cup (250 ml) milk
small piece of onion
1 blade mace
1 cup (40 g) white
  breadcrumbs

1 tablespoon cream
1 tablespoon butter
salt
cayenne pepper

Heat milk until almost boiling, remove from heat, add onion and mace and allow to stand for 15 minutes. Strain milk, return to the saucepan, add crumbs, beat well with fork and stand for 5 minutes with the lid on. Add other ingredients, and serve at once with poultry.

BROWN OR ESPAGNOLE SAUCE

1 stalk celery
1/2 medium carrot
1/2 medium onion
1/2 medium turnip
1 tablespoon butter

1 tablespoon flour
2 cups (500 ml) beef stock or water
1 bacon bone
bouquet garni or pinch of mixed herbs
1/2 tomato (optional)
salt and pepper

Peel and roughly dice celery, carrot, onion and turnip. Heat butter and sauté vegetables until golden brown not burned. Add flour and brown well, stirring constantly, then add stock and stir until boiling. Add bacon bone, bouquet garni and tomato and simmer for 45 minutes. Strain the sauce; reheat and season with salt and pepper to taste. Use as a base for casseroles and braises or as a sauce for roast meat.

CAPER SAUCE

1 tablespoon butter
1 heaped tablespoon flour
1/2 cup (125 ml) stock
1/2 cup (125 ml) milk

1 tablespoon chopped capers
1 tablespoon chopped parsley
salt and pepper

Melt butter, add flour, stir until smooth, then add liquids and stir constantly until boiling. Cook for 2 minutes then add capers, parsley, salt and pepper to taste. Serve with steamed or boiled fish.

CURRY SAUCE

1 medium apple
1 banana
1 small onion
1 tomato, peeled or 1 tablespoon
   tomato paste
1 tablespoon butter
2 tablespoons flour
1/2–1 tablespoon curry powder

1 tablespoon desiccated coconut
1 1/2 cups (375 ml) beef stock
1 tablespoon sultanas
1 tablespoon chutney
1 tablespoon plum jam
1/2 teaspoon salt
1 teaspoon lemon juice

Peel and dice fruit and vegetables. Melt butter; gently sauté onion, flour, curry powder and coconut. Add all other ingredients except lemon juice and stir until boiling. Simmer for 20–30 minutes. Add lemon juice.

Hint This sauce may be used to reheat cold meats, hard-boiled eggs, scallops, crayfish, prawns, tuna or salmon.

DEMI-GLACE
(A GOOD BROWN GRAVY)

1 tablespoon dripping
2 tablespoons flour

2 cups (500 ml) beef stock
salt and pepper

Remove meat from the roasting dish and strain any remaining fat, leaving 1 tablespoon. Add flour and brown over heat, stirring constantly. Add stock gradually and stir until boiling and thickened. Season and serve with roast meat.

HOLLANDAISE SAUCE

4 tablespoons (80 ml) white
  wine vinegar
8 peppercorns
1 bay leaf

3 egg yolks
salt and cayenne pepper
6 tablespoons (120 g) butter

Place vinegar, peppercorns and bay leaf in a saucepan to boil.
When reduced to half quantity, set aside to cool slightly, then
pour over lightly beaten egg yolks. Add the cayenne pepper
and salt. Place eggs in a double saucepan over boiling water
and stir with a wooden spoon, working in butter gradually.
Continue beating until sauce is well mixed and thickened.
Serve with poached fish, eggs or asparagus.

LEMON SAUCE

1 heaped tablespoon cornflour
1 cup (250 ml) chicken stock
3 tablespoons (60 ml) lemon
  juice

1 teaspoon grated lemon rind
1 teaspoon butter
black pepper

In a saucepan, blend cornflour with a little of the cold stock
then add remaining ingredients, mixing well. Heat and stir
constantly until the sauce boils and thickens.

MAYONNAISE

1 egg yolk
1 teaspoon white vinegar
1/2 teaspoon mustard

pinch of white pepper
pinch of salt
150 ml olive oil

In a clean bowl beat egg yolk, vinegar, dry mustard, salt and
pepper. Beating constantly, add olive oil drop by drop, until
the mayonnaise begins to thicken. Then pour the remaining
oil in a thin, steady stream, beating until thick. If mayonnaise
becomes too thick, thin with a little more vinegar. If mayonnaise curdles, beat in a little extra egg yolk.

Variation To make *Tartare Sauce*, to one quantity of Mayonnaise add 1/2 teaspoon chopped parsley, 1 teaspoon chopped gherkin, 1/2 teaspoon chopped capers, 1/2 teaspoon mixed herbs and a pinch of cayenne. Mix well and serve with seafood.

MINT SAUCE

1/2 cup fresh mint leaves
1 tablespoon sugar
2 tablespoons boiling water

1/2 cup (125 ml) white vinegar
salt and pepper

Put mint and sugar in a bowl and crush together with the back of a spoon. Pour boiling water over, add vinegar, salt and pepper. Serve with roast lamb.

MUSHROOM SAUCE

1 cup (80 g) mushrooms, sliced
1 tablespoon butter

1 cup (250 ml) undiluted
  canned mushroom soup
1/4 cup (60 ml) cream or milk

Sauté mushrooms in melted butter until soft. Add soup and cream. Bring to boil, thicken if necessary with a little cornflour made into a paste with cold water. Adjust seasoning.

PESTO

60 g fresh basil
2 cloves garlic
2 tablespoons (30 g) pine nuts
3–4 tablespoons (60–80 ml)
  olive oil

1/4 teaspoon salt
black pepper
50 g Parmesan cheese

Process basil leaves, garlic and pine nuts until finely chopped. Gradually add oil until a thick, creamy paste is formed. Season and fold in Parmesan cheese. Pesto can be used stirred through pasta, or spread on crusty Italian bread.

SATAY SAUCE

1 medium onion, finely chopped
1/4 – 1/2 teaspoon chilli flakes
1/4 teaspoon ground coriander
1/4 teaspoon ground cumin
1 clove garlic, crushed
1 tablespoon peanut oil

1/4 cup (60 ml) water
1/2 cup (125 ml) coconut milk
1/2 cup crunchy peanut butter
1 tablespoon soy sauce
1 teaspoon palm sugar
1 tablespoon lemon juice

Sauté sliced onion, chilli flakes, coriander, cumin and garlic in peanut oil until onion is transparent. Add water, coconut milk and peanut butter, stirring until smooth and boiling. Add soy sauce, sugar and lemon juice and blend.

SEAFOOD COCKTAIL SAUCE

2 tablespoons Mayonnaise
   (see p. 51)
2 tablespoons cream

2 tablespoons tomato sauce
pepper

Blend Mayonnaise and cream and add the tomato sauce gradually. Then add pepper to taste. Chill.

SWEET AND SOUR SAUCE

1 x 425 g can pineapple pieces
1/2 cup (125 ml) vinegar
2 tablespoons tomato paste
1 tablespoon brown sugar
1 tablespoon soy sauce

2 spring onions, sliced
1/2 red capsicum, sliced
1/2 cup (125 ml) water
1 rounded tablespoon cornflour

Combine all ingredients except water and cornflour in saucepan. Bring contents to the boil then add cornflour blended with cold water. Simmer 4–5 minutes. Serve over stir-fried chicken or pork.

Tomato Sauce

6 medium tomatoes
1 teaspoon olive oil
1 clove garlic, crushed
1/2 medium onion, chopped

1 tablespoon tomato paste
1 teaspoon sugar
1 cup (250 ml) vegetable stock
2 teaspoons chopped fresh basil

Peel tomatoes and cut in half. Remove seeds. Chop roughly.
Heat olive oil in a saucepan and gently sauté the garlic and
onion for 2–3 minutes. Add chopped tomatoes, tomato paste,
sugar, vegetable stock and basil. Cook over gentle heat until
the tomato is tender and the sauce thickened. Use with pasta.

∽ Savoury Butters to ∾ Serve with Meat and Fish

Garlic Butter

1/4 cup (60 g) butter
1 clove garlic, crushed

Cream together butter and garlic. Shape into a log and chill.
Slice and serve with steak, chicken or fish or use on sliced
French stick to make garlic bread.

Maître d'Hôtel Butter

1 tablespoon butter
2 tablespoons finely chopped
  parsley

pinch of cayenne pepper
squeeze of lemon juice

Beat butter until creamy, add remaining ingredients. Form
into a log and refrigerate. Slice off pieces as required. Serve
on grilled lamb or steak.

Roquefort Butter

1/4 cup (60 g) butter
30 g blue vein cheese

1 teaspoon lemon juice
2 teaspoons chopped parsley

Cream together butter and cheese, add lemon juice and
parsley. Roll into pats and serve.

♬ SWEET SAUCES ♬

BUTTERSCOTCH SAUCE

4 tablespoons (60 g) brown sugar
1 tablespoon golden syrup
1 tablespoon water
1 tablespoon butter

1 tablespoon cornflour or
   arrowroot
2 tablespoons water
lemon or vanilla essence

Heat brown sugar, golden syrup, 1 tablespoon water and butter in a saucepan until nearly boiling. Mix arrowroot or cornflour with 2 tablespoons cold water and stir into sugar mixture. Stir until boiling, reduce heat and simmer 2–3 minutes. Add essence and serve hot or cold over ice-cream or steamed puddings.

CHOCOLATE SAUCE

$1^1/2$ tablespoons cornflour
2 tablespoons cocoa
cold water
1 cup (250 ml) hot water

$1/4$ cup (65 g) sugar
2 teaspoons butter
1 teaspoon vanilla essence

Blend cornflour and cocoa with a little cold water. Stir into hot water, add sugar and butter. Stir over gentle heat until boiling and thickened. Add vanilla essence. Serve over ice-cream.

CUSTARD SAUCE

1 cup (250 ml) milk
1 egg
1 egg yolk

2 teaspoons sugar
$1/2$ teaspoon vanilla essence
nutmeg

Heat the milk in double saucepan or in a bowl standing over a saucepan of boiling water. Beat egg, egg yolk and sugar together until well mixed. Pour hot milk over egg mixture, stirring quickly. Return to saucepan or bowl, stir with a wooden spoon until it thickens and coats the spoon. Strain at once into a cold basin, add essence when cool and pour into a glass dish. Grate a little nutmeg over the top.

Variation Whip the egg white very stiffly. Add 1 teaspoon caster sugar to it and place in heaps on top of the custard.

HARD SAUCE

3 tablespoons (60 g) butter
3/4 cup (135 g) icing sugar
1 tablespoon boiling water

1/4 teaspoon lemon essence
1/4 teaspoon vanilla essence or
   other essence

Cream butter with a wooden spoon. Add sugar gradually, beating constantly. Add boiling water and continue beating. Add flavouring, chill. Serve with rich plum pudding.

SWEET LEMON SAUCE

1/2 cup (125 g) butter
1/2 cup (125 g) sugar
1 tablespoon cornflour

11/2 cup (375 ml) boiling water
grated rind and juice of 1 lemon

Cream butter and sugar together. In a separate bowl mix cornflour with a little cold water and pour boiling water into it. Add cornflour mixture to the butter and sugar. Stir over heat until thickened. Add lemon juice and rind. Serve with steamed puddings.

SWEET WHITE SAUCE

1 cup (250 ml) milk
1 cup (250 ml) water
1 strip lemon rind

1 bay leaf
1 tablespoon cornflour
1 tablespoon sugar

Bring milk, water, bay leaf and lemon rind nearly to boil. Blend cornflour and sugar with a little cold milk, stir into the hot milk and stir until boiling. Allow to cook 5–7 minutes then remove lemon and bay leaf.

Variations Add nutmeg or cinnamon, chopped glacé cherries or candied peel.

Fish

Important instructions

1. Fish are fresh when:
   - the eyes are bright and prominent;
   - the flesh is firm;
   - the gills are red;
   - the smell is agreeable.
2. Clean fish at once.
3. Soak fish in salted water briefly.
4. Remove scales by scraping from tail to the head with a knife.
5. To skin fish, cut round head, down back across tail, and up front on both sides; free skin at head, and draw down towards tail on both sides.
6. To fillet fish, place one hand firmly on fish; take a knife and place it in opening near head then slide the knife along backbone towards tail, taking the flesh off in one piece.

Sauces to serve with fish

1. Basic White Sauce (see p. 48).
2. Anchovy Sauce (see p. 47).
3. Cheese Sauce (see p. 48).
4. Egg Sauce (see p. 48).
5. Hollandaise Sauce (see p. 51).
6. Mustard Sauce (see p. 49).

Baked Fish

Whole or filleted fish may be baked in the oven. Place in greased baking tray or dish. Sprinkle with salt and pepper, cover with foil and bake in a preheated moderate oven (180°C) for 15 minutes or until cooked. If preferred add a little milk to the baking dish. Another method is to wrap the fish in lightly greased or buttered aluminium foil and place on a tray. The addition of a slice or two of lime or lemon inside the foil further improves this method.

Hints

Prepared fish can be cooked in the microwave for about a quarter of the oven cooking time. Use a microwave dish, add 60 ml milk, salt and pepper.

Fish may also be stuffed (see p. 64).

BOILED BREAM OR SNAPPER
Serves 4

4 small or 1 large fish
1 tablespoon lemon juice or
  1 tablespoon vinegar

1 teaspoon salt
3 sprigs parsley

Trim fins off fish, remove scales and wash well. Add lemon or vinegar, salt and parsley to a saucepan partly filled with boiling water. Add fish and allow to simmer gently. Cook bream 10 minutes, snapper 20–30 minutes. Lift the fish out carefully. Drain and garnish with parsley before serving with Egg or Parsley Sauce (see pp. 48–9).

FISH AND VEGETABLE COUSCOUS
Serves 6–8

FISH AND VEGETABLES

1–1.5 kg fish fillets
3 cloves garlic, sliced
olive oil
2 medium carrots, diced
2 cups (200g) diced celery
1 medium onion, diced
2 leeks, diced

8 ripe tomatoes, skinned and diced
1/4 teaspoon ground cumin
2 teaspoons paprika
4 cups (1 L) fish stock
salt and pepper to taste
4 tablespoons chopped coriander leaves
4 tablespoons chopped parsley

SPICED COUSCOUS

400–500 g instant couscous
water

2–3 tablespoons (40–60 g) butter
1–1 1/2 teaspoons ras el hanout

Cut fish into 16–20 pieces. Sauté garlic in a little olive oil, and add vegetables, cumin and paprika. Cook gently until vegetables are tender, adding a little fish stock if necessary. Add remaining fish stock, simmer until slightly reduced and season to taste. Add fish and simmer until just cooked. Add coriander and parsley a few minutes before serving.

Follow preparation directions on couscous packet. Add butter and *ras el hanout* to couscous and fluff with a fork.

Hints
Canned tomatoes may be used.
Tomato juice or diluted tomato soup can replace fish stock.

FISH CAKES
Serves 4–6

2 cups (500 g) mashed potatoes	*1 egg, beaten*
milk	*breadcrumbs*
1 x 425 g can tuna or salmon	*oil for frying*
salt and pepper	*parsley*

Stir potatoes with a little milk over heat until hot and smooth. Remove all skin and bone from fish, and break it up. Add to potatoes, season to taste, and stir over heat until thoroughly mixed, adding a little more milk if too dry. Let mixture cool. Shape into small round cakes, coat carefully with egg and breadcrumbs, fry in hot oil till lightly browned. Drain well, and garnish with crisply fried parsley.

Hints
Fish cakes can also be baked in the oven.
Cooked fresh fish may be used instead of canned.

FISH CURRY
Serves 4

2 tablespoons (40 ml) oil	*1 x 880 g can tomatoes*
1 medium onion, diced	*1/4 cup (60 ml) water*
2 stalks celery, diced	*2 teaspoons sugar*
1 capsicum, diced	*1 teaspoon salt*
2 teaspoons curry powder	*500 g fish fillets, e.g. whiting or flathead*

Heat oil in large pan, stir in onion, cook until soft, add celery and capsicum, cook for 3 minutes more. Stir in curry powder and cook for 1 minute. Add tomatoes, water, sugar and salt. Bring to boil and simmer on a low heat. Cut fish into bite-sized pieces and place in casserole. Pour sauce over fish and bake uncovered in preheated moderate oven (180°C) for 30 minutes. Serve with bread stick.

FISH IN BATTER

1 cup (150 g) flour	fish fillets
pinch of salt	extra flour
1 teaspoon melted butter or oil	oil
2 eggs, separated	1 lemon, sliced
1 cup (250 ml) milk	

Sift flour and salt together, pour butter or oil into hole in centre of flour. Stir with a wooden spoon. Add egg yolks and milk and mix into smooth paste. Beat the whites of egg to a stiff froth and fold lightly into batter. Allow to stand for some time before using. Wipe fillets dry, dip in flour, then in batter and fry in hot oil. Before serving drain on paper towels and garnish with slices of lemon.

FISH KEDGEREE
Serves 4

500 g cooked or canned fish	2 cups (360 g) cooked rice
1 egg, hard-boiled	1 teaspoon lemon juice
2 tablespoons (40 g) butter	salt and pepper to taste

GARNISH

lemon slices	2–3 sprigs parsley

Flake fish with fork, remove bones, chop hard-boiled egg. Melt butter, add all ingredients. Bake in casserole in a preheated moderate oven (180°C) for 20–30 minutes. Garnish with lemon and parsley and serve hot.

FRIED FISH

Serves 4

500 g fish fillets or cutlets
2 tablespoons (20 g) flour
salt and pepper

1 egg, beaten, or a little milk
breadcrumbs
oil

GARNISH

lemon
parsley

Dip each piece of fish in flour, pepper and salt, then in beaten egg or milk, and lastly in breadcrumbs. Fry in a small amount of hot oil until golden brown. Before serving drain on paper towels and garnish with lemon and parsley.

GRILLED FISH

Clean and dry fish. Preheat griller for 2–3 minutes. Sprinkle fish with salt and brush with melted butter or oil. Place on greased grill rack, grill 2 minutes each side. Reduce heat to half and continue until fish is white and leaves bones easily when tested with a skewer. Garnish with lemon slices and parsley or suitable sauce such as Tartare, Parsley or Hollandaise.

SALMON AND POTATO BAKE

Serves 6

500 g potatoes
1 cup (250 ml) milk
2 tablespoons (40 g) butter
1 medium onion, sliced
1 cup (100 g) chopped celery
180 g mushrooms, sliced
2 tablespoons (20 g) flour

1 cup cooked peas
1 cup (125 g) grated cheese
2 tablespoons chopped parsley
  (reserve a sprig as garnish)
1 x 450 g can salmon
125 g cheese, sliced

Peel and cook potatoes. Mash potatoes and beat well with a little milk. Grease a casserole and line with two-thirds of the mashed potato. Melt butter in a saucepan and cook onion until clear but not brown, add celery and mushrooms and sauté for 5 minutes. Add flour and blend in well. Add remainder of milk gradually, stirring constantly until boiling. Allow to boil for 1 minute. Add cooked peas, grated cheese, chopped parsley and drained salmon. Combine well and pour mixture into potato case. Pipe or spoon remainder of potato around edge of casserole. Top with sliced cheese (can be cut in strips). Heat in moderate oven (180°C) until cheese is slightly browned. Garnish with parsley before serving.

SEAFOOD AND FILLO PARCELS
Serves 6

PARCELS

250 g green prawns
175 g scallops
2 cups (500 g) water
2 spring onions, chopped
1 cup (250 ml) cream

1 clove garlic, crushed
salt and pepper to taste
12 sheets fillo pastry
2$^{1}/_{2}$ tablespoons (50 g) melted
   butter

LEMON SAUCE

1 tablespoon lemon juice
$^{1}/_{3}$ cup (80 ml) cream
2 egg yolks, beaten

1$^{1}/_{2}$ tablespoons (30 g) butter
1 tablespoon chopped chives
salt and pepper to taste

Shell prawns, remove dark veins. Wash and pat dry. Remove dark veins from scallops. Wash and pat dry. Bring water to the boil and add scallops and prawns, cook for 30 seconds then immediately remove from the pan. Strain liquid and reserve $^{1}/_{3}$ cup for the sauce. Mix prawns and scallops with spring onions, cream, garlic, salt and pepper. Divide mixture into 6 portions. Brush 2 sheets of fillo pastry with melted butter and place a portion of the seafood at one end of the sheet. Fold neatly into a parcel shape, place on a greased oven tray and brush the top with a little extra butter. Repeat with remaining seafood and fillo to make 6 parcels. Bake in a moderately hot oven (190°C) for 8–10 minutes or until golden brown.

To make lemon sauce, combine the reserved liquid with lemon juice, cream and egg yolks in saucepan. Heat gently, stirring constantly, until the mixture thickens but does not boil. Gradually stir in the butter. Add chives and season with salt and pepper. Serve parcels with sauce immediately.

Note 450 g of good quality seafood mix can replace scallops and prawns.

SMOKED COD CASSEROLE
Serves 4–6

2 tablespoons (40 g) butter
1/2 cup (50 g) chopped celery
1 small onion, chopped
2 tablespoons (20 g) flour
pepper
2 cups (500 ml) milk

1 x 420 g can celery soup
750 g smoked cod, cooked and
   flaked
1 tablespoon lemon juice
1/2 cup (65 g) grated cheddar
   cheese

Melt butter, add celery and onion. Cook until onion is tender. Blend in flour, pepper, then gradually stir in milk and celery soup. Stir constantly until boiling. Fold in flaked fish and lemon juice. Pour into greased casserole and top with cheese. Bake in preheated moderate oven (180°C) for 30 minutes.

SQUID (OR CALAMARI)
Serves 4

600 g cleaned and prepared
   squid
2 tablespoons (20 g) flour or
   rice flour
2 tablespoons (40 g) salt

1 tablespoon freshly ground
   black pepper
1 teaspoon chilli powder
2–3 tablespoons (60 ml)
   vegetable oil

Cut along each squid so it will open out flat. Dry well with paper towels and cut into 1 cm strips. Mix dry ingredients together in flat dish. Coat pieces of squid with flour mixture. Heat oil in frying pan or wok. Cook squid in batches for 1–2 minutes until golden. Remove with slotted spoon and drain well on paper towels. Serve with chopped parsley and lemon or lime wedges.

Steamed Fish

fillets of whiting, mullet
  or flathead
salt

lemon juice
cayenne pepper
butter

Remove any small bones from fillets, skin if desired. Wash and dry well. Place in well-greased steamer basket. Sprinkle with a little salt, cayenne and lemon juice. Fold fillets in halves and dot with butter. Cover with greased paper and lower the basket into the steamer. Cover and cook over boiling water 7–10 minutes. May also be cooked in pre-heated moderate oven (180°C) for about 15 minutes or in microwave oven for 4 minutes on HIGH.

Stuffing for Fish

4 tablespoons (20 g) breadcrumbs
1 tablespoon chopped parsley
$1/2$ teaspoon thyme
$1/2$ teaspoon marjoram
$1/2$ teaspoon salt

$1/4$ teaspoon pepper
$1/4$ teaspoon nutmeg
1 teaspoon butter
2 tablespoons (40 ml) milk
1 teaspoon lemon rind

Mix all the ingredients together.

Tuna and Noodle Casserole
Serves 4

4 tablespoons (80 ml) oil
250 g egg noodles
1 medium onion, chopped
3 stalks celery, sliced
1 x 425 g can tuna

1 x 420 g can cream of celery
  soup
$1/4$ cup (60 ml) lemon juice
$1/2$ cup (75 g) salted cashew nuts
salt and pepper

Heat oil in frying pan, add the noodles and fry gently until golden. Remove from pan and drain well. Add onion and celery to pan and brown lightly. Mix drained tuna, soup plus a soup can full of water, lemon juice, cashew nuts, salt, pepper, three-quarters of drained noodles and onion and celery. Place in greased casserole, bake in preheated moderate oven (180°C) for 30 minutes. Remove from oven and top with remaining noodles. Return to oven for a further 15 minutes.

TUNA AND VEGETABLE CASSEROLE
Serves 4

1 tablespoon butter
2 tablespoons (20 g) flour
2 cups (500 ml) milk
1/2 cup (65 g) grated cheddar cheese
pinch of cayenne pepper
1 medium onion, finely sliced
1 tablespoon oil

1 stalk celery, diced
1/4 red capsicum, diced
1/2 cup frozen peas
1 medium carrot, diced
1 x 425 g can tuna in brine
1/2 cup corn kernels

TOPPING
1/2 cup breadcrumbs

1/2 cup (65 g) grated cheddar cheese

In a medium saucepan melt the butter over gentle heat and stir in the flour. Blend until smooth and cook for 1 minute. Gradually add and stir in the milk. Bring to the boil, stirring constantly, and cook for 1–2 minutes. Remove from the heat and stir in the cheese and cayenne pepper. Set aside.

Sauté the onion in oil until transparent, add the celery and red capsicum and cook until tender. In a separate saucepan, simmer frozen peas and carrots until tender or microwave on HIGH for 4 minutes. Drain and set aside.

Drain and flake the tuna and stir into the cheese sauce. Mix in all the vegetables. Pour into a casserole dish and sprinkle with breadcrumbs and grated cheese. Bake in a preheated moderate oven (180°C) for 45 minutes.

TUNA PIE

1½ cups (375 ml) white sauce   2 teaspoons lemon juice
1 teaspoon curry powder   1 x 425 g can tuna

TOPPING

2 cups (500 g) mashed potatoes 1 tablespoon grated onion
2 teaspoons butter   1 egg, beaten
1 tablespoon milk   salt and pepper to taste

Make white sauce (see p. 48) then add the curry powder, lemon juice and tuna. Place in greased ovenware dish.

For topping, while potato is still hot, beat in butter, milk, onion, egg and seasoning. Spread lightly over fish mixture and bake in preheated moderate oven (180°C) till golden brown (about 40 minutes).

Poultry and Game

ᖫ Accompaniments ᖬ to Poultry

To add flavour and interest, poultry and game may be stuffed. Use Veal Stuffing for chicken and turkey; Sage and Onion Stuffing for ducks and geese. Sausages and cranberry sauce are often served with turkey, and Bread Sauce (see p. 49) and small Bacon Rolls with chicken. The stuffing recipes below use fresh breadcrumbs; dried breadcrumbs may be substituted but note that 1 cup dried crumbs weighs 100 g.

Bacon Rolls

4 thin bacon rashers

Remove rind from bacon and cut into 5 cm lengths. Roll and thread on to skewers. Grill or bake until fat is clear (5–10 minutes).

Sage and Onion Stuffing

3 onions, finely chopped   *1 tablespoon butter or margarine*
1 tablespoon finely chopped sage *salt and pepper*
1 cup (60 g) fresh breadcrumbs   *1 egg, beaten*

Mix dry ingredients together then bind with egg.

Stuffing for Lamb, Rabbit and Kangaroo

1 cup (60 g) fresh breadcrumbs   *1/2 teaspoon powdered marjoram*
1 tablespoon butter or margarine   *1/2 teaspoon powdered thyme*
1 tablespoon chopped parsley   *1 egg, beaten*

Mix dry ingredients together then bind with egg.

STUFFING FOR VEAL AND POULTRY

1/3 cup (20 g) fresh breadcrumbs
1 tablespoon chopped parsley
1 teaspoon grated lemon rind
1/2 teaspoon salt

1/4 teaspoon pepper
pinch of nutmeg
1 teaspoon butter or margarine
2 tablespoons (40 ml) milk

Mix all ingredients together.

∾ ROASTING POULTRY ∾ AND GAME

ROAST CHICKEN

Wash chicken under tap. It is also important to wash your hands well after handling the chicken. Fill cavity with Sage and Onion Stuffing. Truss, place on baking tray or in roasting dish. Brush over with a little oil, sprinkle with salt/pepper/paprika and cover with aluminium foil or a cover. Bake in a preheated moderate oven (180°C) for 1–1½ hours, depending on size. Remove the cover or foil for the last half hour of cooking, return bird to the oven and allow top of bird to become golden brown.

Hints Prepared vegetables can be placed round the chicken and baked. Allow 45–60 minutes for vegetables.

Trussing poultry compacts the body, so allows more even cooking. Place bird on its breast, fold the skin over the opening at the neck on to the back; turn in the wings, with the ends inside, in the shape of triangles; the points will then keep the loose skin in its place. Push back the leg close to the sides of the bird. Take a trussing needle and a long piece of fine string; pass the needle through the joint of the wing, then through the second joint of the leg, then through the body and other leg and wing. Draw the string through. Turn the bird breast-side down and cross the string over the back, then bring down and tie the leg with the tail firmly together.

Cover the legs with greased foil or paper to prevent over-cooking. If no needle available, two large skewers can be used — one inserted through the leg and body and the second through the wing and body.

Roast Duck

Fill body with Sage and Onion Stuffing (p. 67), roast in pre-heated moderately hot oven (190°C) for 1 1/2 hours or until tender. Serve with Demi-Glace (p. 50), Apple Sauce (p. 48) and vegetables of your choice.

Roast Rabbit

Wash the rabbit and wipe dry. Stuff rabbit (see Stuffing for Lamb, Rabbit and Kangaroo, p. 67) and skewer the shoulders and legs close to the body. Wrap the rabbit in oiled aluminium foil and bake in a preheated hot oven (200°C) for 1 hour. Ten minutes before serving remove foil and return to oven. Remove skewers and serve with Demi-Glace (p. 50), red currant jelly and vegetables of your choice.

Note Rabbit is again becoming popular in the diet. As a general rule it may be substituted for chicken in chicken recipes.

∽ Casserole Dishes ∾

Apricot and Chicken Casserole
Serves 4

8 chicken pieces (about 1 kg)
1 packet Creamy French
  Onion soup

1 x 440 g can apricot nectar
1 x 425 g can mushrooms

Roll pieces of chicken in dry soup mix and place in casserole. Pour over nectar and mushrooms. Cover and cook in a preheated moderate oven (180°C) for 1 1/2 hours.

CHICKEN AND ASPARAGUS
Serves 4

2 tablespoons (40 ml) olive oil
8 pieces chicken (about 1 kg)
1 medium onion, sliced
2 bacon rashers, diced
2 tablespoons flour
1 cup (250 ml) milk

1 cup (250 ml) chicken stock
1 x 340 g can asparagus cuts
1 tablespoon lemon juice
salt and pepper
3/4 cup (90 g) grated tasty cheese
2 tablespoons chopped parsley

Heat oil in pan, add chicken pieces and brown well. Place chicken in ovenproof dish. Add onion and bacon to pan and sauté. Stir in flour, add milk and stock, stirring well until flour is cooked (let it boil for at least a minute). Add asparagus cuts and their liquid, lemon juice and seasoning. Pour over chicken, sprinkle on grated cheese and bake in moderate oven (180°C) for 45 minutes. Sprinkle with parsley before serving.

CHICKEN CASSEROLE WITH ALMONDS
Serves 6

1 kg cooked chicken pieces
3/4 cup boiled rice
1 small onion, chopped
1/2 cup (65 g) slivered almonds
1 x 420 g can cream of chicken
   soup
1 x 420 g can mushroom soup
salt

1 cup (250 ml) Mayonnaise
   (see p. 51)
1 1/2 cups (185 g) diced celery
4 hard-boiled eggs, chopped
2 tablespoons (40 ml) lemon juice
1/2 cup (30 g) fresh breadcrumbs
1 tablespoon (20 g) butter or
   margarine

Dice chicken meat. Combine with other ingredients except breadcrumbs and butter. Place mixture in large casserole and top with breadcrumbs tossed in melted butter. Bake for 30 minutes in preheated moderate oven (180°C).

CHICKEN CURRY

Serves 6

1 kg chicken pieces
2 onions
salt to taste
1–2 teaspoons sugar
1 tablespoon curry powder
1/2 teaspoon chilli power
2 tablespoons (40 ml) oil

2 cloves garlic, crushed
2 stalks lemongrass
500 g sweet potato or potato
1 x 200 ml can coconut milk
1 tablespoon cornflour
1/4 cup (60 ml) cold water

Chop chicken pieces into thirds. Place chicken in large bowl with one finely chopped onion, salt, sugar, curry powder and chilli powder. Mix lightly and leave for 1 hour. In a large saucepan, heat the oil. Add garlic and chicken and fry for 15 minutes until chicken is golden brown. Add enough water to cover chicken. Wash the lemongrass, crush the base, tie stalks together and add to pan. Chop remaining onion coarsely and add. Bring to the boil, turn down heat and simmer for about 30 minutes, until chicken is cooked. Remove lemongrass. While chicken is cooking, peel and dice potato into 3 cm dice. Deep fry for 3 minutes. Add to saucepan and very gently mix. Add coconut milk. Make sure there is enough liquid to just cover the ingredients. Blend cornflour with cold water and add. Stir gently until sauce thickens then let it boil for a minute. Remove from heat. Serve with Vietnamese bread, steamed rice or noodles.

Hint If fried potato is banned in your diet, add diced potato while chicken is simmering.

CHICKEN FOR EASY ENTERTAINING

Use 2 chicken thigh fillets per person. Heat electric frying pan to 180°C. Place a sheet of baking paper in the pan and put chicken thighs in a single layer on the paper. Cook 8–10 minutes, turn the fillets over and cook the other side for a further 8 minutes. Remove immediately to prevent chicken becoming too dry and place in a casserole dish. Pour any juice left in pan over chicken. Add selected sauce from those below to chicken (sauce quantities are sufficient to coat 8 thigh fillets) and keep warm or reheat. Serve with salad or cooked vegetables.

BASIC CHICKEN SAUCE

1 chicken stock cube
3/4 cup (190 ml) water

2 teaspoons cornflour mixed with extra 2 tablespoons cold water

Crumble the stock cube and add to water in a pan. Boil. Add blended cornflour to chicken stock, stirring well and bring to the boil. Pour over chicken. Reheat chicken in moderate oven (180°C) for approximately 30 minutes or microwave oven for 6–8 minutes on MEDIUM.

CREAMY TOMATO SAUCE

1 large or 3 small tomatoes, chopped and peeled
3/4 cup (190 ml) sour cream

1 tablespoon chopped fresh oregano
1 quantity Basic Chicken Sauce

Mix tomato, sour cream and oregano and add to basic sauce. Pour over chicken and reheat.

GINGER AND SOY SAUCE

1 teaspoon ground ginger
2 teaspoons soy sauce

1/2 cup (125 ml) water
1 quantity Basic Chicken Sauce

Mix ginger, soy sauce and water together and add to basic sauce. Pour over chicken and reheat.

HONEY AND PEANUT SAUCE

1/2 cup (180 g) honey
2 tablespoons (40 g) peanut butter
1 teaspoon ground ginger

1/2 cup (80 ml) water
1 quantity Basic Chicken Sauce

Mix honey, peanut butter, ginger and water together and add to basic sauce. Pour over chicken and reheat.

ORANGE AND CHIVE SAUCE

¹/₃ cup (80 ml) orange juice   *1 quantity Basic Chicken Sauce*
2 tablespoons chopped chives

Mix orange juice and chives together and add to basic sauce.
Pour over chicken and reheat.

CHICKEN IN COCONUT MILK SAUCE — OPOR AYAM
Serves 4

1 roasting chicken or 4 chicken   *2¹/₂ cups (625 ml) coconut milk*
*   breasts*   *2 kaffir lime leaves or bay leaves*
1 teaspoon lemon juice   *8 cm stick rhubarb, finely chopped*
¹/₂ teaspoon salt

PASTE

5 shallots or 1 onion, chopped   *¹/₂ teaspoon ground white*
4 cloves garlic, chopped   *   pepper*
5 candlenuts or macadamia   *¹/₄ teaspoon ground or*
*   nuts, chopped*   *   chopped fresh galangal*
1 teaspoon ground coriander   *5 tablespoons (100 ml) coconut*
1 teaspoon ground cumin   *   milk*
                                       1 teaspoon salt

Cut whole chicken into 4 pieces and rub them (or chicken
breasts) all over with lemon juice and half a teaspoon of salt.
Roast the chicken in a moderately slow oven (160°C) for
40–50 minutes. Blend all the ingredients for the paste until
smooth and transfer to a saucepan. Simmer for 5 minutes,
stirring often, then add the 2¹/₂ cups coconut milk. Bring
almost to boiling point, add the chicken, lime leaves and
rhubarb. Simmer for 40–50 minutes. Check for seasoning.
Remove kaffir lime leaves and serve hot with rice and some
cooked vegetables.

Note   Ginger may be used instead of galangal.

CHICKEN IN SOY SAUCE
Serves 6

$^1/_2$ cup (125 ml) soy sauce
$^1/_4$ cup (40 g) brown sugar
$^3/_4$ cup (190 ml) water
4 spring onions, chopped

3 medium dried Chinese
   mushrooms (optional),
   washed and soaked
1 tablespoon chopped fresh ginger
1 roasting chicken, about 1.5 kg
   (size 15)

Put all ingredients except chicken in a large saucepan and bring to boil. Prepare chicken, place in liquid, cover and simmer for 45 minutes–1 hour. Turn chicken occasionally to brown evenly. Remove from heat, let chicken cool slightly, chop into small pieces, arrange neatly on hot platter and pour hot sauce over it.

Hint Leftover sauce may be bottled and stored in the refrigerator.

CHICKEN WITH MUSHROOMS
Serves 4

750 g chicken drumsticks
2 tablespoons (40 ml) oil
1 small onion, sliced
1 clove garlic, crushed

1 x 425 g can cream of mushroom
   soup
$^1/_4$ cup (60 ml) milk
pinch of paprika

Brown chicken in frying pan with oil, then place in casserole. Sauté onion and garlic and add to casserole. Mix soup and milk together and pour over casserole. Sprinkle a little paprika on top. Bake in a preheated moderate oven (180°C) for about 1 hour.

LEMON CHICKEN
Serves 4

500 g chicken breast fillets
1–2 eggs, lightly beaten
1 tablespoon cornflour

oil for frying
4 tablespoons (80 ml) Lemon
   Sauce (see p. 51)

slices of fresh lemon

Cut chicken into bite-sized pieces. Coat with egg and corn-flour. Deep fry in medium hot oil until golden brown, and drain on absorbent paper. Heat lemon sauce (may be thickened with 1 tablespoon cornflour blended with 1/4 cup cold water, added to lemon sauce and boiled for 1 minute) and pour over chicken. Garnish with lemon slices. Serve with boiled rice.

MOROCCAN CHICKEN CASSEROLE
Serves 4–6

1 tablespoon olive oil
1 large onion, sliced
3 cloves garlic, crushed
1/2 teaspoon saffron powder
2 teaspoons paprika
2 kg chicken pieces or 1 large chicken, cut into pieces
2 teaspoons finely grated lemon rind
1 tablespoon lemon juice
1/2 cup (125 ml) chicken stock

1/4 cup (60 ml) water
2 large potatoes, peeled and quartered
3 carrots, peeled and quartered
2 tablespoons chopped parsley
2 tablespoons chopped coriander leaves
100 g olives
salt and freshly ground pepper to taste

Heat oil in saucepan and cook onion, garlic, saffron and paprika until onion is soft. Add chicken, lemon rind and juice and cook until chicken is browned all over. Add stock and water and bring to the boil. Simmer, covered, for 15 minutes, add potatoes and carrots and simmer a further 20 minutes. Stir in herbs and olives, add salt and pepper and simmer for 5 minutes more.

ORANGE CHICKEN
Serves 4

4 pieces chicken
2 tablespoons flour

2 tablespoons paprika
2 tablespoons (40 ml) oil

ORANGE SAUCE

1/3 cup (160 ml) orange juice
2 teaspoons orange rind
2 teaspoons Worcester sauce

1 clove garlic, crushed
salt and pepper

Heat oven to 180°C. Toss chicken in flour and paprika, and place in casserole. Spoon oil over chicken, cover and bake for 30 minutes. Mix together orange sauce ingredients and pour over chicken. Return to oven, bake for a further 30 minutes or until tender, basting occasionally. Serve with salad or vegetables.

Variation Lemon can be used in place of orange.

RABBIT AND CORN CASSEROLE
Serves 4

1 rabbit (600–700 g), jointed
3 tablespoons (60 ml) oil
3 tablespoons (30 g) flour
2 onions, peeled and sliced
3 bacon rashers, chopped
1 cup (250 ml) stock

1 bay leaf
salt and pepper
4 potatoes, peeled and thinly sliced
1 x 420 g can corn kernels
1 x 415 g can tomatoes

Soak rabbit joints in salt water for 1 hour, drain. Toss in flour and fry in hot oil till golden brown. Place in greased casserole. Sauté onions and bacon and put in casserole. In a saucepan heat stock, bay leaf and seasoning; when boiling add to casserole and bake in preheated moderate oven (180°C) for 45 minutes. While casserole is cooking lightly fry potatoes. Remove casserole from oven and top with drained corn, tomatoes and potatoes. Return to oven and bake for a further 45 minutes.

RABBIT OR CHICKEN PIE
Serves 4–6

1 rabbit or chicken
1 tablespoon flour
salt and pepper

1 onion, peeled and sliced
2 cups (500 ml) stock or water

2 hard-boiled eggs

2 bacon rashers, cut into 6–8
  pieces

2 tablespoons chopped parsley

1½ quantity Shortcrust or
  Rough Puff Pastry (see p. 179)

Wash rabbit (or chicken) well and cut into neat pieces. Roll pieces in the flour mixed with the seasoning. Place in saucepan with onion and stock or water, and simmer for 1½ hours. Turn into pie dish to cool, then add sliced egg, bacon and parsley. Roll out pastry into shape of pie dish with 2.5 cm extra all around. Damp edge of pie dish, cut a narrow strip from all around the pastry and place on the wet rim. Wet this strip of pastry with pastry brush and cover with the rest of the pastry. Press edges lightly. Trim edge if necessary and mark at 3 cm intervals, drawing pastry up with knife. Make hole in the centre to allow steam to escape when baking. Glaze with milk or lightly beaten egg yolk and decorate with pastry leaves made from any leftover pastry. Glaze pastry leaves. Bake in a preheated very hot oven (220°C) for 20 minutes.

Sweet and Sour Chicken in Batter

Serves 4

500 g chicken fillets, chopped
  into bite-sized pieces

oil for deep frying

Batter

1 cup (250 g) self-raising flour

salt and pepper

1 egg

½ cup (125 ml) water

Sauce

1 x 440 g can pineapple pieces

2 teaspoons oil

1 cup (250 ml) Chinese pickles,
  sliced

1 tablespoon chopped
  fresh ginger

1 clove garlic, chopped

½ teaspoon salt

2 teaspoons brown sugar

1 tablespoon white vinegar

1 tablespoon cornflour blended
  with ¼ cup (60 ml) cold
  water

For batter, mix flour with a little salt and pepper in a bowl. Make a well in the centre and work in egg. Add water slowly, beating well. Heat oil. Dip chicken pieces in batter and deep fry till golden brown (about 5 minutes). Drain on kitchen paper towel.

For sauce, drain pineapple, retaining juice. Heat oil in pan, lightly fry pineapple, pickles, ginger and garlic. Add salt, sugar, vinegar and pineapple juice. Add cornflour paste to other ingredients, bring to the boil, stirring all the time, and boil for 2 minutes.

Hints   The sauce can be made the day before and reheated when required.

Scallops and pork can be cooked in the same way.

TASTY YOGHURT CHICKEN
Serves 4

500 g chicken fillets
1/2 cup (125 ml) non-fat
* yoghurt*
1 tablespoon lemon juice
1/2 teaspoon curry powder
1/2 teaspoon turmeric
1/4 teaspoon Tabasco sauce
1/2 teaspoon ground ginger

pepper
2 medium onions, sliced
2 teaspoons oil
1 tablespoon plain or
* wholemeal flour*
1 tablespoon desiccated coconut
1/2 cup (125 ml) chicken
* stock*

Remove skin and cut chicken into bite-size pieces. Mix yoghurt, lemon juice, curry powder, turmeric, Tabasco, ginger and pepper in a bowl, and stir in chicken. Allow to stand for some hours or overnight. Cook onions in oil in a saucepan until soft. Add flour and coconut and mix well. Add chicken mixture and stock, and bring the mixture to the boil, stirring well. Transfer contents into a casserole, cover and bake at 150°C for 1 hour.

THAI GREEN CURRY

Serves 4

1 tablespoon vegetable oil	2 chicken breasts, cut in small pieces
4 kaffir lime leaves	1 x 400 ml can coconut milk
1–2 onions, chopped	1 zucchini, sliced
2 teaspoons green curry paste	200 g small broccoli florets

Heat oil. Add lime leaves, paste, chopped onion and sauté for 2 minutes. Add chopped chicken and cook for 2–3 minutes, stirring well. Add coconut milk and simmer for 15–20 minutes. Add sliced zucchini and broccoli florets 5 minutes before serving. Serve with rice.

Hint Add a splash of fish sauce for a more complex Thai taste.

Beef

Recipes for cooking beef may be used for cooking meats such as venison, buffalo and kangaroo, all of which have a low fat content.

Important instructions for cooking meat

Baking Cook in a hot oven (200°C) for 10 minutes, then lower the temperature to 180°C.

Barbecuing Cook food slowly on a rack or metal plate over heat. A popular way for cooking sausages, hamburgers, steak, chops as well as other foods.

Boiling Wash salt meat, then place in cold water and bring slowly to the boil. Allow meat to cool in the saucepan.

Frying There are two kinds of frying. *Dry or shallow frying* is frying in a pan using very little fat, and is suitable for food which requires a considerable time to cook, such as cutlets and sausages. Bacon and egg, pancakes and omelettes are also dry fried. *Deep fat frying* requires a saucepan half full of oil and a frying basket; alternatively thermostatically controlled deep fryers are also available. Heat oil until a haze rises, plunge basket containing food to be fried right into fat and cook until golden brown. Lift out, drain on absorbent paper towel. All meat and fish to be deep fried should have a coating of flour, egg and breadcrumbs or batter.

Grilling A quick method of cooking meat by exposing it to red-hot coals or griller. Used for chops and steak.

Microwaving Is also a good method of cooking roasts and casseroles.

Pressure cooking Inexpensive cuts of meat may be made tender and delicious quickly, and smaller joints roasted or boiled. Stews take about a third of the normal time to cook.

Stewing Economical, as the cheaper parts of meat can be made tender and tasty. First fry the meat in a small amount of oil, then simmer gently in stock or other liquid.

Joints and accompaniments
Roast beef: Yorkshire pudding, horseradish sauce, Demi-Glace, baked vegetables.
Corned beef: Carrots, turnips, parsnips, potatoes, mustard sauce.

Timetable for boiling and roasting
Beef, venison: 15 minutes to each 500 g and 15 minutes over.
Boned meat: 20 minutes to each 500 g and 20 minutes over.
Corned brisket: 30 minutes to each 500 g and 30 minutes over.
Tongue: 2–3 hours, according to size.

Cooking cuts of beef
Bladebone steak: Grill, pan fry, casserole or braise.
Brisket: Usually boned and rolled. If fresh, bake or pot roast; if corned, boil.
Chuck steak: Stew or braise.
Fillet of beef: Usually expensive, roast.
Oyster blade steak: Grill or pan fry.
Roasts: Cut from ribs of beef, sirloin, topside and silverside.
Round steak: If young grill or fry, casserole or braise.
Rump steak: Grill or pan fry — good for stir fry recipes.
Scotch fillet: Grill or pan fry.
Silverside (corned): Boil.
T-bone steak: Grill or pan fry.

BEEF ARGENTINE
Serves 4

2 tablespoons (40 g) butter
500 g rump steak, cut into
   4 serves

1 medium onion, sliced
1 clove garlic, crushed
2 bacon rashers, chopped

2 medium tomatoes, peeled
  and sliced

1½ cups (125 g) mushrooms,
  sliced

1 small green capsicum, seeded
  and finely sliced

1½ cups (375 ml) stock

salt and pepper

Melt three-quarters of the butter in heavy-based pan and brown steaks well. Place meat in a casserole dish. Melt remainder of butter and add onion, garlic, bacon, tomatoes, mushrooms and capsicum. Cook for 5 minutes then add stock and cook for a little longer. Season and spoon mixture evenly over steaks. Cover with foil or lid and bake in a pre-heated moderate oven (180°C) for 35–40 minutes. Serve with a green salad and buttered noodles or hot boiled rice topped with sour cream and sprinkled with chopped chives.

Note   Cheaper cuts of meat may be used in this recipe but must be cooked longer.

BEEF AND MUSHROOM KEBABS
Serves 4

1 tablespoon oil
1 tablespoon soy sauce
1 clove garlic, crushed
2 teaspoons honey

500 g bladebone steak
1 medium onion, cut into eighths
1½ cups (125 g) mushrooms

Mix oil, soy sauce, garlic and honey together to make a marinade. Cut meat into 2.5 cm cubes and marinate for 3 hours or overnight. Thread meat, onion pieces and mushrooms alternately on skewers. Grill until steak is tender, brushing frequently with marinade. Serve with green salad.

BEEF CURRY
Serves 4–6

750 g bladebone or chuck
  steak, cut into 3 cm cubes
1 tablespoon oil
1 large onion, sliced
1 clove garlic, crushed
1 tablespoon flour

2–4 teaspoons curry powder,
  to taste
2 cups (500 ml) water
2 teaspoons powdered beef
  stock or 3–4 stock cubes
1 medium tomato, diced

1 tablespoon tomato paste
1 banana, sliced
1 large apple, diced

1 tablespoon sultanas
salt to taste
1 teaspoon soy sauce

Heat oil in heavy-based saucepan, add meat and brown. Then add onions and garlic and cook until brown. Add flour and curry powder and stir well. Add water and powdered stock, stir until boiling. Cook for 30 minutes, add remaining ingredients, cook for 30 minutes longer or until meat is tender. Serve with boiled rice.

BEEF IN BLACK BEAN SAUCE
Serves 4–6

750 g topside steak
1 tablespoon soy sauce
1 tablespoon vinegar
2 teaspoons cornflour
1 egg white
2 tablespoons (40 ml) oil
6 spring onions, chopped
1 red capsicum, chopped
1 cup (250 g) baby sweetcorn

1 cup (125 g) bean sprouts
1 cup (100 g) trimmed snow peas
1 teaspoon curry powder
1 tablespoon black beans
$1^1/4$ teaspoons sugar
salt
$1^1/4$ cups (310 ml) water
extra 1 tablespoon cornflour

Cut steak into 5 cm long thin strips (it will cut more easily if partly frozen). Combine soy sauce, vinegar, cornflour and egg white in basin. Marinate meat in this for 30 minutes. Add 1 tablespoon oil to wok or heavy-based pan and stir fry meat until brown, then remove from pan. Prepare vegetables, add rest of oil to pan and sauté all the vegetables — apart from black beans — with curry powder for 4–5 minutes. Mash black beans with fork and add sugar, salt and 1 teaspoon of water. Add with meat to pan and fry for 3 minutes. Blend 1 tablespoon cornflour with remaining water, add to pan and stir until boiling, cook for 2 minutes. Serve with boiled rice.

Note Black bean sauce may be bought and used in place of black beans, sugar, salt, water and cornflour.

Beef Pasta Casserole
Serves 6

1 kg steak, cubed
3 tablespoons (30 g) flour
salt and pepper
6 small onions
6 small potatoes
2 tablespoons (40 ml) oil
1 clove garlic, crushed

1 bay leaf
1 x 280 g can tomato paste
1 cup (250 ml) water
1 cup macaroni, or pasta of choice
1 cup (125 g) grated cheddar cheese
1 teaspoon paprika
1 teaspoon butter

Toss meat in seasoned flour. Peel vegetables and cut into uniform pieces. Heat oil in saucepan, add meat and brown well. Add garlic, bay leaf, tomato paste, water and vegetables. Cover and simmer for 1–1 1/2 hours. Place in ovenproof dish. Gradually add the macaroni to a large quantity of boiling salted water and boil for 15 minutes. Drain and place on meat mixture. Combine cheese and paprika and sprinkle on top. Dot with butter. Bake in preheated moderate oven (180°C) until cheese is golden brown.

Beef Spare Ribs Casserole
Serves 6

1 kg beef spare ribs
1 tablespoon oil
1 large onion, chopped
1 cup (150 g) chopped celery
1 clove garlic, crushed
4 cups (1 L) stock

2 teaspoons paprika
salt and pepper
3 large potatoes, peeled and
  cut in eighths
1/4 cup (50 g) rice
1 x 300 g can butter beans

Heat oil in large pan, brown spare ribs well, add chopped onion, celery and garlic, sauté until onion is soft. Place meat in lightly greased casserole. Add stock, paprika, salt and pepper to pan, bring to boil, scraping pan well. Pour stock into casserole, cover with lid or foil and bake in preheated moderate oven (180°C) for 1 hour. Add potatoes and rice to casserole and cook for a further hour, then add drained beans and heat thoroughly. If gravy is too thin, thicken slightly with a little cornflour blended with cold water.

BEEF STROGANOFF
Serves 4–6

750 g frying steak	1 tablespoon flour
2 tablespoons (40 ml) oil	1 cup (250 ml) stock
2 medium onions, chopped	1 tablespoon tomato paste
250 g mushrooms, sliced	salt and pepper
1 clove garlic, crushed	1 cup (250 ml) sour cream

Cut meat into thin strips. Heat oil and fry onions, mushrooms and garlic for 5 minutes. Add steak and brown. Add flour and cook for a minute or so. Stir in stock and tomato paste. Bring to boil, season, and cook for 30 minutes. Add sour cream and heat through.

Note Water and stock cubes may be used instead of stock.

BEEF WELLINGTON
Serves 4–6

1 kg fillet of beef	1 teaspoon mixed herbs
1/2 cup (125 g) butter	500 g Rough Puff Pastry
salt and pepper	(see p. 179)
1 small onion	1 egg yolk
1 1/2 cups (125 g) mushrooms	1 cup (250 ml) stock

Spread 30 g butter over fillet and bake in a preheated hot oven (200°C) for 20–25 minutes until meat is well browned. Remove from oven and cool completely. Chop onion finely and slice mushrooms. Sauté in pan with 30 g butter until tender. Allow to cool. Spread meat with more butter, add cooled vegetables and mixed herbs to top. Roll out pastry to 3 mm thick. Place meat and its topping in centre and wrap pastry round neatly and press edges firmly together. Place in greased baking dish, brush with beaten egg yolk and bake in a preheated very hot oven (220°C) for 12–15 minutes, then reduce heat to 200°C and bake for further 15 minutes or until pastry is golden brown. Add stock to pan juices, cook on high heat to reduce slightly. Strain. Cut wrapped fillet into thick slices and pour stock over. Serve with vegetables such as glazed carrots or broccoli.

Hints

If preferred, the meat can be cut into serving portions, browned for about 2 minutes in a frying pan and individually wrapped as above.

Fillo pastry can be used instead of puff — allow 2 sheets per portion.

CHILLI SPARE RIBS
Serves 4

2 tablespoons (40 ml) soy sauce	*1 teaspoon chopped fresh ginger*
2 tablespoons (40 ml) oil	*1/2 teaspoon chilli powder*
2 tablespoons (40 ml) mustard	*1 clove garlic, crushed*
2 tablespoons (40 ml) lemon juice	*4 large or 8 small spare ribs*

Combine the soy sauce, oil, mustard, lemon juice, ginger, chilli and garlic in a basin. Marinate ribs for at least 2 hours, turning occasionally. May be grilled, basting occasionally during cooking, or baked in a greased pan in a preheated moderate oven (180°C) for about 1 hour, turning once and brushing with marinade. Serve ribs with baked jacket potatoes, glazed carrot ring and a green vegetable.

CORNED BEEF
Serves 10–12

2 kg corned brisket or silverside	*1 tablespoon sugar*
6 peppercorns	*2 small onions*
4 cloves	*4 carrots*
2 tablespoons (40 ml) vinegar	*1–2 turnips or parsnips*

Place meat, peppercorns, cloves, vinegar and sugar in a large pan and cover with cold water. Bring to boil gradually. Cut vegetables into suitable sizes and add. Allow 30 minutes cooking time for each 500 g of meat and 30 minutes over. To serve, garnish with the vegetables and a little of the stock.

Hint   Corned lamb can be cooked in the same way.

HUNGARIAN BEEF GOULASH
Serves 4–6

750 g chuck steak
1/2 cup (125 g) flour
salt and pepper
2 tablespoons (40 ml) oil
1/4 cup (60 g) butter
2 large onions, sliced
1 tablespoon paprika

1 x 440 g can tomatoes
2 tablespoons (40 ml)
  tomato paste
1 cup (250 ml) stock
1 bay leaf
1/2 cup (125 ml) sour cream

Cut meat into cubes and toss in seasoned flour. Heat oil in saucepan, add butter then brown meat well, then add onions and paprika and brown. Add remaining ingredients except cream. Simmer for 2 hours or until meat is tender. Add sour cream and heat gently — do not boil or it will curdle. Serve with new potatoes and a green vegetable.

ORIENTAL BEEF
Serves 4

2 tablespoons (40 ml) oil
1 onion, peeled and cut in
  eighths
4 spring onions, cut into 5 cm
  pieces
2 cups broccoli florets
1 cup (150 g) celery, cut in
  julienne strips
1 cup (200 g) pineapple pieces

1 teaspoon grated fresh ginger
1 clove garlic, crushed
500 g rump steak, cut in thin
  strips
3/4 cup (160 ml) beef stock
1 tablespoon soy sauce
1–2 beef stock cubes
1/4– 1/2 teaspoon Tabasco sauce
1 tablespoon cornflour

Heat half the oil in heavy-based pan and sauté onions for 4 minutes, add broccoli, celery and pineapple and sauté a further 7 minutes, add a little water to soften vegetables if necessary. Remove vegetables and keep warm. Add rest of oil to pan and sauté ginger and garlic for a minute. Add meat, cook for 5–6 minutes. Return vegetables to pan and heat all thoroughly. Combine stock with soy sauce, stock cubes, Tabasco sauce and cornflour. Pour into pan and stir until sauce thickens and coats meat and vegetables. Serve with noodles or steamed rice.

POT ROAST

Serves 4–5

750 g boneless roast or 1 kg standing rib roast
1–2 tablespoons oil

2 cups (500 ml) stock or water
pepper

Heat a little oil in a heavy-based saucepan and brown meat on all sides. Add 1 cup stock and pepper, lower heat and let the meat cook slowly with a close-fitting lid on so that the steam doesn't escape. Turn meat occasionally, adding more stock as it evaporates. Cook for 1¼ hours.

Notes This is a very suitable way of cooking small pieces of meat.

Provided there is room in the pot, vegetables may be added.

ROAST BEEF

Serves 6

1.5 kg roast of choice (rolled sirloin, winged rib, topside, etc.)

1–2 tablespoons oil
salt and pepper

Rinse meat quickly. Put in baking dish. Place in oven pre-heated to 200°C, with lid on dish (foil may be used as a cover). Reduce heat to 190°C after 30 minutes. Cook for 1½–3 hours, according to size of roast. Season meat during cooking. Serve with baked vegetables such as onions, potatoes, pumpkin (placed around meat 1 hour before meat is cooked and turned after 20 minutes), a green vegetable, Yorkshire Pudding, Demi–Glace (see p. 50) and horseradish sauce.

YORKSHIRE PUDDING

1 cup (250 g) flour
2 eggs
1/2 cup (125 ml) milk

1/2 cup (125 ml) water
1 tablespoon oil

Sift flour into basin. Beat eggs and add to flour. Add water and milk a little at a time, beating well with an electric mixer or by hand. Allow mixture to stand for 30 minutes. Heat oil in an ovenproof dish, pour in mixture and bake in a preheated hot oven (200°C) for 20 minutes or until centre is set and top browned. Cut into squares to serve.

SAUSAGE AND BEAN BAKE
Serves 4

500 g sausages
2 tablespoons (40 ml) oil
1 cup (125 g) bacon pieces
2 medium onions, sliced
1 green capsicum, deseeded and
  cut in strips
1 clove garlic, crushed
1 x 780 g can three bean mix

2 tablespoons brown sugar
salt and pepper
1/4 teaspoon ground cloves
1 x 440 g can tomatoes
3 tablespoons (60 ml) tomato
  paste
2 cups (500 ml) stock
1 tablespoon chopped parsley

Boil sausages 5–6 minutes to remove excess fat, cut into chunks. Heat oil, add bacon pieces, onions, green capsicum and garlic. Sauté until vegetables are soft. Place in large casserole. Drain beans, add to casserole with sugar, salt, pepper and ground cloves. Add tomatoes, tomato paste, stock and sausages. Cover and cook in preheated moderate oven (180°C) for 1 hour. Sprinkle parsley on top and serve with vegetables of choice.

Notes This is a suitable recipe for using leftover barbecue sausages.

It may be cooked in the microwave oven on MEDIUM for 15–20 minutes.

SEASONED STEAK

750 g round steak   *1 packet French onion soup*

Cut steak in serving pieces, place on pieces of foil, sprinkle with soup mix. Dot with butter, seal securely. Place on tray, cook in preheated hot oven (200°C) for 45 minutes–1 hour (depending on thickness of meat).

Variations   Sliced tomato, onion rings, mushrooms, sliced capsicums or celery may be added to the foil parcels.

STEAK DIANE
Serves 4

4 slices fillet or rump steak,   *pepper*
*   about 2.5 cm thick*   *2 teaspoons chopped parsley*
butter   *1 tablespoon Worcester sauce*

Beat steak with rolling pin. Heat a thick frying pan, drop in a nut of butter, and while foaming put in the steaks. Cook quickly on both sides, keeping steak flat. Put on to a hot dish, sprinkle lightly with pepper. Reheat frying pan and drop in 1 tablespoon butter. While foaming add chopped parsley and Worcester sauce. Pour over steaks, serve at once.

STEAK AND KIDNEY PIE
Serves 4

500 g round or blade steak   *1 onion (optional), sliced*
2 sheep's kidneys   *1 cup (250 ml) stock or water*
flour   *250 g Flaky Pastry (see*
salt and pepper   *   p. 178), or Rough Puff*
1 tablespoon oil   *   (see p. 179)*

Chop steak and kidneys. Dip into flour seasoned with salt and pepper. Heat oil in pan and sauté meat until slightly brown. Add onion and water or stock. Simmer 45 minutes. Cool and pour into pie dish. Cover with pastry cut to shape and make one or two small holes on top. Brush with milk or egg, flute edges and decorate with leftover pastry made into leaves. Bake in a preheated very hot oven (220°C) for 20 minutes, then reduce heat to 180°C for 15–20 minutes.

Note Steak and Kidney Pudding can be made by using the same filling with 500 g Suet Pastry (see p. 180). Grease a basin and line it with three-quarters of the pastry, add cold filling, moisten edges of pastry and place pastry lid on top, seal edges. Cover with foil, put in saucepan of boiling water (halfway up basin) and steam 2½–3 hours. Add more boiling water if necessary during cooking. Serve with tomato sauce.

STEAK PROVENÇALE
Serves 4

4 spring onions, chopped
1 eggplant, sliced and cut in
  2 cm strips
2 small zucchini, sliced
1 small red capsicum

1 medium green capsicum
4 Scotch fillets
3 tablespoons (60 g) butter
1 tomato, peeled and chopped

Prepare vegetables. Deseed and slice the capsicums thinly. Grill the steak until done as required. While meat is cooking melt butter in a large pan, sauté spring onions, eggplant and zucchini until golden brown, add peppers and tomato and cook for 4 minutes. Serve steaks topped with the vegetable sauce.

Lamb

Recipes for lamb may be used for cooking goat meat (chevon), which has a low fat content.

Joints and accompaniments

Roast mutton: Baked vegetables, Demi-Glace and red currant jelly.

Boiled lamb: Carrots, turnips, capers, onions or parsley sauce.

Roast lamb: Baked vegetables, Mint Sauce or jelly, Demi-Glace.

Timetable for boiling and roasting

Lamb or chevon on the bone: 15 minutes to each 500 g and 15 minutes over.

Boned meat: 20 minutes to each 500 g and 20 minutes over.

Cooking cuts of lamb

Chump chops: Barbecue, grill or pan fry.

Crown roast (rib ends of loin of lamb formed into shape of a crown):   Seasoning placed in centre and baked.

Cutlets (chops with bones trimmed):   Grill, pan fry or coat with egg and breadcrumbs and fry.

Forequarters: Boned and rolled, seasoned and baked or stewed.

Leg chops or steaks (cut from leg):   Grill or fry.

Leg of lamb: Roast; may be boned, stuffed and baked; corned and boiled.

Loin chops: Grill or fry.

Neck chops: Stew.

Rack of lamb: Bake and season with rosemary or herbs of choice.

Shanks: Bake, braise, boil (serve in white sauce).

Apricot and Lamb Casserole
Serves 4–6

1 kg forequarter of lamb, cubed
2 tablespoons (40 ml) oil
2 large onions, sliced
2 cups sliced carrots
1 cup dried apricots or 2 cups
  stewed or canned apricots

2 cups (500 ml) stock
1 tablespoon flour
1 bay leaf
salt and pepper
1 tablespoon chopped mint

Marinade

2 tablespoons (60 g) honey
juice of 1 lemon

1 tablespoon soy sauce
1 clove garlic, crushed

Mix ingredients for marinade, add cubed meat and marinate for 3–4 hours or overnight. Heat 1 tablespoon oil and sauté onions for a few minutes, add carrots and sauté for a few more minutes. Remove from pan, drain meat, heat remaining oil and brown the meat. Place meat in lightly greased casserole. Add onions, carrots and apricots. Blend flour with a little stock, add rest of stock, bay leaf and seasoning and pour over casserole. Cook for 1–1¼ hours in preheated moderate oven (180°C). Remove bay leaf, stir in chopped mint and serve with vegetables of choice.

Baked Savoury Lamb
Serves 4–6

3 meaty breasts of lamb
1½ tablespoons butter
1 large onion, chopped
2 teaspoons curry powder
2 tablespoons (30 g) brown
  sugar

1 apple, chopped
½ cup (90 g) chopped dried
  apricots
1 cup (90 g) chopped celery
1½ cups (375 ml) stock
salt to taste

Trim fat from breasts of lamb. Cut between bones (2 bones per serve) into pieces. Discard ends, which may be used to make stock. Place pieces in a baking dish and bake for 30 minutes in a preheated hot oven (200°C), turning occasionally. While meat is cooking, melt butter in deep pan and sauté onion until soft. Add curry powder, sugar, apple, apricots, celery and stock. Stir until boiling, cover and simmer for 30 minutes. Drain fat from meat, and reduce heat to 180°C. Blend fruit and vegetable sauce in food processor and pour over meat in baking dish. Season with salt. Cover with lid or foil and bake for 45 minutes. Remove lid and cook for further 10 minutes to glaze top. Serve with hot boiled rice or noodles and a green salad.

BOILED LEG OF LAMB WITH CAPER SAUCE
Serves 4–6

1 leg of lamb	1 white turnip, cut into 6–8 pieces
water	4–6 small onions
1 tablespoon vinegar	salt to taste
4 peppercorns	1 quantity Caper Sauce (see p. 50)
2 carrots, cut into 6–8 pieces	

Trim meat. Bring enough water to cover lamb, vinegar and peppercorns to the boil in a large pot. Immerse meat in boiling water, return to boil, cover with lid and reduce heat. Simmer for 2$^{1}/_{2}$–3 hours. Prepare vegetables, cut into suitable pieces and add with salt 30 minutes before serving. Lift meat and vegetables on to a serving dish and serve with Caper Sauce, mashed potatoes and the boiled vegetables plus a green vegetable.

Note Onion or Parsley Sauce may be served instead of Caper Sauce.

🐦 🐦 🐦
Colonial Goose

Ingredients — Leg of mutton, 1 onion, 2 oz butter, 1 egg, 1 lb breadcrumbs, 3 sage leaves, pepper and salt to taste.

Mode — Remove the bone of the leg of mutton. Mince the onion very finely. Mix with breadcrumbs, sage, pepper, salt and butter, bind with the egg, well beaten up. Bake for 1$^{1}/_{2}$ to 2 hours, according to the size of joint.

🐦 🐦 🐦

BONED LEG OF LAMB

Serves 4–6

1 leg of lamb, boned

STUFFING

2 bacon rashers, chopped
1/3 cup (20 g) fresh breadcrumbs
2 shallots, chopped
1 teaspoon chopped parsley
1/2 teaspoon mixed herbs

1/4 teaspoon grated nutmeg
2 tablespoons (40 ml) oil
salt and pepper
1 egg, beaten
milk

For stuffing, mix all dry ingredients together, seasoning with salt and pepper. Moisten with the egg and sufficient milk to bind the whole together. Press the mixture into lamb's cavity and secure the opening. Bake in a preheated oven at 190°C for 2¼–2½ hours. When ready, serve with Brown Sauce (see p. 49) or good gravy and vegetables.

BRAISED CHOPS

Serves 4

500 g forequarter chops
1 tablespoon oil
1 medium onion, cut in rings
1 tablespoon flour
1½ cups (375 ml) stock

salt and pepper to taste
2 stalks celery, diced
1 carrot, diced
1 white turnip, diced

Trim chops, heat oil to very hot in frying pan and fry meat until brown on both sides. Remove meat and fry onion, add flour then, stirring continually, add the stock and heat until the mixture boils and thickens. Add seasoning, return meat to saucepan, and cook gently for 1 hour. Add vegetables and cook 30 minutes longer.

Note The thick outer skin of turnips needs to be removed before dicing.

BRAISED LAMB SHANKS
Serves 4

4 lamb shanks
1 clove garlic
1 tablespoon flour
2 tablespoons (40 ml) oil
1 cup (250 ml) stock
1 bay leaf
salt and pepper

4 carrots, sliced
2 onions, chopped
1 cup (150 g) diced celery
2 tomatoes, peeled and chopped
1 tablespoon chopped fresh mint
1 cup (150 g) frozen peas

Prepare shanks by inserting slivers of garlic into each with a sharp knife, dusting with flour and browning in hot oil in heavy-based pan. Add stock, bay leaf and seasoning to pan. Bring to the boil then lower heat and simmer until shanks are tender — approximately 1¹/₂ hours. Add the carrots, onions and celery to the pan 30 minutes before serving. Add the tomatoes, mint and peas 15 minutes before the cooking is finished. Adjust seasoning if necessary. Serve with steamed new potatoes.

CROWN ROAST OF LAMB
Serves 4–5

1 loin of lamb (12–14 chops),
    jointed by butcher and
    shaped into crown
1 clove garlic, crushed
1 tablespoon oil
juice and rind of 1 lemon
2 cups (120 g) fresh
    breadcrumbs

1 medium onion, finely chopped
¹/₂ cup chopped dried apricots
1 teaspoon mixed herbs or oregano
1 tablespoon chopped parsley
salt and pepper
1 egg, beaten
oil for baking

Trim crown roast if necessary. Mix crushed garlic, oil and 1 tablespoon lemon juice and brush inside and outside of roast with this. Let roast stand for at least 1 hour. Mix together breadcrumbs, onion, apricots, remaining lemon juice and rind, herbs, seasoning and bind it with the beaten egg. Melt oil in pan, place roast in centre of pan and pack stuffing loosely in its centre. Bake in a preheated moderate oven

(180°C); joints under 1.5 kg will take about 1¹/₂ hours, joints over 1.5 kg 2¹/₂–3 hours, but test towards end of time to see if meat is tender. Lift meat on to serving platter and place cutlet frills on bones. Serve with Demi-Glace (see p. 50), baked vegetables, green vegetable and mint jelly or Mint Sauce.

CRUMBED LAMB, VEAL OR MUTTON CUTLETS
Serves 4

4 cutlets (about 500 g)	1 egg, beaten
1 tablespoon flour	breadcrumbs
¹/₂ teaspoon salt	2–3 tablespoons (40–60 ml) oil
¹/₄ teaspoon pepper	

Trim cutlets, mix flour, salt and pepper together and cover each cutlet. Brush with beaten egg and then cover with breadcrumbs. Heat oil in pan and fry cutlets for 5–7 minutes on each side. Drain on kitchen paper towel. Serve with mashed potatoes, vegetables of choice and brown or tomato sauce.

DEVILLED LAMB CUTLETS
Serves 4

2 teaspoons brown sugar	3 tablespoons (90 g) mango
1 teaspoon dry mustard	or fruit chutney
1 teaspoon curry powder	1 tablespoon oil
2 teaspoons soy sauce	8 lean cutlets or lamb chops
1 teaspoon cornflour	(about 500 g)

Combine all ingredients except cutlets. Brush each side of cutlets with mixture and let stand for 1 hour. Set grill at a moderate heat and grill one side for 8–10 minutes. Brush with mixture during cooking. Turn cutlets and grill until cooked, brushing with remainder of mixture. Serve with baked jacket potatoes, vegetables of choice or tossed salad.

JARRED CHOPS
Serves 6

12 small chops (about 1 kg)
2 tablespoons (20 g) flour
1 tablespoon brown sugar
$^1/_4$ teaspoon pepper
$^1/_2$ teaspoon salt

3 tablespoons (60 ml) tomato sauce
2 tablespoons (40 ml) Worcester sauce
1 tablespoon vinegar
1 cup (250 ml) water

Remove superfluous fat from chops, roll in flour, season with sugar, pepper and salt, and place in casserole. Mix all liquid ingredients together well and pour over chops. Place in pre-heated moderate oven (180°C), and cook about $1^3/_4$ hours.

LAMB AND BACON CASSEROLE
Serves 6

2 cups (250 g) bacon pieces
6 large barbecue lamb chops
   (about 500 g)
1 large onion, sliced
$1^1/_2$ tablespoons flour
2 cups (500 ml) chicken stock

2 teaspoons Worcester sauce
1 tablespoon tomato chutney
salt and pepper
1 cup (150 g) chopped celery
$^1/_2$ cup chopped green capsicum
2 tablespoons chopped parsley

Fry bacon in heavy-based pan, remove with slotted spoon. Fry chops until lightly browned on both sides and remove. Sauté onion until lightly browned, add flour, stir well and cook for 1 minute then add stock, stirring well until boiling. Add sauce, chutney and seasoning to taste. Place bacon, lamb, celery and capsicum in casserole, pour sauce over and bake for 2 hours in moderate oven (180°C). Stir parsley in just before serving. Serve with mashed potatoes, rice or pasta.

LAMB CHOPS WITH PLUM SAUCE
Serves 4

$^1/_2$ cup (125 ml) Plum Sauce
   (see p. 286) (if too thick dilute
   with lemon or orange juice)
1 clove garlic, crushed
1 teaspoon ground cumin

3 cups (250 g) sliced
   mushrooms
1 tablespoon butter or oil
4 forequarter or barbecue
   chops

Mix plum sauce, fruit juice if necessary, garlic and cumin and heat in small saucepan. Brush chops with marinade and let stand for 2 hours. Sauté mushrooms in butter or oil until cooked. Barbecue or sauté chops, basting frequently with sauce. Serve with mushrooms, green salad and garlic bread.

Note   Plum jam diluted with orange juice may be used instead of sauce.

LAMB MOGULAI
Serves 4

500 g cubed lamb
2 tablespoons (40 g) ghee or oil
1 x 350 g can Curry Sauce
2 tablespoons (40 ml) natural
   yoghurt

2 tablespoons (25 g) ground
   almonds
fresh coriander leaves

Fry meat in ghee or oil until golden brown, add the sauce and allow to simmer until meat is tender, adding a little water if necessary. Stir in yoghurt and almonds just before serving and scatter some coriander leaves on top. Serve with rice and vegetables of choice.

LEMON CURRIED CHOPS
Serves 4

8 lamb loin chops (about 675 g)
$^1/_3$ cup (80 ml) lemon juice
3 teaspoons curry powder
1 teaspoon salt

$^1/_4$ teaspoon sugar
4 tablespoons (80 ml) oil
4 medium potatoes, peeled
2 medium onions, sliced

Remove excess fat from chops. Mix together the lemon juice, curry powder, salt and sugar. Brush mixture over chops, stand 2 hours. Peel potatoes, cook whole in boiling salted water for 7 minutes, drain and cut into slices. Peel onions, slice thinly. Heat oil in large frying pan, fry drained chops until brown and tender; 5 minutes before chops are cooked, add sliced potatoes and onion rings to one side of pan and fry until golden. Serve with pan juices.

Mallee Lamb Casserole

Serves 6

2 tablespoons (40 ml) oil
1 kg boned forequarter lamb, cubed
1 small onion, diced
1 clove garlic, crushed
3/4 cup (135 g) dried apricots
1/2 cup (90 g) sultanas
1/2 cup (75 g) chopped celery

1/2 teaspoon dried rosemary
2 tablespoons flour
2 cups (500 ml) water
1 packet chicken noodle soup
salt and pepper
chopped parsley

Heat oil and brown meat, place in casserole. Add onion and garlic to pan and cook until soft, add to casserole, then add apricots, sultanas, celery and rosemary. Add flour to pan, brown well and add water and soup. Stir well, scraping pieces off pan and bring to the boil. Add to casserole. Cook for 1¹/2 hours in preheated moderate oven (180°C). Adjust seasoning and sprinkle with parsley.

Rack of Lamb

Serves 4–6

2 large racks of lamb
  (about 1 kg)
1 tablespoon French mustard
1 tablespoon soy sauce
1 tablespoon chopped fresh
  rosemary
1 clove garlic, crushed

1 tablespoon lemon juice
1 tablespoon apricot or plum
  jam
1 cup (250 ml) stock
salt and freshly ground black
  pepper

Score fat side of meat with a sharp knife in a criss–cross pattern. Combine mustard, soy sauce, rosemary, garlic, lemon juice and jam and baste lamb on all sides, reserving any leftover marinade. Let stand for at least 1 hour. Mix stock with remaining marinade. Place lamb on a rack in a baking dish and pour stock into dish. Bake uncovered in a preheated moderate oven (180°C) for 30 minutes, basting frequently with liquid in pan. Cover loosely with foil and cook 30 minutes longer, continuing to baste well. Lift meat to serving plate and allow to stand for a few minutes covered with foil. Slice thickly. Reduce liquid by boiling rapidly, adjust seasoning and pour over meat. Serve with minted new potatoes, glazed carrots, broccoli and mint jelly.

SATAY LAMB
Serves 4

1 tablespoon oil
500 g cubed lamb
1 clove garlic, crushed
1 teaspoon grated fresh ginger

6 spring onions, cut into
  2.5 cm pieces
4 tablespoons (120 g)
  commercial satay sauce
1 tablespoon soy sauce

Heat oil in a heavy-based large pan or wok. Add lamb, garlic and ginger and stir fry until meat is browned and nearly cooked. Add spring onions to pan and stir fry for 3–4 minutes. Add satay and soy sauces and toss over heat for 2 minutes. Serve with boiled rice or noodles and green salad or coleslaw.

SHASHLIK WITH RICE PILAF
Serves 4–6

1 kg cubed lamb
6 small onions
250 g small mushrooms

1 green capsicum
3 tomatoes, quartered

MARINADE

1 clove garlic, crushed
1/4 cup (80 ml) oil
2 tablespoons (40 ml) vinegar
  or lemon juice

1 small onion, finely chopped
salt and pepper

Combine ingredients for marinade, add lamb, mix well and refrigerate overnight. Thread meat on skewers and brush with marinade. Prepare vegetables: peel and halve onions, wipe mushrooms and remove stems; cut capsicum in half, remove seeds and cut into 2.5 cm strips. Thread vegetables alternately on skewers, brush with marinade. Grill skewers, turning frequently and brushing with marinade, until cooked. Serve with Rice Pilaf (see opposite).

Rice Pilaf

1 tablespoon oil
4 spring onions, chopped
2 cups (400 g) long-grain rice
4 cups (1 L) chicken stock

$^1/_2$ cup (90 g) frozen peas
1 tablespoon melted butter
$^1/_2$ cup (90 g) sultanas
$^1/_4$ cup (30 g) peanuts

Heat oil in saucepan, add spring onions and sauté until soft. Add rice and stir well for a few minutes. Add boiling chicken stock and cover tightly. Cook until liquid is absorbed and rice tender. Stir in peas until hot. Turn rice into heated dish, separate grains with fork and stir in melted butter, sultanas and peanuts.

Spanish Chops
Serves 4

2 teaspoons oil
4 chump chops (about 500 g)
1 large onion, sliced
2 stalks celery,
  cut in 2.5 cm pieces
1 green capsicum, seeded and
  sliced

150 g mushrooms, sliced
3 medium tomatoes, peeled
  and sliced
$^1/_2$ teaspoon dried basil
$^1/_2$ teaspoon dried oregano
1 tablespoon chopped parsley
salt and pepper to taste

Heat oil in large heavy-based pan. Add chops and cook on medium heat for 5 minutes per side. Remove chops. Reduce heat and cook onion, celery and capsicum gently until soft. Add mushrooms, tomatoes, herbs and seasoning and cook until vegetables are soft. Add chops and heat through. Serve with boiled rice or noodles.

Spiced Lamb Chops
Serves 4

8 loin chops (about 675 g)
2 teaspoons oil

500 g fresh stir fry vegetables or
  1 x 500 g packet frozen
  stir fry vegetables

MARINADE

2 tablespoons (40 ml) soy sauce	1 clove garlic, crushed
1 tablespoon honey	1/2 teaspoon ground ginger
1 tablespoon vinegar	1 teaspoon oregano

Mix together soy sauce, honey, vinegar, garlic, ginger and oregano and brush chops with mixture. Let stand for 1 hour. Heat griller. Grill chops, basting with sauce, 5 minutes on each side or until cooked as desired. While meat is grilling, heat oil in wok and stir fry vegetables for 3–4 minutes, add any remaining basting mixture to vegetables and heat through. Serve with chops.

TASTY CUTLET PARCELS
Serves 4–6

8 lamb cutlets	125 g mushrooms, chopped
salt and pepper	1 cup frozen or fresh cooked spinach
2 teaspoons butter	4 sheets puff pastry
1 onion, finely diced	2 tablespoons chutney
1 carrot, grated	1 egg, beaten
2 stalks celery, diced	

Preheat griller to high and preheat oven to 220°C. Season cutlets and grill on both sides but do not cook through. Set aside. Melt butter, sauté all vegetables until soft and allow to cool. Cut pastry sheets in half. Place a little of vegetable mixture in centre of each piece. Lay a cutlet on top, add some chutney to each cutlet, divide rest of vegetable mixture between parcels, then fold pastry over enclosing cutlet but leaving bone exposed. Seal edges and brush with beaten egg. Bake on lightly greased tray in hot oven (200°C) for 20 minutes, until pastry is golden brown. Serve with salad of choice. Tomato sauce may be served also.

Veal

If veal is unobtainable, yearling beef may be substituted in these recipes.

Joints and accompaniments

Roast veal: Boiled ham or bacon, Demi-Glace, sliced lemon, stuffing, baked vegetables.

Timetable for boiling and roasting

Veal: 25 minutes to each 500 g and 25 minutes over.

Cooking cuts of veal

Cutlets: Grill or pan fry.
Loin chops: Grill or fry.
Leg of veal: Roast.
Forequarter of veal: Bake.
Veal steaks: Used for schnitzels, veal Parmigiana.
Veal shanks: Osso buco (shanks cut in suitable pieces).

Fillet of Roast Veal
Serves 4–6

*1.5 kg fillet of veal
  (boned by butcher)
1 quantity Stuffing for Veal
  and Poultry (see p. 68)*

*oil for baking
1–2 lemons, cut into wedges*

Wipe and trim joint if necessary. Fill cavity with stuffing. Close cavity with skewers and tie in shape with string. Add oil to pan. Cover joint loosely with foil and bake in pre-heated moderate oven (180°C) for 2 hours, basting frequently. Serve with baked vegetables and a green vegetable, Demi-Glace (see p. 50), bacon or ham rolls and garnish with lemon wedges.

Osso Buco
Serves 4

4 veal shanks, sawn into
    thick slices
2 tablespoons flour
salt and pepper
1 tablespoon butter
1 tablespoon oil
1 clove garlic, crushed
1 large onion, finely chopped
3 medium tomatoes, peeled
    and diced

1½ cups (375 ml) stock
2 tablespoons (60 g) tomato
    paste
1 teaspoon oregano
1 teaspoon dried basil
few drops Tabasco sauce
1 teaspoon grated lemon rind
1 teaspoon chopped parsley

Coat meat with flour seasoned with salt and pepper. Heat butter and oil in heavy-based saucepan. Brown meat well then add garlic, onion, tomatoes, stock, tomato paste and herbs. Place lid on saucepan and simmer for 1½ hours. Add a few drops of Tabasco sauce and adjust seasoning. Place osso buco in serving dish and sprinkle with grated lemon rind and chopped parsley. Serve with mashed potato and vegetables of choice.

Schnitzels with Cream Sauce
Serves 4

4 x 100 g veal steaks
1 tablespoon flour
salt and pepper
3 tablespoons (60 g) butter
2 tablespoons (40 ml) oil

1 small onion, sliced
180 g mushrooms, sliced
½ cup (125 ml) chicken stock
½ cup (125 ml) cream

Pound steaks until thin then dip in seasoned flour. Heat butter and oil in frying pan, add steaks and sauté until golden brown, then reduce heat and cook until tender. Remove veal and set aside, keeping warm. Add a little extra butter to pan and sauté onion until soft, then add mushrooms and cook for 3–4 minutes. Add any remaining flour and stir until smooth. Cook for 1 minute then add stock and cream and stir until boiling. Adjust seasoning, spoon over steaks. Serve with vegetables of choice.

Veal and Ham Rolls

Serves 4

4 veal steaks (about 400 g)
4 thin slices ham
2 teaspoons dried sage
1 tablespoon oil

^{3}/4 cup (190 ml) chicken stock
1 tablespoon tomato paste
1 teaspoon Worcester sauce
salt to taste

Garnish

chopped parsley

Pound steak until thin. Place a slice of ham on each steak, sprinkle with ^{1}/2 teaspoon sage. Roll steaks up and fasten with small skewers. Heat oil in pan. Sauté rolls until brown on all sides. Combine stock, tomato paste and sauce and pour over rolls. Simmer, covered, for 1–1^1/2 hours, until meat is tender. Remove meat and keep hot. Boil pan juices on high until reduced, spoon over rolls. Garnish with chopped parsley. Serve with mashed potatoes and vegetables or salad of choice.

Veal Cordon Bleu

Serves 4

4 slices Gruyere or cheddar
  cheese
4 slices ham (half the size of veal)
4 large veal steaks (about 400 g)
1^1/2 tablespoons flour

salt and pepper
1 egg, beaten
^{1}/3 cup (35 g) dried
  breadcrumbs
3 tablespoons (60 g) butter

Cut cheese to same size as the ham. Put a piece each of ham and cheese on one half of each piece of veal, fold veal pieces over to make neat sandwiches. Dip in seasoned flour, then in beaten egg and roll in breadcrumbs. Fry steadily in butter on both sides until veal is crisp and golden. Lower heat and cook gently to make sure the ham and cheese are hot.

Veal or Beef Olives
Serves 4

750 g fillet of veal or
  bladebone steak
8 thin bacon rashers
1 quantity Stuffing for Veal
  and Poultry (see p. 68)

2 cups Brown Sauce (see p. 49)
1 tablespoon butter
salt and pepper

Cut thin slices of veal. Place a slice of bacon on each piece of veal, spread on a thin layer of stuffing, roll up tightly and fasten securely. Melt butter in pan, put in the veal olives, and fry till lightly browned. Pour away butter, heat Brown Sauce and add. Cover closely and simmer for $1^{3}/4$–2 hours.

Variation For beef olives omit the bacon.

Veal Parmigiana
Serves 8

1 kg veal
2 tablespoons flour
salt and pepper
1 egg, beaten
$1/2$ cup (50 g) dried
  breadcrumbs

1 tablespoon grated Parmesan
  cheese
oil
250 g mozzarella cheese, sliced
1 x 800 g can tomatoes
oregano

Cut veal into thin slices, roll in seasoned flour. Dip in beaten egg and coat with breadcrumbs and Parmesan cheese. Fry veal in a little oil until golden brown. Slice mozzarella cheese. Place layers of veal, tomato and cheese in ovenproof dish, finishing with a topping of oregano. Bake in preheated moderate oven (180°C) for 1 hour.

WIENER SCHNITZEL

Serves 6

6 thinly cut veal steaks
(about 750 g)
2 tablespoons flour
salt and pepper
1 beaten egg

$1/2$ cup (30 g) fresh
breadcrumbs
oil for frying
2 tablespoons (40 g) butter

GARNISH

lemon slices

capers

Flatten veal steaks with rolling pin or meat mallet until very thin. Cut each in half or leave whole. Chill. When cold dip each first into seasoned flour, then into beaten egg and finally into breadcrumbs. Press with heel of hand to firm the coating on. Place on a flat tray and chill again for at least 30 minutes.

Heat sufficient oil to cover base of heavy frying pan. Add butter and when hot add veal. Cook until golden brown, turning during cooking. Serve hot with slices of lemon and a few capers as garnish. Schnitzels may be served with tomato-flavoured gravy.

HAM AND PORK

JOINTS AND ACCOMPANIMENTS

Roast pork: Sage and Onion Stuffing (see p. 67, baked vegetables, Apple Sauce (see p. 48), Demi-Glace (see p. 50).

TIMETABLE FOR BOILING AND ROASTING

Pork: 25 minutes to each 500 g and 25 minutes over.

Ham or pickled pork: 25 minutes to each 500 g and 25 minutes over.

COOKING CUTS OF PORK

Fillet (thick end of leg): Roast.

Forequarter: Roast.

Leg chops: Grill or pan fry.

Loin chops: Grill or fry.

Leg of pork: Roast.

Pork fillet (cut from inside of loin — use for special pork dishes): Roast.

Pork steaks: Grill, fry or stir fry.

ᏯᏗ HAM ᏯᏗ

BAKED HAM

1 ham   *water*

3 cups flour

GLAZE

1/2 cup (75 g) brown sugar   *1 teaspoon mixed spice*

1 cup (250 ml) pineapple juice

Make a flour and water pastry. Wrap ham in it and bake at 190°C, allowing 15–20 minutes for each 500 g. When cooked strip off pastry and skin will come off also. Combine glaze ingredients and spread over ham after skin has been removed. Return to oven for 30 minutes, basting every 10 minutes.

BOILED HAM

5 kg ham
2 turnips
3 onions

1 head celery
1 tablespoon mixed herbs
1 cup (100 g) dried breadcrumbs

Put ham into large saucepan with sufficient water to cover and gradually bring to the boil. Add washed and peeled vegetables and herbs and simmer until ham is tender — a 5 kg ham needs about 4½ hours. Let it remain in water until nearly cold. Take out of saucepan, strip off skin and rub breadcrumbs over it.

HAM STEAKS AND CIDERED PEACHES
Serves 4

1 tablespoon butter
4 ham steaks
2 tablespoons brown sugar
¼ teaspoon cinnamon

1 x 825 g can peach halves,
    drained and syrup reserved
4 tablespoons (80 ml) cider
    vinegar

Heat butter in pan. Fry ham steaks on both sides until brown. Sprinkle with sugar and cinnamon. Spoon over 4 tablespoons of the peach syrup and the vinegar. Add peach halves, cut side downwards. Cover and simmer for 10 minutes.

Note   Ham steaks may be glazed before cooking with a mixture of 1 teaspoon prepared mustard and 2 tablespoons honey (60 g) or 1 teaspoon prepared mustard and 2 tablespoons (60 g) marmalade mixed together.

Ham Steaks with Apples

1 ham steak

1 teaspoon oil

1 apple

1 tablespoon butter

2 teaspoons brown sugar

Snip edges of ham steaks to prevent curling. Heat oil in heavy-based frying pan. Sauté ham on each side for 4–5 minutes. Remove steaks and keep warm. Cut each apple (cored but not peeled) into quarters. Melt butter in pan, add apples and sauté until golden. Turn, sprinkle with a little brown sugar and cook until soft. Serve on top of steaks, accompanied by green or tossed salad.

Variations

Ham steaks may also be served with spiced Apple Sauce (add ½ teaspoon mixed spice to recipe on p. 48) or Mushroom Sauce (see p. 52).

Ham Steaks and Pineapple: Allow 1 slice pineapple (fresh or canned) per person.

Ham Steaks with Spiced Pears: Allow 2 pieces of Spiced Pear per serve.

Spiced Pears

8 pear pieces, stewed or canned

½ cup (125 ml) pear syrup

½ cup (60 ml) white vinegar

6 whole allspice

2 cloves

½ cinnamon stick

Place pears, syrup, vinegar and spices in a saucepan, bring to boil and simmer for 5 minutes. Pour into a serving dish and cover. Leave overnight. Serve with steaks, and vegetables of choice or salad.

✌ PORK ✌

BAKED PORK CHOPS OR MEDALLIONS OF PORK
Serves 4

1 x 425 g can crushed pineapple
4 medium potatoes
1 tablespoon brown sugar
salt
ground black pepper
4 pork chops (about 700 g) or
   medallions of pork
4 lean bacon rashers

Lightly grease baking dish, place pineapple in bottom, lay thinly sliced potatoes on top of pineapple. Sprinkle with brown sugar, salt and pepper. Place chops (with rind removed and fat trimmed) or medallions on top. Season with pepper. Arrange rindless lean bacon on top. Cover with lid or foil, bake in preheated moderate oven (180°C) for 1 hour. Remove lid and bake another 10–15 minutes to brown. Serve with Barbecue Sauce and vegetables of choice.

CRUMBED PORK SCHNITZELS
Serves 4

4 pork leg schnitzels
   (about 600 g)
2 tablespoons flour
salt and pepper
1 egg, beaten
1 cup (100 g) dried breadcrumbs
oil for frying

Trim meat if necessary, coat in seasoned flour, dip in beaten egg and press breadcrumbs on firmly. Use a fairly deep frying pan or electric frypan, add oil to approximately 0.5 cm depth and heat. Add schnitzels and fry at least 20 minutes until golden brown, turning occasionally. Serve with French fried potatoes and vegetables of choice or tossed salad.

Note For special occasions serve with Spiced Peach Slices or Spiced Mango Slices.

SPICED PEACH SLICES

1 x 440 g can peach slices   2 teaspoons brown sugar
stick of cinnamon

Put peaches and their juice in saucepan with cinnamon and sugar. Boil gently for 5 minutes and then remove cinnamon stick. Serve hot with schnitzels.

SPICED MANGO SLICES

1 x 425 g can mango slices   1 tablespoon tomato sauce
1/2 cup mango syrup   1 tablespoon fruit chutney
1 teaspoon powdered chicken stock

Drain mango slices, reserving syrup. Combine 1/2 cup mango syrup, powdered chicken stock, tomato sauce and fruit chutney. Bring to the boil then add mango slices and simmer for 2–3 minutes.

LOIN OF PORK
Serves 4–6

2 kg loin of pork   3 apples
2 tablespoons (40 ml) oil   6 small onions
6 medium potatoes   1 quantity Demi-Glace
    (see p. 50)

Score pork skin in narrow lines and brush with oil. Bake in preheated moderately hot oven (190°C) for 40 minutes. Quarter and peel potatoes, apples and onions and add to the meat. Cook gently for 1¹/4 −1¹/2 hours longer. When ready, arrange vegetables and apples on hot dish, place the meat in centre, and serve gravy separately.

PORK, APPLE AND SAUERKRAUT
Serves 4

500 g shoulder of pork   3 medium potatoes, peeled and
2 tablespoons (40 ml) oil   sliced
1 small onion, diced   1¹/2 cups (375 ml) apple juice
1 x 410 g can sauerkraut   2 teaspoons brown sugar
2 apples, cored and cut in chunks   salt and pepper

Cut meat into cubes. Heat oil in pan and brown meat. Place meat in casserole. Cook onion in pan until soft, then add sauerkraut, apples, potatoes, apple juice, sugar and seasoning. Add to casserole, cover with lid or foil and bake in preheated moderate oven (180°C) for 2 hours.

PORK CHOPS
Serves 4

1 tablespoon oil	2 tablespoons flour
4 pork chops (about 500 g)	6 sage leaves
1/2 apple, diced	1 1/2 cups (375 ml) water
1 medium onion, chopped finely	pepper and salt

Heat oil in frying pan. Fry chops brown on both sides and set aside. Fry apple and onion together till brown. Sprinkle the flour over vegetables, stir, add chopped sage and water. Stir until it boils. Season to taste. Return chops to gravy and simmer for 20 minutes.

PORK SPARE RIBS WITH PLUM SAUCE
Serves 4–6

750 g pork spare ribs

MARINADE

1 medium onion, chopped	1 clove garlic, crushed
2 tablespoons (40 ml) soy sauce	1 teaspoon five-spice powder
2 tablespoons (60 g) honey	2 tablespoons (40 ml) oil
2 tablespoons (40 ml) lemon juice	pinch of black pepper

PLUM SAUCE

1 tablespoon oil	1/2 cup (125 ml) stock
1 small clove garlic, crushed	2 teaspoons soy sauce
1 small onion, chopped	few drops Tabasco sauce
1 teaspoon grated fresh ginger	1 tablespoon cornflour blended
1 cup (250 ml) plum sauce	with a little cold water

Remove rind and excess fat from ribs. Mix ingredients for marinade together. Place ribs in marinade and leave for at least 3 hours.

To make sauce: heat oil in saucepan and sauté garlic, onion and ginger gently until soft. Add plum sauce, stock, soy sauce and a few drops of Tabasco. Mix well with marinade, add blended cornflour and simmer for 5 minutes.

Put spare ribs in a lightly greased pan in a preheated moderate oven (180°C) and cook for 20–25 minutes, brushing well with plum sauce from time to time and turning ribs once. Serve ribs with saffron rice and vegetables or salad of choice.

PORK STEAKS WITH LEMON SAUCE
Serves 4

rind of *1/2 lemon*
juice of 1 lemon
1 clove garlic, crushed
1/2 teaspoon ground cumin
4 pork leg steaks

salt and black pepper
1 tablespoon oil
1 cup (250 ml) chicken stock
1/2 cup (125 ml) condensed
   cream of chicken soup

GARNISH
parsley sprigs

Mix lemon rind and half the juice, garlic and cumin together. Spread on both sides of the steaks, season with black pepper and salt, let stand for 1 hour at least. Lightly oil and heat a heavy-based pan, add meat and lightly brown on each side. Add rest of juice and half the stock. Simmer gently without a lid for 20 minutes. Remove pork and keep warm on serving platter. Add rest of stock and chicken soup to pan. Let boil for a few minutes to reduce. Adjust seasoning then pour around steaks. Serve with mashed potatoes, broccoli, glazed carrots and garnished with parsley sprigs.

PORK STEAKS WITH ORANGE SAUCE

Serves 4

1 tablespoon oil
4 midloin butterfly steaks (about 500 g)
2 teaspoons brown sugar
2 teaspoons vinegar
1 large orange, rind cut in thin strips and juiced
water
1¹/2 cups (375 ml) chicken stock
1 tablespoon cornflour blended with a little cold water
freshly ground black pepper

Smear heavy-based frying pan with oil, add steaks, cook until golden brown on each side. Remove meat from pan and keep warm. Add sugar and vinegar to pan and cook until sugar browns (do not burn). Place strips of orange rind in a small saucepan, cover with water and boil for 1 minute, then drain. Add stock, orange juice and rind to frying pan and cook until sauce has reduced a little, scraping pan during cooking to get all the meat juices. Add blended cornflour, stir until sauce boils and thickens. Add pepper if desired. Pour sauce over steaks. Serve with vegetables of choice or salad.

ROAST BELLY OF PORK WITH SAGE AND APPLE STUFFING

Serves 4–6

1 kg belly pork, in one piece

STUFFING

1 large onion, finely chopped
1 tablespoon butter
1 cooking apple, grated
1¹/2 cups (90 g) fresh breadcrumbs
1 egg, beaten
1 teaspoon dried sage
2 teaspoons grated lemon rind
salt and pepper

Bone meat and remove excess fat. Chop onion finely and sauté in butter until soft. Add all stuffing ingredients and mix well. Cut a pocket through the centre of pork. Fill cavity with stuffing, fasten opening with skewers. Rub skin of pork with a little salt, place in lightly greased dish with skin side up. Bake in a preheated hot oven (200°C) for 30 minutes, then reduce heat to moderate (180°C) and cook for 1 hour or until tender. Serve with Demi-Glace (see p. 50), Apple Sauce (see p. 48), baked vegetables and a green vegetable.

ROAST LEG OF PORK AND CRACKLING
Serves 6

2 kg leg of pork
Sage and Onion Stuffing
  (see p. 67)

1 cup (250 ml) water
salt

Bone leg and remove rind for crackling (butcher will do this). Fill cavity with stuffing. Place on rack in baking dish, add water to baking dish and bake in a preheated moderate oven (180°C) for 3–4 hours. If necessary add water to pan during cooking. An oven bag may be used for rindless roast. Rub rind with salt and bake in a preheated very hot oven (220°C) until blistered and crisp for crackling. Serve with Demi-Glace (see p. 50), Apple Sauce (see p. 48), baked vegetables and a green vegetable.

ROAST PORK LOIN WITH MINTED FRUITY STUFFING
Serves 4–6

1.5 kg pork loin, boned and rolled
(boned shoulder pork may be used)

STUFFING

1 small onion, finely chopped
1 tablespoon oil
1½ cups (90 g) fresh
  breadcrumbs
2 apples, finely chopped
½ cup (90 g) dried apricots,
  chopped

grated rind and juice of 1 orange
1 tablespoon chopped mint
½ teaspoon ground ginger
salt to taste
1 egg, beaten

Sauté onion in oil until soft. Add remainder of ingredients for stuffing and mix well. Unroll pork loin and ensure that

119

rind is well scored. Place stuffing down centre of loin, re-roll and tie or skewer into shape. Rub rind with salt, place on rack in roasting pan and roast in a preheated very hot oven (220°C) for 30 minutes. Reduce heat to 180°C and bake for a further 1¹/₂ hours or until juices are clear when meat is tested with a skewer. A little water may be added to pan during cooking. Gravy should be made in pan in order to use all the pan juices. Serve with Demi-Glace (see p. 50), baked vegetables and a green vegetable. Apple Sauce (see p. 48) may be served if desired.

STUFFED BUTTERFLY PORK STEAKS
Serves 4

2 tablespoons (40 g) butter	¹/₂ cup (30 g) fresh breadcrumbs
4 spring onions, finely chopped	4 butterfly steaks (about 500 g)
125 g mushrooms, finely chopped	2 tablespoons seasoned flour
2 teaspoons chopped parsley	1 tablespoon oil
salt and pepper	1 cup (250 ml) chicken stock

Melt 1 tablespoon butter in saucepan and sauté spring onions until soft. Add mushrooms and parsley, season with salt and pepper. Cook for a few minutes, add breadcrumbs, mix well then let cool. Place quarter of the mushroom mixture on each steak, fold over and fasten with small skewers. Roll pork in seasoned flour. Heat remaining butter and oil in a saucepan, add steaks and brown well on each side. Add stock, cover and simmer for 20–25 minutes. Serve with gravy made from pan juices and vegetables of choice.

Minced Meat

Basic Mince
Serves 4

2 cups (500 g) minced steak
1 large onion, chopped

salt and pepper
1/2 tablespoon flour

Heat heavy-based saucepan, add mince, onion and salt and pepper. Stir until steam rises, place lid on pan and simmer for 30 minutes. Take off heat, add any flavouring desired and flour. Stir and boil for 1–2 minutes.

Note Sliced vegetables can be added before simmering. Cooked pasta or rice can be added at the end, to make a satisfying meal.

Aberdeen Sausage
Serves 6

2 cups (500 g) minced steak
6 bacon rashers, finely chopped
2 cups (120 g) fresh breadcrumbs
1 egg, beaten

salt and pepper
1 teaspoon Worcester sauce
1/2 cup (50 g) dried
   breadcrumbs

Mix all ingredients well except for dried breadcrumbs. Make into a roll like a sausage and roll up in aluminium foil. Steam for 2 hours. Allow to cool and roll in dried breadcrumbs.

Note If preferred, the 'sausage' may be placed in a floured pudding cloth and boiled for 2 hours.

Baked Hawaiian Burgers
Serves 6

2 cups (500 g) minced steak
1 medium onion, peeled and
   grated or processed

2 medium potatoes, peeled and
   grated or processed
2 tablespoons flour

1 teaspoon dried oregano
  or mixed herbs
salt and pepper

1 egg, beaten
extra flour

TOPPING

1 medium onion, sliced
1 green capsicum, deseeded
  and sliced

1 x 200 g can sliced pineapple
2 tablespoons (40 ml) tomato
  sauce

Mix meat, onion, potatoes, flour, herbs and seasoning
together. Add egg and mix well. Wet hands and shape into 6
patties, coat in flour and place in greased baking dish. Place
sliced onion on each patty, then green capsicum and top
with pineapple slice. Mix 1/2 cup (125 ml) pineapple juice
with tomato sauce. Pour some over each patty and baste
occasionally with sauce while baking for 40–45 minutes in
preheated moderate oven (180°C). Serve with creamed
potatoes, carrot straws and peas.

CHOW MEIN
Serves 4

2 cups (500 g) minced steak
2 tablespoons (40 ml) oil
1 small onion, chopped
1/2 medium green cabbage,
  chopped

2 tablespoons (30 g) rice
2 teaspoons curry powder
2 packets chicken noodle soup
250 g French beans, sliced
21/2 cups (625 ml) water

Lightly brown mince in hot oil in saucepan. Add all other
ingredients. Cook for 20 minutes.

CHEESY BEEF PIE
Serves 4–6

2 cups (500 g) minced steak
1 tablespoon tomato paste
2 tablespoons (60 g) chutney
1 small onion, grated
1 clove garlic, crushed

1 teaspoon dried oregano
1/2 cup (50 g) dried breadcrumbs
1 egg, beaten
salt and pepper

1 tablespoon butter or oil

1 clove garlic, crushed

1 small zucchini, thinly sliced

125 g mushrooms, finely sliced

185 g cream cheese

2 eggs

salt and pepper to taste

2 tablespoons grated Parmesan
cheese

Combine mince, tomato paste, chutney, onion, garlic, oregano, breadcrumbs, egg and seasoning. Press firmly into a well-greased 23 cm pie plate, hollowing out the centre a little. Bake in preheated hot oven (200°C) for 10 minutes, remove from oven.

Heat butter in pan, add garlic, zucchini and mushrooms. Sauté for 3–4 minutes, stirring well. Beat cream cheese until smooth, beat in eggs, then add vegetables, season to taste. Spoon mixture over beef, smooth top and sprinkle with cheese. Bake in preheated moderate oven (180°C) for about 30–35 minutes, until set. Serve hot with gravy or tomato sauce and vegetables of choice or cold with salads.

CHILLI CON CARNE
Serves 4

2 onions, chopped

2 tablespoons (40 ml) oil

2 cups (500 g) minced steak

1 cup (150 g) diced celery

1 x 780 can red kidney beans

1 x 415 g can tomato soup

2 teaspoons brown sugar

salt

1/2 teaspoon chilli powder

Sauté onion in oil until clear, add meat and celery and sauté until meat changes colour, add remaining ingredients, simmer for 30 minutes. Serve with boiled rice or buttered noodles.

HAMBURGERS
Serves 6–8

4 cups (1 kg) minced steak

2 cups (500 g) sausage mince

1 teaspoon nutmeg

1 teaspoon allspice

1/2 teaspoon powdered cloves

salt and pepper

Mix meats together. Add spices, salt and pepper. Use large ice-cream scoop to shape hamburgers. Place on hot plate or in frying pan and press flat. Cook 5 minutes either side.

KOFTE
Serves 4

2 slices white bread, crumbled
2 cups (500 g) minced steak
1/2 teaspoon salt
1/4 teaspoon pepper

3 tablespoons (60 ml) oil
1/2 teaspoon garlic salt
21/2 cups (625 ml) tomato
purée

Mix bread, mince, salt and pepper. Form into small balls and brown in hot oil. Place in shallow dish. Add garlic salt to purée and pour over meatballs. Cover. Bake for 15 minutes in a preheated moderate oven (180°C).

LASAGNE
Serves 4–6

1 tablespoon oil
1 onion, chopped
2 cups (500 g) minced steak
1 clove garlic, crushed
125 g mushrooms, sliced
salt and pepper
1/2 cup (125 ml) stock

1 x 440 g can tomatoes
2 tablespoons (60 g) tomato paste
11/2 tablespoons (30 g) butter
3 tablespoons (30 g) flour
11/2 cups (375 ml) milk
11/2 cups (190 g) grated tasty cheese
200 g instant lasagna sheets

Heat oil, brown onion and meat lightly, add garlic, mushrooms, seasoning, stock, tomatoes and tomato paste. Bring to boil and simmer for 15 minutes. Make cheese sauce by melting butter, adding flour then gradually stirring in milk until sauce is smooth and cooked then finally add 1 cup cheese. Grease a deep baking dish. Put a third of lasagne sheets on the bottom, then a third of meat mixture and a third of cheese sauce. Continue with layers ending with cheese sauce. Sprinkle remainder of grated cheese on top. Bake in a moderate oven (180°C) for 30 minutes.

LASAGNE VERDI AL FORNO
Serves 4

¹/3 packet (175 g) green pasta
1 cup (250 g) minced steak
1 small onion, chopped
¹/4 cup grated carrot
1 stalk celery, diced
1 tablespoon olive oil
¹/2 teaspoon salt
¹/4 teaspoon pepper

1 teaspoon flour
2 tablespoons (60 g) tomato paste
2 quantities Basic White Sauce
   (see p. 48)
1 cup (125 g) grated Parmesan
   cheese
butter

Bring a large pan of salted water to the boil and cook pasta for about 12 minutes, until tender, then drain. Sauté meat and vegetables in oil until brown and season. Blend flour and water into tomato paste and add to meat. Cook over low heat until sauce thickens. Make a double quantity of Basic White Sauce. Grease shallow baking dish and line it with a layer of pasta. Cover with meat sauce, spreading it thinly. Moisten generously with white sauce. Cover with cheese. Continue layering until all is used, finishing with sauce and cheese. Dot with butter. Bake 10 minutes in an oven preheated to moderate heat (180°C) and then increase heat to 200°C for 35 minutes.

LIMA BEAN HOT POT
Serves 4

3 cups (600 g) lima beans,
   soaked overnight
¹/2 cup (60 g) bacon pieces
1 onion, chopped
1 green capsicum, deseeded
   and chopped
1 cup (150 g) chopped celery

2 cups (500 g) minced steak
1 x 420 g can corn kernels
100 g mushrooms, sliced
2–3 tomatoes, chopped
pinch of chilli powder
salt

Drain beans, put in pan, cover with water and cook for 20 minutes, then drain. Fry bacon until crisp. Add onion, capsicum and celery and cook till tender. Add meat, stir until lightly browned. Add beans and remaining ingredients.

Transfer to a greased casserole, cover and bake in a preheated moderate oven (180°C) for 1–1½ hours.

MEAT LOAF
Serves 8

2 cups (500 g) minced steak
2 cups (500 g) sausage mince
½ cup bacon pieces or
   2 bacon rashers, diced
½ cup (50 g) dried breadcrumbs
1 large onion, chopped

2 teaspoons salt
pepper to taste
1 teaspoon Worcester sauce
1 tablespoon tomato sauce
2 tablespoons (40 ml) water
1 tablespoon chopped parsley

Mix all ingredients well together and form into a loaf shape. Wrap in aluminium foil or put in greased loaf tin and bake in preheated moderate oven (180°C) for 1–1½ hours.

Note This mixture may also be made into hamburgers or used for stuffing marrows (after removing seeds).

MEXICAN HOT POT
Serves 4–6

1 tablespoon oil
2 cups (500 g) minced steak
1 onion, diced
1 clove garlic, crushed
2 teaspoons paprika

½ cup (125 ml) tomato paste
2 tablespoons (60 g) chutney
1 x 440 g can baked beans
1 x 440 g can tomato vegetable
   soup

Heat oil, brown meat, onion and garlic. Add remaining ingredients. Stir until boiling, reduce heat and simmer for 35 minutes.

Note Half cup each cooked diced carrot and peas may be added.

Mezzotti
Serves 4–6

2 cups (500 g) minced steak
2 onions, sliced
1 tablespoon oil
1 green capsicum, deseeded
 and cut in strips
2 cups (300 g) diced celery

1 cup (100 g) diced carrot
2 beef stock cubes
1 x 425 g can mushrooms
1 x 415 g can tomato soup
250 g shell pasta

Garnish
chopped parsley

Brown meat and onions in hot oil, add capsicum, celery, carrot and beef cubes, sauté few more minutes then add mushrooms and tomato soup. Bring to the boil and simmer for 45 minutes. Cook pasta in boiling salted water, drain and add to meat just before serving. Sprinkle with parsley.

Hints
1 teaspoon stock powder concentrate may be used instead of 2 stock cubes.
Quantities may be doubled.
This recipe freezes well.

Mince Italiana
Serves 4

1 large onion, sliced
1 clove garlic, crushed
2 tablespoons (40 ml) oil
2 cups (500 g) minced steak
2 teaspoons Worcester sauce
1 teaspoon dry mustard
1 teaspoon curry powder

1/2 teaspoon mixed spice
pinch of nutmeg
salt and pepper
200 g spaghetti
2–3 tablespoons grated
 Parmesan cheese

Sauté onion and garlic in oil. Add meat and lightly brown then add rest of ingredients except spaghetti and cheese. Cook spaghetti in boiling salted water until just tender. Strain and mix into meat. Place in a casserole, sprinkle top with grated cheese and brown in oven.

MOUSSAKA
Serves 4

2 tablespoons (40 ml) oil
2 cups (500 g) minced steak
   or lamb
2 large onions, chopped
6 medium tomatoes, peeled
   and chopped

salt and pepper
1 small eggplant, sliced thickly
1/4 cup (60 ml) extra oil
2 eggs, separated
1 quantity Cheese Sauce
   (see p. 48)

Heat oil in a saucepan and fry meat until brown. Add onions, tomatoes, salt and pepper. Mix well and simmer for 10–15 minutes. Sauté eggplant in extra oil until tender. Place alternate layers of eggplant and meat mixture in a greased ovenproof casserole. Beat egg yolks. Make cheese sauce, remove it from heat and add beaten egg yolks. Whisk egg whites until stiff and gently fold into sauce. Pour cheese sauce over casserole and bake in a preheated moderate oven (180°C) for 30–40 minutes. Serve with a tossed green salad.

PORCUPINE MEAT BALLS
Serves 4–6

3 cups (750 g) minced steak
1/2 cup (120 g) uncooked rice
1 large onion, chopped
1 teaspoon mixed herbs
1 teaspoon salt

1/4 teaspoon pepper
1/4 cup (60 ml) milk
1 x 415 g can tomato soup
1 cup (250 ml) water

Mix meat, rice, onion, herbs, seasoning and milk together. Shape into small balls, brown in a little oil. Heat tomato soup and water to the boiling point, drop balls into liquid, cover and simmer gently for 30 minutes.

RISSOLES
Serves 4

2 cups (500 g) cooked meat,
   minced
1/2 teaspoon mixed herbs

2 tablespoons fresh breadcrumbs
1 tablespoon chopped parsley
1 egg, beaten

¹/₂ cup (125 ml) stock   *pepper and salt*
2 cups (300 g) flour   *oil for frying*

COATING

2 tablespoons flour seasoned   *1 egg, beaten*
with salt and pepper   *1 cup (60 g) fresh breadcrumbs*

Mix all ingredients apart from oil and those for Coating in a bowl. Shape into 8–12 balls the size of a small apple. Coat with seasoned flour then with egg and breadcrumbs, pressing crumbs on well. Shallow fry for 20 minutes, turning until golden brown all over. Drain on kitchen paper towel, serve with Demi-Glace (p. 50) and vegetables of your choice.

SHEPHERDS PIE
Serves 4

2 cups (500 g) minced   *2 tablespoons (40 ml) tomato*
   cooked meat   *sauce*
1 small onion, grated   *¹/₂ cup (125 ml) water*
salt and pepper   *2 cups (500 g) mashed potato*
¹/₂ teaspoon mixed herbs

GARNISH
parsley sprigs

Combine meat, onion, seasoning, herbs, tomato sauce and water. Place in pie dish, and spread potato on top. Bake in a preheated oven at 180°C for 20 minutes, until golden brown on top. Garnish with parsley.

SILVER PORK PATTIES
Serves 4

2 cups (500 g) minced pork   *1 tablespoon flour*
1 onion, grated   *salt and pepper*
1 apple, peeled and grated   *1 egg, beaten*
1 teaspoon dried sage   *flour seasoned with salt*
                                          and pepper

Mix meat, onion, apple, sage, flour and seasoning with egg. Shape into patties and coat with seasoned flour. Fry in a little oil in pan over a moderate heat until golden brown on both sides and cooked through. Serve with mashed potatoes, Apple Sauce (p. 48) and vegetables of choice.

SPAGHETTI BOLOGNAISE
Serves 4

1 tablespoon oil	salt and pepper
1 onion, chopped	1 teaspoon oregano
1 clove garlic, crushed	1 cup (250 ml) water
2 cups (500 g) minced steak	250 g spaghetti
1 x 440 g can tomatoes	4 tablespoons (40 g) grated
	tasty cheese

Heat oil in saucepan, add onion, garlic and meat and stir until lightly browned. Add tomatoes, seasoning, oregano and water and simmer for 30 minutes. Cook spaghetti in boiling salted water for 12 minutes or until tender. Drain spaghetti and serve immediately with meat sauce. Sprinkle grated cheese on top of each serve.

Hint   2 tablespoons tomato paste and 1–2 (200 g) fresh tomatoes may be used instead of canned tomatoes.

SWEET AND SOUR MEATBALLS
Serves 4–5

2 cups (500 g) minced steak	1–2 tablespoons oil
1/2 cup (50 g) dried breadcrumbs	1 cup (150 g) chopped celery
1 onion, chopped	1 carrot, cut in straws
1 tablespoon chopped parsley	1 cup sliced green beans or peas
2 teaspoons stock powder	1 cup (200 g) pineapple pieces
1 egg, beaten	

SAUCE

3 tablespoons (60 ml) vinegar	1 teaspoon salt
3 tablespoons (60 g) brown sugar	2 teaspoons cornflour
2 tablespoons (40 ml) soy sauce	8 tablespoons (160 ml)
	pineapple juice

Mix meat, crumbs, onion, parsley and stock powder together, add egg and mix well. Form into balls the size of a walnut. Brown well in hot oil, add vegetables and pineapple and sauté for a few minutes. Make sauce: put vinegar, sugar, soy sauce, pineapple juice and salt in a pan, blend cornflour with a little cold water and mix in, then bring to the boil and stir until sauce thickens. Put meatballs in a casserole, pour sauce over and cook in a preheated moderate oven (180°C) for 50–60 minutes, stirring occasionally. Serve with boiled rice.

SWEET CORN BAKE
Serves 4–5

2 cups (500 g) minced meat	*1 x 415 g can tomato soup*
2 large onions, chopped	*1 x 420 g can sweet corn kernels*
1 tablespoon oil	*250 g cooked noodles*

Brown meat and onions in oil in saucepan. Transfer contents to a 3 litre casserole. Add corn, tomato soup and noodles. Cook, covered, in a preheated moderate oven (180°C) for 30 minutes.

Variation Sliced or grated mozzarella cheese can be put on top before baking if desired.

TINI CARLOW
Serves 2–3

1 cup (180 g) boiled rice	*1 small onion, diced*
1 cup (250 g) minced meat	*2 tablespoons (40 ml) milk*
1 tablespoon grated cheese	*2 eggs, beaten*
pinch of thyme	*salt and cayenne pepper*
1/2 tablespoon chopped parsley	*1/2 cup (50 g) dried breadcrumbs*

Grease a pie dish and sprinkle with a third of the breadcrumbs, setting aside rest of crumbs. Mix remaining ingredients together and fill pie dish, then sprinkle top with reserved breadcrumbs. Bake for 30 minutes in a preheated moderate oven (180°C). Turn out on to a hot dish and serve with Demi-Glace (see p. 50). If preferred, the mixture may be put in ramekins and baked for 15–20 minutes.

Variety Meats

Variety meats, or offal, are the internal organs of animals used for food — brains (lamb), liver (lamb or calf), kidney (lamb, calf, ox, pig), heart (sheep or ox) and tongue (lamb or ox). They are less expensive than other meats but are very nutritious, easily digestible and make a welcome change.

Cooking variety meats
Brains (lamb): Pan fry or steam.
Kidneys (lamb, calf, ox and pig): Pan fry.
Lamb's fry or **calf's liver**: Pan fry.
Oxtail: Stew or as flavouring for soup.
Sweetbreads (lamb, calf): Fry or stew.
Tripe (ox): Fry or boil.
Tongues (ox and lamb): Boil.

Baked Lamb or Ox Heart

1 lamb heart per serve or 500 g ox heart (usually sold whole)

Stuffing
1 cup (60 g) fresh breadcrumbs　*salt and pepper*
1 onion, finely chopped　*1 egg, beaten*
1 teaspoon mixed herbs

Wash heart(s) well and soak for 30 minutes in cold, salted water. Rinse well and dry. Fill with stuffing and bake in preheated moderate oven (180°C) until tender. Serve with Demi-Glace (see p. 50), baked vegetables and a green vegetable.

Note Lamb hearts may be sliced and fried. See recipe for Liver and Bacon (opposite).

BOILED TONGUE

1 ox tongue or 4 sheep tongues   3 cloves

Wash tongue(s) well, and put in saucepan with cloves. Cover with water. Bring to boil and simmer until tender, about 2–3 hours for ox tongue, a little less for lamb. Remove skins. Serve hot with Parsley Sauce (see p. 49). If served cold, press into a mould. Cover with plate with heavy weight on top.

BRAINS AND BACON
For each serve

1 set lamb's brains (about 85 g)   dried breadcrumbs
flour seasoned with salt and pepper   oil
1 egg, beaten   1 bacon rasher

GARNISH
parsley

Soak brains in salted water for 10 minutes. Place in saucepan with fresh water and a little salt, bring to boil then strain. Remove skin and blood vessels, coat with seasoned flour, dip in egg and roll in breadcrumbs, coating well. Heat a little oil in a pan and gently fry brains until golden brown on each side (7–10 minutes). Serve with grilled bacon, garnish with parsley sprig.

Variation Sweetbreads can be used instead of brains; allow 100 g per serve.

LIVER AND BACON
Serves 4

1 lamb's fry (about 500 g)   3 tablespoons (60 ml) oil
2 tablespoons flour seasoned   1 1/2 cups (375 ml) stock
*   with salt and pepper   4 bacon rashers*

GARNISH
1 tablespoon chopped parsley

Wash liver, remove skin if necessary and slice into thin pieces. Coat in seasoned flour then fry in hot oil for 5–6 minutes each side. Lift liver on to a hot plate and keep warm. Pour away most of the oil, add remaining flour and stir until brown. Then add stock and stir until it thickens. Grill bacon. Serve liver with gravy and bacon. Garnish with parsley.

LIVER AND BACON CASSEROLE
Serves 4

375 g calf or lamb's liver
2 tablespoons flour seasoned
  with salt and pepper
1 tablespoon oil or butter
2 onions, sliced

4 tomatoes, peeled and sliced
1 carrot, cut in rings
1 stalk celery, sliced
3/4 cup (125 g) bacon pieces
1 cup (250 ml) stock

GARNISH
2 teaspoons chopped parsley

Wash, skin and slice liver, roll in seasoned flour and brown in hot oil. Remove from pan then sauté onion until clear. Arrange liver, vegetables and bacon in casserole. Add stock. Cook in a preheated moderate oven (180°C) for 1–1¼ hours. Garnish with parsley.

SCALLOPED BRAINS
Serves 6

6 sets lamb's brains (500 g)
1 large onion
3 sage leaves
3 cups (750 ml) White Sauce
  (see p. 48)

juice of 1 small lemon
salt and pepper
breadcrumbs
butter

GARNISH
parsley

Wash brains well and place in saucepan with onion and sage. Cover with cold water and add salt. Bring to boil, cook for 10 minutes. Strain, remove skin and blood vessels, dice and add to white sauce. Add lemon juice and adjust seasoning. Grease a shallow casserole, sprinkle with breadcrumbs, add brain mixture and cover with breadcrumbs. Dot with butter and brown in a preheated moderate oven (180°C) for about 10–15 minutes. Garnish with parsley.

TRIPE AND ONIONS
Serves 4

500 g tripe	*1 teaspoon butter*
1 large onion, sliced	*pinch of cayenne pepper*
1 teaspoon salt	*1 1/2 tablespoons cornflour*
1 1/2 cups (375 ml) milk	*1 tablespoon chopped parsley*

Blanch tripe by covering with cold water in saucepan, bring to boil. Pour off water then add fresh water, onion and salt. Cook until tender (about 1 1/2 hours). Strain off water, cut tripe into 2 cm pieces. Put tripe in a saucepan with milk, butter and cayenne, bring to boil, add cornflour blended with a little cold milk, stir until it thickens and cook for 2 minutes. Add parsley. Serve on hot plates with triangles of toast.

🐑 🐑 🐑
Sheep's Head Hash

Mode — Cut the meat neatly from the bones. Take a cupful of the stock or soup it has been boiled in, and a small cup of milk, 1/4 teaspoon Worcester sauce, 1 oz (or 1 dessertspoonful) butter, 1 dessertspoonful flour. Blend and mix thoroughly the stock with the other ingredients. Set all over the fire, and stir and leave for 10 minutes till the sauce is the thickness of cream, and then add the hashed meat, and simmer for 1/4 of an hour. Serve hot with sippets of toast.

🐑 🐑 🐑

STIR FRY RECIPES

Stir fry recipes are becoming more and more popular in Australia for various reasons. Provided the ingredients are available they are simple and straightforward to make.

COOKING STIR FRIES

It is possible to make stir fries in frying pans but a wok is even better because it is made of thin iron so can be heated quickly to a high temperature. Woks are also available in copper, stainless steel and non-stick materials but the cheaper iron wok works more efficiently than an expensive stainless steel one.

The coating film of a new iron wok should be removed before use by filling the wok with water, adding 2 tablespoons bicarbonate of soda and boiling for 15 minutes to soften it and then using a scouring pad to remove it. Then season the wok by drying it well, placing over a gentle heat and wipe over with a wad of kitchen paper towel dipped in vegetable oil. Repeat with more paper and oil until paper remains clean. Allow wok to cool. It is now ready to use.

After use, soak the wok in water and rub gently with a mop or cloth using detergent and hot water. DO NOT use an abrasive. Make sure the wok is absolutely dry to prevent rusting. Do not worry if your wok turns black.

Note Follow makers' instructions for care of types of woks other than iron.

Long wooden chopsticks can be used for cooking stir fries, and are very good for separating noodles. A good way to test if the oil is hot enough for cooking is to see if bubbles appear when you put the ends of wooden chopsticks upright in the oil. A slotted curved spatula also works well. Only use wooden or plastic utensils on non-stick woks to avoid scratching the surface.

HINTS ON STIR FRIES

- Vegetables are cut into small pieces so can be cooked quickly and therefore they retain their flavour and nutrients better — they should be 'crisp' tender.
- Frozen vegetables may be used but will not be as crisp as the fresh ones.
- 500 g meat or fish will provide 6–7 serves.
- Both meat and fish should be in bite-size pieces.
- Meat is cut in strips across the grain.
- If trying to cut down on fat use an oil spray (in some recipes meat can be dry-fried). Otherwise use an oil with a high smoking point such as canola or peanut.
- For the diet-conscious it is now possible to buy salt-reduced soy sauce.

STIR FRIED VEGETABLES

A variety of vegetables may be used. After peeling, vegetables are thinly sliced and cut into strips or coarsely grated. Broccoli and cauliflower are cut into small pieces or florets and stems sliced diagonally. Vegetables such as asparagus, spring onions and snake beans are cut into small lengths. Heat a small amount of oil in a wok and stir fry lightly and quickly for 2 minutes until 'crisp' tender.

BEEF WITH OYSTER SAUCE

Serves 4

1 1/2 teaspoons cornflour
1/2 cup (125 ml) beef stock
2 tablespoons (40 ml) oyster sauce
1 clove garlic, crushed
1 teaspoon sugar
1 tablespoon peanut oil

350 g rump steak, thinly sliced
250 g French beans, topped, tailed and sliced
1 small red capsicum, deseeded and finely sliced
1 cup (120 g) bean sprouts

Blend cornflour in a little cold stock. Mix with the rest of the stock, oyster sauce, garlic and sugar. Heat the wok well. Add oil and stir fry the beef in batches over high heat for

2 minutes or until it browns. Add beans and capsicum and stir fry for a further minute. Add the cornflour mixture to the wok and cook until mixture thickens and boils for a minute. Stir in the bean sprouts and serve immediately.

CASHEW-NOODLE STIR FRY
Serves 4

250 g dried egg noodles
2 tablespoons (40 ml)
  vegetable oil
2/3 cup (100 g) cashew nuts
3 cm piece fresh ginger, peeled
  and grated

1 bunch baby bok choy
  (about 750 g), shredded
3 tablespoons (60 ml)
  oyster sauce
2–3 teaspoons lemon juice

Cover noodles with boiling water, stand for 5 minutes, drain and set aside. Heat 1 tablespoon oil in wok or large frying pan, stir fry nuts until golden brown. Remove from pan and set aside. Add rest of oil, grated ginger and bok choy. Stir fry over high heat for 2 minutes. Stir in noodles and oyster sauce until hot. Season with lemon juice. Sprinkle toasted nuts on top.

CHICKEN AND NOODLE STIR FRY
Serves 4

500 g Hokkien noodles
2 skinless chicken breast fillets
  (about 250 g), cut in thin strips
2 teaspoons cornflour
1 tablespoon soy sauce
1 teaspoon sugar

2 tablespoons (40 ml)
  vegetable oil
2 cloves garlic, crushed
4 shallots, chopped
1 tablespoon oyster sauce
2 cups (250 g) mung bean
  sprouts

GARNISH
1/2 red capsicum, thinly sliced

Separate noodles, place them in a bowl and cover with boiling water. Drain. Prepare chicken, blend cornflour with soy sauce in a bowl, add sugar and 2 teaspoons oil. Stir in chicken and marinate for 10 minutes. Heat remaining oil in a wok, add garlic, stirring till golden. Add shallots and chicken, stir fry for 2 minutes. Add noodles, any remaining marinade and oyster sauce, and stir fry for 4–5 minutes. Add bean sprouts and stir fry till heated. Scatter capsicum slices on top.

CHILLI CHICKEN STIR FRY
Serves 6

4 spring onions, sliced
1 clove garlic, crushed
4 chicken breast fillets (about 500 g), sliced finely
1/4 cup (60 ml) sweet chilli sauce
1/4 cup (60 ml) tomato paste

2 1/2 cups (250 g) trimmed snow peas
1 zucchini, sliced into matchstick-size pieces
2 red capsicums, sliced into matchstick-size pieces
500 g cooked pasta or noodles

Heat a wok over a high heat and stir fry onions, garlic and chicken for 3–4 minutes until chicken is browned. Add sauce, paste and vegetables and stir fry for 2–3 minutes more; vegetables should still be crisp and chicken cooked through. Serve over hot pasta or noodles, or add to wok and stir through.

DUCK AND ORANGE STIR FRY
Serves 4

1 Chinese barbecued duck (about 2 kg)
1 tablespoon oil
1 onion, sliced finely
2 cloves garlic, crushed
2 teaspoons grated fresh ginger
1 tablespoon grated orange rind

2/3 cup (165 ml) orange juice
1/4 cup (60 ml) chicken stock
2 teaspoons soft brown sugar
2 teaspoons cornflour
1 bunch baby bok choy (about 750 g), leaves separated
1 orange, segmented

Cut duck into bite-sized pieces. Reserve and thinly slice some crispy skin for garnish. Heat the wok well, add oil and stir fry onion for 3 minutes. Stir in garlic and ginger for 1–2 minutes. Add rind, juice, stock and sugar and bring to the boil. Blend cornflour with a little cold water. Add to the wok, stir until mixture boils and thickens. Add duck pieces to wok and simmer for 2 minutes. Remove contents from wok and keep warm. Place bok choy in the wok with 2 tablespoons water. Cover and steam until leaves are just wilted. Arrange bok choy on serving dish, spoon duck on top and garnish with orange segments and crispy duck skin.

FRIED NOODLES
Serves 4

1/2 onion, cut in wedges
1 clove garlic, crushed
1 x 420 g can champignons, sliced
1 small carrot, cut in strips
1/2 bunch bok choy, chopped
2 spring onions, chopped
1/2 bunch coriander

250 g chicken fillet
2 tablespoons (20 g) cornflour
1 tablespoon sesame oil
1 cup (250 ml) cooking oil
1 x 225 g packet Chinese Crispy Noodles
1/2 x 420 g can baby corn, drained
salt

Prepare onion, garlic, champignons, carrot, bok choy, spring onions; chop most of the coriander but reserve some leaves. Cut chicken into 2 cm strips. Mix 1 tablespoon cornflour and sesame oil with chicken. Heat some cooking oil in a frying pan and when hot, fry noodles a small amount at a time, until crisp. Arrange on a large serving platter. Remove oil from pan and cool.

Heat 2 tablespoons of the oil in a wok. Fry garlic, add chicken mixture and fry for 2 minutes. Add champignons, carrot and corn and fry for 2 minutes. Add salt, bok choy and spring onions and fry for another 3 minutes. Then add the remaining tablespoon cornflour blended with a little cold water. Once sauce thickens, remove from heat and serve on top of fried noodles. Garnish with reserved coriander.

MANDARIN BEEF
Serves 4

350 g rib eye steak or topside, finely sliced
2 teaspoons soy sauce

2 teaspoons mandarin juice
1 teaspoon chopped fresh ginger

1 teaspoon sesame oil
oil for cooking
pepper
2 teaspoons dried mandarin or
   tangerine rind

extra 2 teaspoons soy sauce
2 teaspoons sugar
1 1/2 teaspoons cornflour
4 tablespoons (80 ml) beef stock

GARNISH
small strips of fresh mandarin peel

Place the meat in a bowl. Mix the soy sauce, juice, ginger and sesame oil, add to the meat. Toss well and leave to marinate for 15 minutes. Heat the wok, add oil and stir fry meat for 2 minutes until browned all over. Add pepper, dried rind, extra soy sauce and sugar and stir fry for about a minute. Blend cornflour in a little cold stock, add remaining stock. Pour into the wok, stir until it boils and thickens. Serve with noodles or over hot cooked rice. Garnish with a few strips of fresh mandarin rind.

DRIED MANDARIN PEEL
Use a vegetable peeler to remove peel thinly. Cut the strips into small pieces, removing any pith. Spread out on a baking tray and dry in a preheated moderate oven (180°C) for 15 minutes. Peel can also be spread on kitchen paper towel and dried in the microwave oven for 4 minutes. If stored in an airtight container it will keep well for months. Three mandarins will yield about 1/3 cup of dried peel.

MA POR TOFU
Serves 4

3 teaspoons cornflour
2 teaspoons soy sauce
1 teaspoon oyster sauce
1 clove garlic, sliced
1 cup (260 g) pork mince
1 tablespoon oil
3 teaspoons red bean chilli paste

3 teaspoons preserved bean curd
750 g tofu, drained and cubed
2 spring onions, sliced diagonally
extra 3 teaspoons oyster sauce
extra 2 teaspoons soy sauce
1 1/2 teaspoons sugar

Mix the cornflour with the two sauces and garlic in a bowl. Stir in the mince and leave for 10 minutes. Heat the oil in the wok, add the mince and stir fry for 5 minutes. Add the chilli paste and bean curd and cook for 2 minutes. Add the remaining ingredients and stir fry for 3–5 minutes.

MEE GORENG
Serves 4

1 large onion, chopped
2 cloves garlic, finely chopped
2 red chillies, seeded and chopped
2 cm piece fresh ginger, grated
350 g Hokkien noodles
2 tablespoons (40 ml) oil
500 g prawns, shelled

250 g rump steak, finely sliced
4 spring onions, chopped
1 carrot, cut into matchsticks
2 stalks celery, cut into matchsticks
1 tablespoon kecap manis
1 tablespoon soy sauce
1 tablespoon tomato sauce

Process, or pound with a mortar and pestle, the onion, garlic, chilli and ginger until they form a paste. Separate the noodles, heat the wok until very hot, add 1 tablespoon oil and stir fry the noodles until hot. Put on a serving platter and cover to keep warm. Add remaining oil and stir fry the paste until golden. Add the prawns, steak, spring onion, carrot and celery and stir fry for 2–3 minutes. Add the kecap manis, soy and tomato sauces and season well. Serve immediately over the noodles.

Note Kecap manis is sweet Indonesian soy sauce. If it is not available use soy sauce sweetened with some brown sugar.

MONGOLIAN LAMB

500 g lamb backstrap, cut in
thin strips
2 tablespoons (40 ml) peanut oil
2 cloves garlic, crushed
2 spring onions, sliced

2 tablespoons (40 ml) soy sauce
1/3 cup (85 ml) hoisin sauce
2 tablespoons (40 ml) sweet
chilli sauce
2 teaspoons toasted sesame
seeds

Heat wok and 1 tablespoon oil. Stir fry lamb in batches, adding a little more oil if necessary. Remove lamb from wok.

Add 1 tablespoon oil and stir fry garlic and spring onions for 2 minutes. Remove from wok. Add soy sauce, hoisin sauce and sweet chilli sauce to wok, bring to the boil and simmer for 3–4 minutes. Return meat and vegetables to wok, toss in sauce and serve sprinkled with toasted sesame seeds.

PORK AND APPLE STIR FRY
Serves 5–6

500 g pork fillet, cut in strips
2 tablespoons (40 ml) oil
1 large onion, finely sliced
2–3 Granny Smith apples,
  cut in thin wedges
1 tablespoon soft brown sugar

2 cloves garlic, finely shredded
2 tablespoons (40 ml) hoisin
  sauce
1 tablespoon chopped fresh sage
1/2 cup (125 ml) cream
salt and pepper

Prepare pork. Heat oil in wok. Add onion and apple and sauté. Sprinkle with brown sugar and stir fry for 4 minutes. Remove from wok. Reheat the wok and stir fry the garlic and pork (in batches) over high heat for 2 minutes until the meat turns white. Return all the meat to the wok, stir in all the other ingredients. Serve immediately with rice or noodles.

Hint Fat-reduced yoghurt can be used instead of cream.

PUMPKIN AND CASHEW STIR FRY
Serves 4–6

2 tablespoons (40 ml) oil
1 cup (150 g) cashew nuts
1 leek, white part only, sliced
2 teaspoons ground coriander
2 teaspoons cumin
2 teaspoons brown mustard seeds

2 cloves garlic, crushed
1 kg butternut pumpkin,
  peeled and cubed
3/4 cup (190 ml) orange juice
1 teaspoon soft brown sugar

Heat wok, add 1 tablespoon oil and stir fry nuts until golden, then drain them on paper towels. Stir fry leek 2–3 minutes and remove from wok. Reheat wok, add remaining 1 tablespoon oil and stir fry coriander, cumin, mustard seeds and garlic for 2 minutes. Add pumpkin and stir fry for 5 minutes.

Add orange juice and sugar. Bring to the boil and cook for 5 minutes. Stir in the leek and most of the cashews. Sprinkle remaining cashews on top.

SATAY PORK STIR FRY
Serves 4

1¹/2 cups (300 g) rice
1 tablespoon oil
325 g pork fillet, cut in strips
1 bunch baby bok choy (about
  750 g), stems sliced, leaves
  chopped

1 quantity Satay Sauce (see p. 53)
1 cup (100 g) trimmed snow peas
1 cup (120 g) bean shoots
¹/4 cup coriander leaves

Cook rice in rice cooker or boil in 3 cups water in saucepan for about 15 minutes. Heat 2 teaspoons oil in a wok over high heat until very hot. Add pork and stir fry in 2 batches for 2–3 minutes. Add bok choy stems and stir fry for another minute. Add satay sauce, snow peas, bok choy leaves and stir fry 2–3 minutes). Serve rice in serving bowls with satay pork on top. Garnish with bean shoots and coriander.

Hint If in a hurry use a 410 g can or jar of ready-made satay sauce.

SEAFOOD WITH SPINACH AND PLUM SAUCE
Serves 4–6

150 g squid tubes
1 bunch spinach
2 tablespoons (40 ml) oil
500 g raw prawns, peeled
  and deveined
400 g cleaned scallops

1–2 red chillies, deseeded and
  finely chopped
2 cloves garlic, crushed
¹/2 cup (125 ml) plum sauce
1 teaspoon soft brown sugar
2 tablespoons (40 ml) lime juice
3 spring onions, sliced

Rinse squid, pat dry with paper towels and slice into rings. Rinse spinach, remove stalks and chop leaves. Heat wok, add spinach (wet so it does not stick to wok) and toss till wilted. Transfer to serving dish. Reheat wok, add 1 tablespoon oil and stir fry squid, prawns and scallops in batches until they turn opaque and are cooked. Remove all seafood from wok and set aside. Heat remaining oil in wok and stir fry chillies and garlic for 1–2 minutes. Add the plum sauce, brown sugar and lime juice, bring to boil, and simmer for 4–5 minutes. Return the seafood to wok, add spring onions, coating them with the sauce and serve on top of the spinach.

Vegetables

Vegetables are a rich source of complex carbohydrates and dietary fibre. They supply vitamins and minerals in our daily diet and must be stored, prepared and cooked with care. Soaking and prolonged cooking should be avoided.

Important instructions

- Buy vegetables in season for economy and freshness.
- Store green vegetables and salad vegetables in plastic bags in the crisper in the lower part of the fridge.
- Potatoes and onions should be kept in a dark, well-ventilated cupboard. Discard potatoes that show any sign of going green.
- Buy small quantities at a time and use quickly to avoid loss of vitamins and spoilage.
- Prepare vegetables as close to cooking time as possible. Never soak vegetables in water for lengthy periods before cooking, as water-soluble vitamins will be lost.

∽ Cooking Vegetables ∾

- Use a heavy-based saucepan with a tight-fitting lid. Add water to saucepan to a depth of 3 cm, bring to the boil, add prepared vegetables, replace lid. When water returned to boiling, turn heat to low and allow to simmer gently until the vegetables are just tender. Serve as soon as possible after vegetables are cooked.
- Cook vegetables until just tender. They should retain some crispness and natural colour after cooking. New season vegetables will cook more quickly than vegetables that have become over-mature or woody. Adjust your cooking time accordingly.

- After cooking, any excess vegetable cooking water may be drained and used in sauces, gravy and soups.
- Microwave cooking is a quick, low-water method of cooking which retains vitamins. Cooking times vary according to the power of the microwave oven and the quantity of vegetables being cooked. Check your operating manual. Steaming and pressure-cooking are also quick and nutritious methods of cooking vegetables.

VEGETABLE	METHOD OF PREPARATION	COOKING AND SERVICE
Artichokes, globe	Choose heavy plump heads, with a good green colour. Wash well, trim away bottom leaves.	Salted, boiling water. Cook with lid off for 20 minutes. Serve with melted butter.
Artichokes, Jerusalem	Wash and peel, cover with cold salted water.	Boil for 20 minutes or until tender. Serve with white sauce, or melted butter.
Asparagus	Choose firm, even-sized stems. Remove woody, lower ends, peel any thicker skin on the lower ends, tie in bundles for a steamer, or lie flat in a saucepan, tips lying in one direction.	Microwave, steam or boil, just covered in water for 5–10 minutes or until just tender. Serve with a little melted butter and lemon juice or a drizzle of extra-virgin olive oil.
Beans, broad	Shell beans from pods. Very young broad beans may be sliced as French beans.	Microwave, steam or cook in 3 cm of boiling water for 10 minutes or until just tender. Serve with a little melted butter. **Variation** Serve with finely diced fried bacon.
Beans, French	Select firm, green, crisp beans. Rinse. Top and tail, removing any string. If small, leave whole. If larger, slice diagonally.	Steam, microwave or cook just covered in boiling water for 7–10 minutes. Serve with salt, freshly ground pepper and butter. **Variation 1** Sauté with a little crushed garlic and butter. **Variation 2** Serve with a sprinkle of slivered almonds.

VEGETABLE	METHOD OF PREPARATION	COOKING AND SERVICE
Bok choy	Select crisp, dark green leaves with no signs of yellowing. Trim the base of the stems off and wash well to remove any grit. Slice coarsely.	Steam, microwave or simmer in a few tablespoons of water or stir fry in a little oil until wilted. Serve sprinkled with a little soy sauce.
Broccoli	Always select dark, compact flower heads with no yellowing or open flowers. Trim the woody stem leaving 3–6 cm florets. Rinse under running water.	Cook in 3 cm boiling water for 5–10 minutes or until just tender. Serve with a squeeze of lemon juice or herb butter. **Herb butter** 2 tablespoons butter, $1/2$ clove garlic, crushed, 2 teaspoons lemon juice, $1/8$ teaspoon oregano, pinch of salt, black pepper. Combine all ingredients over heat and pour over broccoli.
Brussels sprouts	Select uniform size, with a good green colour. Trim and remove outer leaves. Cut a cross in the base. Wash well.	Steam, microwave or boil in 3 cm of boiling water for 5–10 minutes. Drain, serve with nutmeg.
Cabbage	Select firm cabbage with no limp outer leaves. Remove hard centre stalks, shred finely.	Cook over gentle heat without water (enough will remain from rinsing). Cook for a few minutes or until just translucent. **Variation** Cabbage can be sautéed with a little diced bacon.
Capsicums, red, green or yellow	Select firm, shiny capsicums free from wrinkling. Cut in half; remove core, seeds and any white membrane.	Slice and use in stir fries. Dice and add to casseroles or salads or leave whole, blanch, fill with savoury meat filling and bake.

VEGETABLE	METHOD OF PREPARATION	COOKING AND SERVICE
Carrots	Choose crisp, well-formed carrots. Wash, scrape if necessary, cut into rings, matchsticks or dice as desired. Baby carrots may be cooked whole.	Place in boiling water and cook for 5–10 minutes. **Note** Carrots burn easily, take care. **Variation** Serve with a little butter, brown sugar and ginger.
Cauliflower	Choose firm white, compact heads free from discolouration. Break into florets, leave a 3 cm stem. Rinse under running water.	Steam, microwave or boil in 3 cm boiling water for 10–12 minutes. Serve with white sauce to which a little nutmeg has been added, or with cheese sauce.
Celery	Look for celery with fresh, unwilted leaves and stems that snap easily. Wash and remove coarse strings before using.	Use in salads or as snacks. Slice and use in stir fries. Cook in 3 cm boiling water for 5 minutes. Drain and serve with white or cheese sauce.
Chinese broccoli	Select dark green leaves and closed flower buds, with no wilting or yellowing. Rinse well. Peel any thick stems and chop coarsely.	Steam or boil young, tender shoots. Use in stir fries.
Chinese cabbage	Choose firm, pale green cabbage. Wash and shred.	Cook as for cabbage or use in stir fries.
Choko	Choose firm, pale green chokoes. Wash, cut in half, and remove seed. Slice or cut into wedges.	Cook in a little water or butter over heat until tender 7–8 minutes.
Corn	Buy corn with fresh green husks and plump pale yellow kernels. Remove the husk and silk, wash, trim, top and tail and leave whole or cut into 6–8 cm sections.	Cook in boiling water to cover for 15–20 minutes or until tender. Serve with melted butter, pepper and salt. To microwave: leave husk in place and cook on HIGH for 3 minutes per cob. Remove husk and silk and serve.
Eggplant (aubergine)	Choose dark purple, firm glossy skin. Wash, cut into 1 cm slices, sprinkle with salt and allow to drain for a few minutes. Rinse off salt.	Dip slices of eggplant in flour or egg and breadcrumbs and fry gently on both sides in butter or olive oil. Alternatively, brush with a little oil and grill.

VEGETABLE	METHOD OF PREPARATION	COOKING AND SERVICE
Leeks	Choose crisp, green leaves and firm white bulb. Cut in half lengthwise and wash well to remove all grit.	Cook in boiling salted water until tender 5–10 minutes. Drain well and serve with butter and pepper or white sauce. Sliced leeks may be sautéed in a little butter and freshly ground black pepper until tender.
Mushrooms	Available as buttons, caps and flats. Trim stalks and wipe over with a damp cloth. Leave whole or slice. Check your greengrocer for Swiss brown, oyster, shiitake and enoki mushrooms.	Cook flats in butter for a few minutes until tender. Season with salt and pepper, Slice caps or leave button mushrooms whole. Use in stir fries and pasta sauces. Mushrooms can be grilled or barbecued.
Parsnips	Select firm, well-shaped parsnips. Peel and slice into rings. Quarter lengthwise to remove core if old and coarse. If roasting cut into 5 cm lengths.	Cook in 3 cm boiling water for 10–15 minutes or until tender. May be roasted or baked. **Variation** Cook with carrots and serve mashed together. Add butter and ground pepper.
Peas	Shell peas (remove from pod).	Cook in 3 cm of boiling water with mint and 1 teaspoon sugar until tender.
Snow peas and sugar snap peas	Select firm bright green peas. Top and tail shells and remove strings. Wash well.	Stir fry in a little oil taking care not to overcook. Alternatively blanch and use in salads.
Potatoes	Select firm, even-sized potatoes free from damage or green discoloration. Wash to remove dirt, peel and cut into even-sized pieces. Washed potatoes need not be peeled.	Cook covered in salted water for 20 minutes or until tender. Serve with melted butter, chopped parsley or mint.

VEGETABLE	METHOD OF PREPARATION	COOKING AND SERVICE
Potatoes baked in their jackets	Select potatoes without damage. Scrub well.	Prick each potato several times with a skewer. Bake in a moderately hot oven (190°C) for 1–1½ hours. Cut an X on top and serve with a knob of butter, or sour cream and chives.
Mashed potatoes	Prepare as for potatoes.	Cook in boiling water until tender, and drain. Mash well, add butter, salt and pepper. Mix with sufficient milk to make potatoes light and fluffy. Reheat if necessary.
Roasted potatoes	Prepare as for potatoes.	Parboil for 5 minutes. Drain. Heat 2 tablespoons oil in roasting dish. Turn potatoes in hot oil, bake for 20–30 minutes in 220°C oven. Turn once during cooking. Drain and serve.
Pumpkin and vegetable marrow	Select heavy, firm pumpkins. Peel pumpkin or marrow and remove seeds. Cut into serving-sized pieces.	Pumpkin may be boiled, microwaved or roasted as for potatoes. Pumpkin may be cut into cubes or slices, placed on a pie plate with a little chopped bacon, covered with foil and cooked in a moderate oven (180°C) for 30–45 minutes.
Silver beet and spinach	Select leaves that are green and not wilted. Wash thoroughly to remove all traces of grit. Cut green leaves from stalk. Shred leaves coarsely. **Note** White stalks of silver beet can be sliced and cooked separately.	Sufficient water will cling to washed leaves so no extra should be needed. Place in a saucepan and cover with a lid. Cook gently for 5 minutes or until leaves are just wilted. Serve with melted butter, salt and pepper or with grated nutmeg.
Squash	Choose firm smooth squash free from blemishes. Wash and trim stem end.	Cook in 3 cm of boiling water until tender. Larger squash may be sliced and simmered or stir fried.

| --- | --- | --- |
Swede	Wash and peel thickly. Dice or slice.	Cook until tender. Mash with butter, pepper and cream.
Sweet potato	Select firm and free from blemishes. Peel and cut into pieces.	Cook in 3 cm of boiling water for 15–20 minutes or until tender. Serve with a little melted butter or mash with butter and black pepper. May also be baked.
Tomatoes	Select firm, plump, red tomatoes. Wash and remove the woody core from the top of the tomato. Cut in half, sprinkle with a little sugar, salt and pepper and $1/2$ teaspoon butter.	Grill cut side up 5–10 minutes.
Turnips, white	Select small to medium firm turnips. Wash, peel thickly, and cut into quarters.	Cook in boiling water for 15 minutes. Drain and serve with butter and black pepper.
Zucchini	Choose firm, glossy skin. Wash, trim off top and tail and slice.	Sauté, steam, stir fry or bake. Can be boiled in a little water until just tender.

CAULIFLOWER AU GRATIN
Serves 4

1/2 cauliflower
1 quantity White Sauce
  (see p. 48)

1/2 cup (60 g) grated cheese
3 tablespoons (30 g) dried
  breadcrumbs

Separate cauliflower into florets and steam or microwave until just tender. Arrange in an ovenproof dish. Pour white sauce over cauliflower and top with grated cheese and breadcrumbs. Cook in a preheated hot oven (200°C) for 10 minutes until cheese is melted and lightly browned.

Chinese Broccoli in Oyster Sauce

Serves 4

1 bunch Chinese broccoli
3 tablespoons water
2 tablespoons oyster sauce

1 tablespoon peanut oil
1 teaspoon sugar

Wash Chinese broccoli, removing mature or tough stems and leaves. Tie into a bundle with string. Bring water to a fast boil in a wok. Add vegetables, bring back to the boil and cook for 2 minutes. Strain vegetables and cut into bite-sized lengths. Arrange in a serving dish. Put 3 tablespoons water in the wok, add oyster sauce, peanut oil and sugar and bring to the boil. Pour over the Chinese broccoli and serve.

Note Other green vegetables, e.g. asparagus, can be cooked in the same way.

Devilled Carrots

Serves 6–8

500 g carrots
2 tablespoons (40 g) butter
1 tablespoon brown sugar

1 teaspoon mustard
3 shakes cayenne pepper
pinch of salt

Wash and scrape carrots, cut into sticks 1 cm thick by 7 cm long. Melt butter and cook carrots gently for 5 minutes. Add all other ingredients and cook for 10 minutes or until tender.

Glazed Vegetables

Serves 4–6

Mixture 1

1 cup (150 g) sliced carrot
1 cup (150 g) sliced celery

1 cup (100 g) broccoli florets
1 cup (120 g) sliced zucchini

Mixture 2

1 cup (150 g) sliced carrot
1 cup (150 g) sliced parsnip
1 cup (150 g) thinly sliced swede

1 cup (150 g) sliced celery
1 cup (100 g) broccoli florets
1 cup (120 g) quartered squash

Glaze

2 tablespoons (40 g) butter	2 teaspoons brown sugar or honey
1 tablespoon lemon juice	salt and pepper
1 teaspoon grated lemon rind	chopped parsley or chives

To make glaze, place all ingredients except parsley or chives in a small saucepan and boil for 5 minutes. Cook mixed vegetables of choice until tender in lightly salted water, then drain. Pour glaze over vegetables and sprinkle with chopped parsley or chives.

MACEDOINE OF VEGETABLES
Serves 4

1 medium carrot	2 level teaspoons cornflour
1 medium parsnip	1/2 cup (125 ml) milk
1 medium turnip	1/2 cup (125 ml) vegetable water
1 cup (150 g) green peas	salt and pepper
1 cup (100 g) cauliflower	chopped parsley
or broccoli florets	

Prepare and dice carrot, parsnip and turnip. Cook all vegetables in lightly salted water for 10 minutes then drain, reserving water. Make a thin white sauce by blending cornflour with a little cold milk, then combine with rest of milk, vegetable water and seasoning, and heat, stirring constantly until boiling. Remove from heat. Pour white sauce over vegetables, sprinkle with chopped parsley.

POTATOES DUCHESSE
Serves 6–8

500 g potatoes	pinch of nutmeg
1 egg	salt and pepper to taste
1 tablespoon butter	

Peel and boil potatoes as per chart. Drain and push potatoes through a sieve. Beat egg and retain 1 teaspoon for glazing. Beat potatoes with butter, nutmeg, salt, pepper and rest of egg until fluffy. Pipe into rosettes on a greased oven tray. Glaze with egg. Brown in a preheated hot oven (200°C) for 10 minutes.

Potato Fans
Serves 4

4 medium potatoes   tasty or Parmesan cheese
60 g butter, melted   black pepper

Peel potatoes thinly, cutting a slice from the base of each to make potatoes sit evenly. Slice potatoes thinly and carefully almost through to the base. Brush liberally with butter, sprinkle with cheese and black pepper. Place on a greased shallow dish and bake for 50–60 minutes in a preheated moderate oven (180°C).

Potato Wedges
Serves 4–6

6 potatoes   spray oil
2 tablespoons Cajun seasoning

Cut washed but unpeeled potatoes in half then into wedges. Toss wedges in Cajun seasoning. Spray an oven tray with oil and arrange wedges. Spray wedges with a generous coating of oil and bake in a preheated very hot oven (220°C) for 35–40 minutes or until crisp.

Ratatouille
Serves 4–8

2 small eggplants   1 clove garlic
2 large onions   2 tablespoons (40 ml) oil
4 medium tomatoes   salt and pepper
1 green capsicum   chopped parsley
2 medium zucchini

Peel and slice eggplant, sprinkle with salt and let stand for 30 minutes, then rinse and drain. Peel and slice onions and tomatoes, deseed and slice capsicum, slice zucchini, crush garlic. Heat oil in a large casserole in a preheated moderate (180°C) oven. Add all vegetables and season with salt and pepper to taste. Cover with a lid or foil and bake for 35 minutes. Sprinkle with chopped parsley. Serve hot with a meat dish or hot or cold as an entrée.

Notes Four button squash can be used instead of zucchini. Ratatouille may be cooked in a large saucepan on the stove top.

Sayur Lodeh — Vegetables in Coconut Milk
Serves 4–6

This recipe may be used for most vegetables separately or for a mixture of vegetables.

500 g vegetables
2 tablespoons (40 ml) peanut oil
1 onion, chopped
2 teaspoons chopped garlic
1 fresh chilli, deseeded
1 teaspoon dried shrimp paste

1 stalk lemongrass, bruised
2 cups (500 ml) vegetable or chicken stock
1 cup (250 ml) coconut milk
salt and pepper
1 tablespoon lemon or lime juice

Cut vegetables into bite-sized portions. Heat oil in wok or saucepan and fry onion until soft. Add garlic, chilli and shrimp paste, mixing well. Add lemongrass, stock and coconut milk. Simmer uncovered for a few minutes, then add vegetables and cook until just tender. Add salt and pepper to taste. Stir in lemon or lime juice and serve hot.

Scalloped Potatoes
Serves 4–6

500 g potatoes
3 tablespoons flour
salt and freshly ground pepper to taste

1 cup (250 ml) milk
2 tablespoons (40 g) butter

Peel potatoes and cut into thick slices. Put flour, salt, pepper and potatoes into a large paper bag and shake well. Put potatoes into a greased casserole. Heat milk and butter together and pour over potatoes. Cover casserole, bake in a preheated moderate oven (180°C) for 1 hour, the final 15 minutes with lid off to allow top to brown.

STUFFED CABBAGE
Serves 6

6 large cabbage leaves
1 cup (250 g) minced steak
1 cup (250 ml) cooked rice
1 small onion, chopped

pinch of mixed herbs
salt and pepper
1 cup (250 ml) tomato soup or
   juice

Wash leaves and pour boiling water over them. Allow to
cool. Combine mince, rice, onion, herbs and seasoning and
place some in the centre of each cabbage leaf. Fold leaf to
form a parcel and secure with toothpicks. Place in a greased
casserole, pour over soup or tomato juice and bake 45 minutes–1 hour in preheated moderate oven (180°C).

TOMATO AND ONION PIE
Serves 4

4 tomatoes
1 onion
1/2 cup (30 g) fresh breadcrumbs

2 teaspoons butter
salt and pepper

Wash tomatoes and slice them thickly. Peel and slice onion.
Grease pie dish and layer tomato and onion slices. Sprinkle
with breadcrumbs. Dot with butter and season to taste. Bake
in a preheated moderate oven (180°C) for 45 minutes.

VEGETABLE BAKE
Serves 4–6

1 onion, sliced
1 carrot, sliced
1 1/2 cups (180 g) green
   beans, sliced
1 1/2 cups (150 g) broccoli or
   cauliflower florets

1 1/2 cups (225 g) celery, sliced
1/2 cup (125 ml) vegetable
   stock
1 tablespoon chopped parsley
   or fresh oregano

Lightly grease casserole. Place most of the onion slices in
bottom of the casserole then layer each vegetable. Top with
a few slices of onion. Pour vegetable stock over and season

with parsley. Cover with a lid or foil and bake for 45–50 minutes in a preheated moderately hot oven (190°C).

Note Any combination of vegetables may be used.

VEGETABLE ROGAN JOSH
Serves 4–6

*500 g mixed vegetables (try a
selection of potato, sweet potato,
capsicum, eggplant, peas
or broccoli)*

*1 onion, chopped
2 tablespoons ghee or oil
1 x 360 g can Rogan
Josh Curry Sauce*

Cut vegetables into large dice and parboil. Fry onion in ghee or oil until golden brown, then fry remaining vegetables for 3 minutes. Add sauce and simmer until vegetables are tender. Serve with rice or flat bread.

Note Rogan Josh Curry Sauce can also be used with turkey, lamb or beef.

Salads and Salad Dressings

A perfect salad looks cool and inviting, and ingredients that are blended with skill and imagination make it tasty and nutritious. Fruit and vegetables must be fresh and of best quality.

Important instructions

- The salad bowl may be rubbed with a clove of garlic.
- Do not add dressing to green salad until required or lettuce will lose its crispness.
- Dry lettuce by shaking in a cloth or using a salad spinner.
- Hard-boiled eggs will not discolour if placed in boiling water and boiled for 10 minutes. Remove from heat, crack the shell or peel and plunge into cold water.
- A wide range of colourful and decorative salads may, with imagination, be made from assortments of salad greens, fruit and raw and cooked vegetables. Add cold meats, fish, eggs or cheese.
- Parsley keeps fresh and green longest if stored in a covered jar in the refrigerator.
- Top salads with a sprinkling of toasted pine nuts, sesame seeds or pumpkin seeds for a little extra crunch.

Salad vegetables

Alfalfa sprouts: Fine, mildly flavoured, pale green sprouts.
Baby spinach leaves: Small vivid green leaves of English spinach.
Bean shoots: Larger in size than alfalfa sprouts, mung bean sprouts have a sweet, nutty flavour.

Coral lettuce: Has finely frilled, lacy, bright green or brown leaves.

Cos lettuce: Has crisp, elongated green leaves.

Endive: Has long, lacy green leaves with a distinct flavour.

Iceberg lettuce: Crisp, tightly curled, pale green leaves; the traditional lettuce.

Mesclun mix: A blend of various lettuce and spinach leaves.

Mignonette: Has soft, gently curled green or brown leaves and a mild flavour.

Oak leaf lettuce: Has soft green or brown leaves and a mild flavour.

Radicchio: Has a crisp, deep-red leaf and a strong, bitter flavour.

Rocket: A dark green vegetable with peppery flavoured leaves.

Snow pea shoots: Bright green, leafy shoots with a gentle flavour.

Watercress: Dark green, leafy sprays of a peppery flavoured plant.

Whitlof or witlof: Small, compact white leaves.

Australian Salad

Serves 6

6 tomatoes	*1 tablespoon chopped nuts*
salt, pepper, sugar	*1 teaspoon chopped parsley*
4 tablespoons chopped lettuce	*1 spring onion, chopped*
3 tablespoons (30 g) grated cheese	*1/2 teaspoon cayenne pepper*
1 tablespoon chopped pineapple	*Mayonnaise Dressing (see p. 167)*

Wipe tomatoes, cut off tops and scoop out centres. Sprinkle with salt, pepper and sugar. Mash tomato pulp and mix it with chopped lettuce, cheese, pineapple, nuts, parsley and spring onion. Fill tomatoes with the mixture, top with a little cayenne and mask with mayonnaise. Serve chilled on a crisp lettuce leaf.

BEAN SALAD

Serves 6

1 x 300 g can three bean mix
1 x 300 g can lima beans
2 cups (250 g) green beans
1 salad onion

1 tablespoon chopped parsley
Mayonnaise or French
 Dressing (see p. 167)

Drain three bean mix and lima beans, cook green beans and cool. Slice onion into rings. Mix all together with parsley and enough dressing to moisten.

BEETROOT

1 bunch beetroot
2 cm piece fresh ginger
600 ml vinegar
200 g sugar

2 teaspoons salt
1 teaspoon black peppercorns
1 teaspoon mustard seed

Wash beetroot and place unpeeled in a large saucepan. Cover with water. Bring to the boil. Simmer until tender — about an hour. Peel ginger and crush. Simmer ginger, vinegar, sugar, salt and spices together for 5 minutes. Cool and strain, reserving the vinegar. When beetroot are cooked, peel, cut into slices or dice, pack into jars and cover with boiling vinegar. Seal and refrigerate.

Note Beetroot can be set in a mould by warming 2 cups pickling liquid and mixing with 1 tablespoon gelatine. Pour over the beetroot, chill and allow to set.

CAESAR SALAD

Serves 6

1 cos lettuce
3 slices white bread
pepper
6 bacon rashers
3 hard-boiled eggs

$^{1}/_{4}$ cup (30 g) Parmesan
 cheese shavings
6 anchovies
Caesar salad dressing

Break apart the cos lettuce and remove any coarse outer leaves. Tear into large pieces and place into a serving bowl. To make croûtons, trim crusts off bread and dice into 1 cm squares. Spread on a baking tray, sprinkle with pepper and bake in a moderate oven until browned then allow to cool. Dice bacon and fry until crisp; drain well. Slice hard-boiled eggs. Gently mix bacon, anchovies, hard-boiled eggs and Parmesan with lettuce. Sprinkle with croûtons and top with dressing before serving.

CARROT SALAD

1 tablespoon gelatine
1/4 cup (60 ml) cold water
1 cup (250 ml) boiling water
1/4 cup (60 g) sugar
2 tablespoons lemon juice

2 1/2 tablespoons (50 ml) vinegar
1 cup crushed pineapple
1/2 cup (50 g) finely grated carrot
1 tablespoon chopped mint
2 teaspoons chopped chives
    (optional)

Soak gelatine in cold water for 5 minutes, then dissolve in boiling water with sugar, add lemon juice, vinegar and drained, crushed pineapple. Chill until syrupy then add carrot, mint and chives. Set in a flat dish. When set cut into squares to serve.

COLESLAW

4 cups (400 g) shredded cabbage
1 cup crushed pineapple
1 cup (150 g) finely diced celery
1 cup (100 g) grated carrot
1/4 cup (25 g) chopped walnuts
1 small onion, diced
2 tablespoons chopped chives

1/2 red capsicum, deseeded and
    finely diced
1 cup (250 ml) Mayonnaise
    Dressing (see p. 167)
salt and freshly ground black
    pepper, to taste

Prepare all vegetables and nuts, toss together well with mayonnaise. Serve.

GREEK SALAD

Serves 6

250 g fetta cheese	1 small red onion
5 tomatoes	1/2 cup pitted black olives
1/2 continental cucumber	1/2 red capsicum

DRESSING

1/2 (125 ml) cup olive oil	1 teaspoon sugar
1 clove garlic, crushed	oregano to taste

Cut fetta cheese into squares, dice tomatoes coarsely, slice continental cucumber, slice red onion finely, halve olives and dice red capsicum. Combine in a bowl. Mix all dressing ingredients in a jar and shake well. Pour over salad before serving.

GREEN SALAD

1 butter lettuce	1 Lebanese cucumber
1 cup (120 g) green beans	1/2 green capsicum
2 stalks celery	1 cup alfalfa or bean sprouts
3 spring onions	French Dressing (see p. 167)

Prepare lettuce and tear into small pieces. Place in glass bowl. Slice and blanch green beans, slice celery, onions, cucumber and capsicum. Place on lettuce in layers. Add sprouts and sprinkle with French dressing.

MANGO AND AVOCADO SALAD

1 butter lettuce	1/2 cup alfalfa sprouts
1 mango	French Dressing (see p. 167)
1 avocado	croûtons (optional)
1 punnet cherry tomatoes	

Wash and separate lettuce leaves, cut mango into pieces, slice avocado and put these in a serving bowl. Add cherry tomatoes, alfalfa and sprinkle with dressing. Top with a sprinkling of croûtons if desired.

Orange and Onion Salad

3 oranges
1 onion

French Dressing (see p. 167)
chopped parsley

Peel and slice oranges, peel and slice onion. Arrange in layers. Add about 2 tablespoons dressing and sprinkle with parsley.

Potato Salad

4 cups (600 g) diced potato
1 onion

1 cup (150 g) cooked peas
2 tablespoons chopped mint

Dressing

1 hard-boiled egg, finely chopped
²/3 cup (160 ml) cream
¹/3 cup (80 ml) vinegar

1 tablespoon sugar
salt and pepper to taste

Cook potato until just tender, drain and add finely chopped onion, peas and mint. Mix together and add dressing. Mix carefully. Serve chilled.

Rice Salad

3 cups cooked rice
1 small onion, finely chopped
1 x 130 g can corn kernels
¹/4 red capsicum, finely chopped
¹/4 green capsicum, finely chopped

pineapple to taste
¹/2 cup (50 g) peanuts or
   cashew nuts (optional)
French or Mayonnaise
   Dressing (see p. 167)

Blend ingredients together. If using nuts, add just before serving. Use French dressing or mayonnaise as desired.

Roasted Vegetable Salad

150 g jap pumpkin
olive oil spray
salt

cayenne pepper
2 red onions
1 eggplant

1 red capsicum
1 yellow capsicum
1 zucchini

1 tablespoon toasted sesame
 seeds
French Dressing (see p. 167)
 made with balsamic vinegar

Preheat oven to 220°C. Peel and cut pumpkin into chunks, place in a roasting pan and spray with olive oil. Sprinkle with salt and cayenne and roast for 30 minutes. Quarter onions, cut eggplant and capsicum into pieces and add to the baking tray. Return to the oven for 15 minutes. Slice zucchini and add to the tray. Bake for a further 10 minutes. Remove vegetables from the oven and cool slightly. Place on a serving platter, sprinkle with sesame seeds and top with French dressing made with balsamic vinegar.

SPINACH SALAD

6 cloves garlic
3/4 cup (180 ml) French
 Dressing (see p. 167)
6 bacon rashers
3 hard-boiled eggs
200 g spinach leaves

1 x 190 g can water chestnuts
100 g mushrooms
1/2 cup (75 g) chopped spring
 onions
1/4 cup (25 g) cashew nuts
salt and pepper

Marinate garlic in French dressing for several hours. Dice bacon and fry until crisp. Peel and chop eggs. Tear up any large spinach leaves. At serving time, sprinkle eggs and bacon over spinach. Add water chestnuts, mushrooms, spring onions and cashews. Remove garlic from dressing and pour over salad. Add salt and pepper to taste, toss and serve at once.

TABBOULEH

1 cup fine burghul
3 large tomatoes, chopped
1 onion (or 2 spring onions)
 finely chopped
4 cups flat leaf parsley, finely
 chopped

1/4 cup fresh mint, finely
 chopped
1/4 cup olive oil
1/4 cup lemon juice
teaspoon salt, to taste

Wash burghul in cold water, drain well, squeezing out excess water. Spread tomato over burghul and refrigerate for 30 minutes. Add onion, parsley and mint. Dress with olive oil, lemon juice and salt just prior to serving.

TOSSED SALAD

1 clove garlic
1 lettuce
1/2 small cucumber
3 spring onions
4 red radishes

1/2 green capsicum
1 cup (150 g) sliced celery
French Dressing (see p. 167)
1 tomato
2 teaspoons chopped parsley

Rub inside of bowl with cut garlic. Tear lettuce into small pieces and add to bowl. Slice cucumber, onion, radish and capsicum and add to lettuce with celery. Sprinkle with dressing, toss lightly and garnish with tomato wedges and parsley.

WALDORF SALAD

2 large apples, chopped
1 1/2 cups (225 g) diced celery
3/4 cup (75 g) walnut pieces

1/2 cup (125 ml) Mayonnaise
  or Boiled Salad Dressing
(see p. 167)

Combine all ingredients, mix lightly and serve immediately.

ZUCCHINI SALAD

3 zucchini
2 tomatoes
1 small onion

1 tablespoon chopped chives
French Dressing (see p. 167)

Dice all vegetables. Blend together, serve with French dressing.

✍ DRESSINGS ✍

BOILED SALAD DRESSING

2 teaspoons butter
2 teaspoons sugar
1 teaspoon dry mustard
1/2 teaspoon salt

1 egg
1/2 cup (125 ml) milk
2 teaspoons vinegar

Put butter, sugar, mustard and salt in basin, stir until mixed, beat egg slightly and add. Stir well then add milk. Put in top of double saucepan, heat and stir until all ingredients are well blended. Remove from heat and add vinegar very slowly; return to heat and cook until the consistency of custard. This dressing will keep for several weeks if refrigerated.

FRENCH DRESSING

1 clove garlic
1/4 cup (60 ml) vinegar
    or lemon juice
3/4 cup (190 ml) salad oil

1/4 teaspoon salt
1/4 teaspoon pepper
1/4 teaspoon paprika

Slice garlic and soak in vinegar for 10 minutes, strain. Place vinegar and remaining ingredients in a jar, cover tightly and shake well. Use as required.

MAYONNAISE DRESSING

2 egg yolks
1 teaspoon French mustard
1/2 teaspoon salt
pinch of pepper

2 1/2 cups (625 ml) safflower
    or olive oil
1 tablespoon tarragon vinegar
1 tablespoon cream

Put yolks in a basin with mustard, salt and pepper, and stir quickly with wooden spoon. Add oil at first drop by drop, then more quickly and at intervals a few drops of vinegar. If beaten well, the mixture becomes the consistency of whipped cream. Lastly add the cream, stirring all the time. If the dressing is too thick, add a little cold water.

QUICK SALAD DRESSING

1–2 teaspoons mustard
$^{1}/_{4}$ teaspoon salt

1 x 395 g can sweetened
condensed milk and an equal
quantity of vinegar

Mix mustard and salt with a little of the vinegar, add condensed milk, and using the same can to measure, pour in an equal amount of vinegar, stirring all the time. Allow dressing to stand for a few minutes after it is thoroughly mixed. This dressing keeps well in the refrigerator.

SPECIAL DRESSING (FOR THE DIET CONSCIOUS)

1 tablespoon skim milk powder
1 tablespoon vinegar
$^{1}/_{4}$ teaspoon dry mustard

artificial sweetener equal to
4 teaspoons sugar
salt and pepper

Shake well together. Use on salads.

THOUSAND ISLAND DRESSING

1 cup (250 ml) Mayonnaise
Dressing (see p. 167)
$^{1}/_{4}$ cup (60 ml) cream
1 teaspoon tomato sauce

1 tablespoon chopped stuffed
olives
2 teaspoons chopped green
capsicum
1 tablespoon chopped chives

Mix all ingredients together. Chill.

FAST AND TASTY SAVOURIES

To assist in the preparation of these recipes, keep on the shelves or in the refrigerator packaged and canned foods such as pasta, tomatoes, soups, fruit salad, sweet corn, mushrooms, potato chips, asparagus, fruit and tomato juices. Store bacon and grated cheese in the freezer and make use of frozen foods such as peas, spinach and pastry. Processing canned or home-cooked vegetables with a carton of chicken or vegetable stock can make a delicious soup. Potato chips can replace mashed potatoes as a topping on casseroles.

BRUSCHETTA
Serves 4

1 loaf ciabatta bread
4 roma tomatoes
1/2 red onion, finely chopped
1 tablespoon chopped basil

salt and pepper
olive oil
2 teaspoons balsamic vinegar

Slice ciabatta loaf and toast slices until well browned. Dice roma tomatoes finely and mix together with onion, basil, salt and pepper. Drizzle olive oil over each slice of toast, sprinkle with vinegar and top with tomato mixture.

CHEESE SAVOURIES
Serves 4–6

1 cup (120 g) grated cheese
1 egg
mustard

salt and pepper
4–6 slices bread, buttered
2 bacon rashers

Combine cheese, egg and flavourings and spread on slices of buttered bread. Cut into finger lengths and place on a baking tray. Sprinkle with chopped bacon. Bake in a pre-heated hot oven (200°C) for 7–10 minutes.

CHEESE SOUFFLÉ
Serves 2–4

1 cup (250 ml) milk	*salt and pepper*
1 cup (60 g) fresh breadcrumbs	*cayenne pepper*
1 cup (120 g) grated cheese	*2 eggs*

Boil milk and pour over breadcrumbs. Add cheese and seasonings. Separate eggs and stir yolks into the breadcrumb mix. Beat egg whites until soft peaks form and fold gently into the mixture. Place into a greased ovenproof dish and bake in a preheated moderate oven (180°C) for 20–30 minutes.

CURRIED EGGS
Serves 4

4 eggs, hard-boiled	*1 teaspoon curry powder*
1 tablespoon oil	*1 teaspoon desiccated coconut*
1 small onion, chopped	*pepper and salt*
1 apple, chopped	*1 cup (250 ml) stock or water*
1 tablespoon tomato sauce	*few drops of lemon juice*
2 teaspoons flour	*1 tablespoon sultanas or raisins*

Peel eggs and cut in half. Heat oil and fry apple and onion until brown. Add tomato sauce, flour, curry powder, coconut, pepper and salt and stir until well browned. Add the stock, lemon juice and sultanas or raisins and stir until mixture thickens. Simmer for about 30 minutes. Add eggs to the curry and allow to heat without boiling. Lift out and arrange on a hot dish surrounded with steamed rice. Decorate with slices of lemon or parsley.

FRENCH TOAST

eggs	*butter or spray oil*
milk	*maple syrup or cinnamon*
sliced bread	*sugar*

For each egg use ¼ cup (60 ml) milk. Beat eggs and milk together. Dip each slice of bread into this mixture and cook bread in a frying pan sprayed with a little oil or coated with a little melted butter. Cook both sides until golden brown and serve immediately with maple syrup or cinnamon sugar.

Note This makes a very tasty savoury if salt and pepper is added to the mixture and the syrup or sugar is omitted.

FRIED RICE
Serves 4

4 cups cooked rice (see note)
1½ tablespoons vegetable oil
2 eggs
½ cup (75 g) cooked shrimps (see note) or ½ cup (90 g) diced bacon

1 cup (150 g) cooked green peas
1 cup (150 g) canned bamboo shoots, sliced
1 cup (100 g) bean shoots
2–3 spring onions, sliced
1 tablespoon light soy sauce

Fork rice over to break it up. Heat 1 tablespoon oil in wok or large frying pan. Beat eggs. Reduce heat to moderate, pour in eggs and cook until just set. Remove egg and cut into slices. Heat a little extra oil; sauté shrimps or bacon for 2 minutes. Add peas, sliced bamboo shoots and bean shoots and, stirring, cook 2 minutes. Add rice and heat through. Add cooked egg, sliced onion and soy sauce. Mix thoroughly and serve piping hot.

Notes 1⅓ cups (270 g) uncooked rice will produce 4 cups cooked rice.

Do not allow rice to cool at room temperature; instead refrigerate immediately, as cooked rice can develop food-poisoning bacteria.

The shrimps can be fresh, frozen or canned.

Other vegetables and meats can be used, such as baby sweet corn, chicken and barbecue pork.

Frittata
Serves 6

15 g butter
1 tablespoon olive oil
3 rindless bacon rashers
1 potato, sliced

1 cup (150 g) frozen peas
6 eggs
1 cup (120 g) grated tasty cheese

Heat butter and oil together in a frying pan. Dice bacon coarsely and sauté in pan for 2 minutes. Add potato slices and cook for a further 5 minutes, stirring occasionally. Stir in peas. Lightly beat eggs and pour over vegetable mixture. Top with grated cheese. Cook frittata over gentle heat for 10–12 minutes or until almost firm. Brown the top of the frittata by sliding the frying pan under a preheated grill for 2–3 minutes. Serve hot or cold.

Macaroni Cheese
Serves 4

1 cup (100 g) macaroni
2 cups (500 ml) White Sauce
  (see p. 48)
1/2 cup (60 g) grated cheese

salt and pepper
extra grated cheese
breadcrumbs
cayenne pepper

Garnish
chopped parsley

Sprinkle macaroni into a large saucepan half filled with boiling, salted water. Boil until tender (12–15 minutes). Drain and rinse. Stir the grated cheese into the white sauce and season to taste. Stir the macaroni into the sauce and pour into a greased, ovenproof dish. Top with a layer of grated cheese and breadcrumbs. Sprinkle with a little cayenne. Brown in a preheated moderately hot oven (190°C) for about 20 minutes. Garnish with chopped parsley.

MIXED GRILL

lamb's kidneys
tomatoes
sausages

lamb chops
bacon rashers

Trim and halve kidneys. Remove woody core from tomatoes and halve. Place sausages, chops, bacon, kidneys and tomatoes under preheated griller, turning when necessary. Serve with fresh crusty bread or potato chips.

MUSHROOMS
Serves 4

When choosing mushrooms for this dish, try some of the newer varieties available in the markets, including Swiss browns and oyster mushrooms.

500 g mushrooms
2 tablespoons (40 g) butter
pepper and salt

slices of toast
parsley
4 bacon rashers

Wipe mushrooms clean or if using field mushrooms, peel and wash. Cook mushrooms in butter until just tender. Season. Serve on slices of toast, sprinkled with a little parsley and garnished with grilled bacon.

PUMPKIN AND FETTA QUICHE
Serves 6–8

500 g pumpkin
1/2 red capsicum
1 onion
1 teaspoon oil
2 bacon rashers, diced
1 clove garlic, crushed

250 g fetta cheese
3 eggs, lightly beaten
1/3 cup (80 ml) cream
pepper
6 sheets fillo pastry
30 g butter, melted

Peel pumpkin and steam or microwave until tender. Place red capsicum under grill, skin side up, and cook until skin is blackened. Place capsicum in a paper bag until cool and peel away the blackened skin, remove seeds and slice. Peel and slice onion, place in a small saucepan with oil and cook gently over low heat until soft and brown, add diced bacon and fry until crisp, add garlic and fry a little longer. Mash pumpkin and push fetta cheese through a sieve. Put pumpkin and cheese in a bowl, add lightly beaten eggs, cream and pepper. Stir in onions and bacon.

Fold each sheet of fillo to form a square, brush with melted butter and fit into a quiche pan. Repeat with each sheet's stacking one on top of the other. Pour pumpkin mixture over and top with strips of capsicum. Bake in a preheated moderate oven (180°C) for 30 minutes or until filling is set.

RISOTTO

Serves 6

6 cups (1.5 L) chicken stock
50 g butter
1 onion, chopped
2 cloves garlic, crushed
2 cups (400 g) arborio rice
1 x 250 g can sweet corn
   kernels

1 red capsicum
1 cup (150 g) peas
$1/3$ cup (80 ml) sour cream
$1/3$ cup grated Parmesan cheese
3 tablespoons chopped coriander
salt and pepper

Heat stock in a saucepan, cover and keep at low simmer. Melt butter in a large saucepan. Add onion and garlic and cook for 4–5 minutes or until soft. Stir in the rice. Add $1/2$ cup of hot stock, stirring constantly over medium heat until liquid is absorbed. Add another $1/2$ cup, then add corn, peas and capsicum. Continue adding stock $1/2$ cup at a time until all the stock is absorbed and rice is tender and creamy. Remove from the heat and add parmesan, sour cream and coriander. Season with salt and pepper and serve.

SAVOURY TULIPS

12–24 slices fresh bread
$1/2$–1 cup (125–250 g) butter

savoury filling (e.g. thick white
   sauce flavoured with chicken
   and leek, or salmon, corn and
   bacon, or brain and walnut, or
   smoked oyster)

Cut crusts off bread slices, cut slices into quarters and spread with softened butter. Push bread slices into patty tins, buttered side down. Bake in a preheated moderate oven (180°C) for 15 minutes until lightly coloured. Remove from oven, allow to cool, fill with savoury filling. Serve either cold or reheated. Bread cases can be made ahead of time and stored in an airtight tin or frozen. Cases can also be made using squares of mountain bread or wonton wrappers.

STUFFED CAPSICUMS
Serves 4

4 green capsicums
3 tomatoes
1 tablespoon butter
1 tablespoon chopped onion
1 teaspoon prepared mustard

1 cup (180 g) cooked rice
1 x 85 g can tuna
salt and pepper
grated cheese

Cut a slice from the stem end of each pepper and remove the seeds. Peel and chop tomatoes. Parboil peppers in boiling salted water for 5 minutes. Melt butter in saucepan, fry onion until tender. Stir in tomatoes and mustard and cook for 5 minutes. Add rice and tuna. Season to taste. Spoon mixture into peppers and sprinkle with grated cheese. Bake in a preheated moderate oven (180°C) for 15–20 minutes.

STUFFED TOMATOES
Serves 4

4 large tomatoes
2 bacon rashers
10 g butter
2 spring onions, chopped
1 clove garlic, crushed
1 stalk celery, diced

1 x 130 g can sweet corn
    kernels
1/3 cup (20 g) fresh
    breadcrumbs
1/4 cup (30 g) grated cheese
2 shakes cracked black pepper

Slice tomatoes in half, scoop pulp out from each half and chop finely. Dice bacon and fry until crisp. Drain. Add butter to the pan and fry onion, garlic and celery. Mix together drained corn, breadcrumbs, cheese, bacon, tomato pulp, pepper, onion, garlic and celery. Spoon filling into tomato halves, stand in an ovenproof dish and bake in a preheated moderate oven (180°C) for 15 minutes.

WELSH RAREBIT

Serves 4

4 slices bread
1 tablespoon (20 g) butter
1 cup (120 g) tasty cheddar cheese
3 tablespoons (60 ml) milk

$^1/_2$ teaspoon mustard
salt and pepper
1 teaspoon Worcester sauce

Make toast and butter it. Keep hot. Put grated cheese, milk, mustard, salt, pepper and Worcester sauce in a saucepan (preferably in a double saucepan). Heat very gently until ingredients are well blended and mixture is creamy. Pour over toast and brown under a hot grill. Serve with a sprig of parsley.

YELLOW RICE

Serves 4

$^2/_3$ cup (130 g) rice
$^1/_2$ cup (125 ml) milk
$1^1/_2$ teaspoons turmeric
$^1/_2$ cup (90 g) raisins

$^1/_4$ cup (45 g) brown sugar
1 tablespoon butter
1 teaspoon salt

Cook rice in water until grains are tender. Dissolve turmeric in milk. Place all ingredients in saucepan and heat. Serve with stir fries or casseroles.

Pastry, Pies, Quiches and Tarts

Important instructions

- Rub shortening in with fingertips, roll pastry lightly, and make in a cool place.
- The less water used, the shorter the crust will be.
- The less flour used in rolling out, the lighter the crust will be.
- Most pastries are improved by being kept cool. Refrigerate if possible before cooking.
- Preheat oven.
- If using glass ovenware, allow extra cooking time.
- Tarts cooked without a filling should be pricked to prevent their rising.
- Use suet pastry for boiled meat and fruit puddings and dumplings, shortcrust pastry for fruit pies and tarts, flaky and puff pastry for meat pies and slices.
- Some pastries can be made quickly and easily using a food processor.
- Commercially prepared pastries and pre-cooked pastries are available for those in a hurry.

Choux Pastry
Makes about 30 small puffs or 12 éclairs

¹/₂ cup (125 g) butter or margarine   1 cup (150 g) plain flour
1 cup (250 ml) water   4 eggs, beaten

Filling
1 cup (250 ml) cream, whipped   icing sugar

Sift flour. Put butter in water, heat until it has melted then bring to the boil. Add flour, beat well until mixture is smooth. Cook 2 minutes until mixture is shiny and forms one lump. Cool for a few minutes, then add beaten eggs gradually, beating well with a wooden spoon with each addition (spoon should stand in mixture). Place on wet trays in small spoonfuls for puffs or lengths for éclairs (see notes below) and bake in a preheated very hot oven (220°C) for 15 minutes then reduce heat to 190°C — large shapes need a little longer than small ones. Small puffs take 30–40 minutes to cook in all, and éclairs 45–50 minutes. When taken from the oven make a small slit on the side to release steam.

Notes

Choux Puffs: Fill choux puffs with 1 cup (250 ml) cream that has been whipped and dredge tops with icing sugar.

Chocolate Eclairs: Pipe hot pastry mixture on to wet tray in 8 cm lengths (use sharp knife to cut off pastry). Fill with 1 cup (250 ml) cream that has been whipped and ice with 1 quantity Chocolate Glacé Icing (see p. 237).

Profiteroles au Chocolat: Fill 30 small puffs with 1 quantity Confectioners' Custard (see p. 187) or 1 cup (250 g) ricotta cheese combined with 1 tablespoon (15 g) icing sugar. Pile on serving dish and pour over Chocolate Sauce (see below) just before serving.

CHOCOLATE SAUCE
(MICROWAVE RECIPE)

2¹/2 tablespoons (50 g)   ¹/3 cup (80 ml) milk, lukewarm
  butter or margarine   1¹/2 tablespoons (30 g) sugar
120 g dark chocolate   1 teaspoon vanilla essence

Melt butter and chocolate in a 1 L jug or bowl on HIGH for 1–2 minutes. Stir in milk, sugar and essence and stir for 2 minutes until well blended. Cook on HIGH for 1 minute. Stir then serve.

FLAKY PASTRY

1 cup (150 g) plain flour   ¹/2 cup (125 g) butter
1 cup (150 g) self-raising flour ¹/2 cup (125 ml) water

Sift flours together and divide butter into 4 equal parts, then rub one part lightly into the flour using fingertips. Mix into an elastic dough with the water, turn onto a lightly floured board or clean kitchen surface and knead lightly. Roll as square as possible, spread on a third of butter remaining, leaving a margin of 5 cm all round. Sprinkle lightly with flour, fold into 3 even folds, turning so that the open ends are toward you, and roll one way — away from you, and with a light even pressure. Use the remaining 2 parts of butter in the same way. The idea is to trap air in between the rolls and folds, which will expand when cooked and make the pastry light and flaky. Give the dough one last roll to whatever shape is required.

HOT WATER PASTRY

2 tablespoons (40 ml) boiling water
1/2 cup (125 g) butter

1 1/2 cups (225 g) plain flour
1/2 teaspoon baking powder

Pour water over butter, stir till smooth. Add sifted dry ingredients and mix well. Chill for 30 minutes, then roll out.

ROUGH PUFF PASTRY

1 cup (150 g) plain flour
1 cup (150 g) self-raising flour
1 egg yolk

few drops of lemon juice
1/2 cup (125 g) butter
1/2 cup (125 ml) water

Sift flours together, beat the egg and add the lemon juice to it. Cut the butter into the flour in pieces the size of a walnut. Mix into a dough with egg mixture and water, turn on to a lightly floured board and knead lightly. Roll into a square and fold in three. Turn pastry so that fold is to the left. Roll into a rectangle. Rolling and folding is repeated three times to entrap air and mix butter evenly. Cover and refrigerate until ready to use.

SHORTCRUST PASTRY

1 cup (150 g) plain flour   *½ cup (125 g) butter*
1 cup (150 g) self-raising flour *½ cup (125 ml) water*

Sift flours together, rub in butter with the fingertips. Pour the water into the centre slowly, making a stiff dough that will leave the side of the bowl quite cleanly. Turn it on to a slightly floured board and knead lightly with the tips of the fingers and thumbs. Turn rough side down and roll to size required.

SUET PASTRY

1 cup (150 g) plain flour   *½ cup (90 g) suet*
1 cup (150 g) self-raising flour   *(or Suet Mix)*
                      water

Sift flours together, shred suet and mix with flour. Mix slowly with enough water to make a very stiff paste. Knead very lightly on lightly floured board, roll out. May be boiled, steamed or baked.

Note 250 g packets of Suet Mix are available.

SWEET PASTRY

1 cup (250 g) butter   *1 egg, beaten*
5 tablespoons (50 g) icing sugar *3 cups (450 g) self-raising flour*

Cream butter and icing sugar together, add beaten egg, then sifted flour. Work the mixture until smooth. Refrigerate until ready to use.

∽ Savoury Pies ∾

Bacon and Egg Pie
Serves 6

1 quantity (500 g) Shortcrust
  Pastry (see p. 180)
6 bacon rashers
6 eggs

salt and pepper
1 tablespoon chopped parsley
beaten egg mixed with
  a little milk

Line a deep pie dish with half the shortcrust pastry. Trim rind from bacon and chop roughly. Place on pastry. Break eggs over bacon, sprinkle with salt and pepper and parsley. Dampen edge of pastry with water. Cover with remaining pastry, sealing edges. Glaze with a little egg and milk. Make a hole in centre of top with a skewer. Bake 10 minutes in preheated hot oven (200°C) then 20–25 minutes at moderate heat (180°C).

Cornish Pasties
Serves 6

200 g minced steak
1 potato, diced
1 small onion, chopped
1/2 white turnip, diced
1/2 carrot, diced

2 teaspoons chopped parsley
salt and pepper
1 quantity (500 g) Shortcrust
  Pastry (see p. 180)
milk

Mix meat, vegetables and parsley together, and season. Divide pastry into 6 equal parts. Knead each part into a ball and roll each into a circle the size of a small plate or saucer. Place an equal portion of meat mixture on each round. Damp the edge. Fold over and press the edges together. Raise the pastry, letting it rest on the middle of the round, and bend the edges into deep curves. Brush with a little milk. Place on a greased baking tray. Bake for about 10 minutes in a preheated hot oven, 200°C, then at moderate, 180°C, for 20–25 minutes.

PORK PIE
Serves 8–10

1 kg lean pork
$^{1}/_{2}$ cup (125 ml) cold water
$^{3}/_{4}$ cup (190 g) lard

4 cups (600 g) plain flour
salt and pepper
1 egg, beaten

Cut pork in small pieces, put in pan with water and bring to the boil. Pour off the water on to lard. Sift flour into a bowl, pour on the lard and hot water slowly, stirring all the time to make the dough. Leave until cool, turn on to floured board and knead for 4–5 minutes. Cut off a quarter of the dough for top. Roll out remainder and line a buttered pie dish. Season the meat with salt and pepper and fill the pie. Roll the quarter of dough into a round and cover pie, moisten and seal the edges. Cut the leaves out of any left-over pastry, make a small hole in the middle of the top, and decorate with the leaves. Brush with beaten egg and bake in a preheated moderate oven (180°C) for 2 hours.

QUICHE
Serves 3–4

PASTRY

120 g plain flour
2 tablespoons (40 g)
  butter or margarine

1$^{1}/_{2}$ tablespoons (30 ml)
  iced water
1 egg yolk

BASIC FILLING

1 medium onion
1 tablespoon butter or margarine
2 eggs

salt and pepper
1 cup (250 ml) milk
$^{1}/_{2}$ cup (60 g) tasty cheese

Rub butter into flour. Work into a firm dough with water and egg yolk. Roll out and line quiche pan. Refrigerate for at least 30 minutes. Place a piece of greaseproof paper covered with tablespoon of rice or dried lentils over pastry. Bake in preheated moderate oven (180°C) for 7 minutes. Remove paper and rice. Bake a further 3 minutes. Cool.

Make filling: slice onion, sauté in margarine until soft but do not brown. Beat eggs, season, add milk and grated cheese. Mix well. Place onion rings on prepared pastry base, gently pour mixture over. Bake in preheated hot oven (200°C) for 10 minutes, then at 180°C for 20–25 minutes.

Variations

Asparagus Quiche: Add 1 x 340 g can asparagus cuts, drained.
Crab Quiche: Add 1 x 95 g can crab meat, drained, 1 tablespoon chopped parsley, 1 tablespoon lemon juice.
Quiche Lorraine: Add 60 g chopped and sautéed bacon.
Spinach Quiche: Add 125 g chopped spinach and 1/2 teaspoon grated nutmeg.
Sweet Corn Quiche: Add 1 x 95 g can creamed corn, 6 chopped spring onions or 1 chopped green capsicum, and top with 1 sliced tomato.

Note Mini quiches make ideal finger food.

SEAFOOD PIE
Serves 4–6

1 x 425 g can tuna or salmon
2 tablespoons (40 g) butter
  or margarine
125 g mushrooms, sliced
1 small onion, chopped
1 clove garlic, crushed
1/2 teaspoon dried oregano

2 tablespoons (20 g) plain flour
1 1/2 cups (375 ml) milk
2 tablespoons (40 ml) lemon
  juice
salt and pepper
500 g Rough Puff Pastry
  (see p. 179)

Flake fish, removing any skin and bones (optional). Heat butter and sauté mushrooms, onion, garlic and oregano until tender. Add flour, cook for 1 minute then gradually add milk, stirring until thick. Fold in flaked fish, add lemon juice and seasonings. Roll out two-thirds of the pastry and line pie dish (20–23 cm diameter). Add filling, and top with remainder of pastry. Trim edges, seal and flute. Make pastry leaves for top, brush with milk and bake in hot oven (200°C) until golden brown for about 40 minutes.

Note 500 g cooked fish may be used instead of canned fish.

⤳ Sweet Recipes ⤳
Almond Cheesecakes

Pastry

2 cups (300 g) plain flour
1/2 cup (125 g) sugar
1 tablespoon (20 g) butter or margarine
2 eggs
water if required

Filling

1 egg
1/2 cup (125 g) sugar
1 tablespoon (20 g) butter or margarine
almond essence to taste
1 tablespoon desiccated coconut

Make the pastry by rubbing butter into the flour and sugar using fingertips, and mixing into a stiff dough with eggs and water if required. Roll out pastry and using a biscuit cutter, cut out rounds and line patty tins. Beat egg, sugar and butter to a cream, add almond essence and coconut. Put 1 teaspoon mixture in each patty tin, and bake in a preheated moderate oven (180°C) for 10 minutes.

Apple Pie
Serves 6

6 apples, peeled and sliced
4 cloves
3 tablespoons (60 g) sugar
500 g Flaky Pastry (see p. 178)
or Shortcrust Pastry (see p. 180)
extra sugar

Place apples in a pie dish with sugar and cloves in layers. Cover dish with pastry, glaze with water and sprinkle with sugar. Bake in a preheated hot oven (200°C) for 30 minutes, reducing heat if necessary after 15 minutes.

Apple Slice

1/2 cup (125 g) butter or
  margarine
1/2 cup (125 g) sugar
1 egg, beaten
1 1/2 cups (375 g) self-raising
  flour
1 teaspoon cinnamon
1 teaspoon ground ginger
1 teaspoon mixed spice
4 apples, peeled, sliced and
  stewed

Cream butter and sugar together, add beaten egg and sifted dry ingredients. Chill dough for at least 30 minutes before use. Divide dough in two. Line lamington tray with half. Put warm apple on this and cover with rest of dough. Glaze with water and sugar. Bake in preheated moderate oven (180°C) for 40 minutes.

Note Canned pie apple may be used.

BAKED APPLE BASKETS
Serves 4

4 apples (about 500 g)	*2 teaspoons butter*
1 quantity (500 g) Shortcrust Pastry (see p. 180)	*2 tablespoons (40 g) sugar*
	4 cloves or nutmeg

Peel and core each apple. Roll out pastry into a large square and cut into 4 squares large enough to cover each apple. Place an apple on each square, fill up apple hole with sugar, a little butter and a clove or a pinch of nutmeg. Brush edges of pastry with water. Gather edges of square together over each apple. Place apple baskets on a baking tray. Glaze with water and sugar. Bake in oven preheated to 220°C for 30 minutes, reduce heat to 180°C and continue baking until the apple is soft when tested with a skewer.

CUSTARD TART
Serves 6

1/2 quantity (250 g) Shortcrust Pastry (see p. 180)	*2 tablespoons (40 g) sugar*
1 1/2 cups (375 ml) milk	*3 drops vanilla essence*
2 eggs	*nutmeg*

Line a pie dish with shortcrust pastry. Warm milk, beat eggs and sugar, then add milk and vanilla essence. Gently pour custard into pie dish. Sprinkle with nutmeg. Place pie dish on oven tray. Bake in preheated hot oven (200°C) for 15 minutes, reduce heat to 180°C and cook until custard is firm and the pastry is cooked.

FRUIT PIE (RHUBARB, PLUM, PEACH OR APRICOT)

Serves 4

500 g fruit
1/4 cup (60 g) sugar
2 tablespoons (40 ml) water

1/2 quantity (250 g)
Shortcrust Pastry (see p. 180)

Prepare fruit, cutting into suitable sized pieces, and put in pie dish. Add sugar (rhubarb will require more than other fruit) and water. Cover with shortcrust pastry. Glaze top with water and sprinkle on sugar. Make hole in centre. Bake in preheated moderate oven (180°C) for 30–40 minutes.

LEMON MERINGUE PIE

Serves 4–6

1/2 quantity (250 g) Rough
  Puff Pastry (see p. 179) or
  Shortcrust Pastry (see p. 180)
1 tablespoon butter or
  margarine
6 tablespoons (120 ml) water

rind and juice of 1 lemon
1 tablespoon cornflour
4 tablespoons (80 g) sugar
2 eggs, separated
2 tablespoons (40 g) caster sugar

Line a pie dish with pastry. Melt the butter in small pan, add the water with grated rind and juice. Blend cornflour with a little cold water, and add to pan. Stir in sugar and well-beaten egg yolks. Bring to the boil. Pour mixture into pie dish and bake in preheated moderate oven (180°C) for 10 minutes, reduce heat to 120°C and bake for a further 20 minutes. Beat egg whites until stiff, add caster sugar gradually and beat until thick. Pile meringue on pie, return to oven and brown top slightly.

Note A bought pastry shell can be used and saves work.

MILDURA MINCE TART

Serves 6

1 cup (180 g) sultanas
1 cup (180 g) currants

1/2 cup (65 g) nuts
1/2 cup (90 g) grated apple

rind of 1 lemon
sugar

1 quantity (500 g) Shortcrust
Pastry (see p. 180)
icing sugar

Mince fruit and nuts together finely, sprinkle with sugar. Divide thinly rolled pastry into equal halves and put one pastry sheet on a greased baking tray. Spread with mixture. Top with remaining pastry. Cut into squares and bake 10–15 minutes in a preheated moderate oven (180°C). When cold dredge with icing sugar.

VANILLA SLICE
Makes 18

1 quantity (500 g) Flaky Pastry (see p. 178)
1 quantity Confectioners' Custard (see below)
1 quantity Soft Icing (see p. 238)

Make the pastry. Roll out thinly and divide in two. Lay pastry on a tin sprinkled with water and mark into squares with sides about 8 cm long. Bake in a hot oven (200°C) till well risen and underside is cooked. Cut into squares. When cold, sandwich two squares together with custard then coat tops of squares with icing.

Note Four sheets of commercially prepared pastry can be substituted for the Flaky Pastry. Each sheet should be cut into 9 squares.

CONFECTIONERS' CUSTARD

2 tablespoons (40 g) butter
3 tablespoons (30 g) flour
1 cup (250 ml) milk

1 egg, beaten
2 tablespoons (40 g) sugar
1 teaspoon vanilla essence

Melt butter in pan, add flour and stir till smooth. Add milk, stir till boiling and cook for 1 minute. Cool slightly, add beaten egg, sugar and essence.

Note Confectioners' Custard is used in Vanilla Slice, but can also be used in tarts or flans.

Hint To get a more yellow appearance substitute custard powder for flour.

Sandwiches

Sandwiches have taken on a new dimension with the arrival of so many new breads and fillings on the market. Try slicing and wrapping your favourite sandwich fillings in some of these breads. Choose from:

Ciabatta: Crisp, crusty Italian-style loaf.
Foccacia: Flat Italian loaves, can be split and filled. Delicious toasted.
Mountain bread: Place fillings at one end of this thin, flat bread and roll up to make a wrap.
Naan: Indian bread. Split and fill or use with dips.
Pita bread: Split and wrap fillings, or halve and fill pockets.
Pumpernickel: Danish, dark rye bread. Top with savoury fillings.
Roti: Round Indian flat bread often made with potato. Roll up fillings or use with dips.
Sourdough: A dense, yeast-free loaf, good for sandwiches and toast.
Tortilla: Mexican flat bread. Use to wrap fillings.

Try spreading sandwiches with tasty, low-fat dips such as hummus and tzatziki or use reduced-fat cream cheese, avocado or Mayonnaise instead of butter. For a stronger flavour try a little tapenade or pesto.

As a butter stretcher, beat butter and add up to 1 cup slightly warmed milk to 500 g butter.

Sandwich Fillings

Try any of the breads listed above with the following fillings.
- Cream cheese, smoked salmon, red onion rings and capers.
- Turkey slices with cranberry sauce, lettuce and alfalfa sprouts.

- Ham, mustard, semi sun-dried tomatoes and tasty cheddar cheese.
- Olive tapenade, salami, sliced onion, red capsicum and mozzarella cheese.
- Avocado, lettuce, slices of chicken and roma tomato.
- Curried hard boiled eggs and shredded lettuce.
- Sliced silverside, mustard, cucumber and tomato.
- Roasted eggplant, semi sun-dried tomatoes, baby spinach leaves and cheese.
- Bacon, lettuce and tomato with Mayonnaise.
- Roast beef and horseradish sauce.
- Finely chopped chicken, diced celery and chopped almonds with cream cheese.
- Crunchy peanut butter, sultanas, alfalfa sprouts and thin slices of apple.
- Cream cheese, sultanas, grated carrot.

Ribbon Sandwiches

Butter a slice of bread, spread with sliced ham, add another slice of bread buttered on both sides. Cover with gherkin spread, add another slice of bread buttered on both sides. Cover with slices of tomato and lettuce. Top with slice of buttered bread. Flatten well and cut into finger lengths. Other combinations of fillings may be used.

Super Sandwich Loaf

1 day-old unsliced loaf
1 x 440 g can sliced pineapple
250 g cooked chicken, minced
1/2 stalk celery, finely diced
1 tablespoon chopped green olives
Mayonnaise (see p. 51)

4 hard-boiled eggs
3 tablespoons (60 ml) milk
250 g cream cheese
cayenne pepper
1/2 cup chopped walnuts

Drain pineapple. Remove crusts from loaf and cut lengthwise twice. Spread one layer with filling of minced chicken blended with celery, olives and mayonnaise to moisten. Peel and mash boiled eggs with a little mayonnaise. Spread the second layer with mashed eggs. Stir milk into the cream cheese, add cayenne pepper to taste then nuts and 2 slices of pineapple, cut into small pieces. Spread top and sides of loaf with this cheese. Garnish loaf with remaining pineapple and extra chopped walnuts and stuffed olives. Chill 3 hours. Slice and serve.

✍ FILLINGS ✍

CHEESE SPREAD

2 tablespoons (40 g) butter
1 cup (120 g) grated cheddar cheese
mustard

125 g cream cheese
1 tablespoon tomato sauce
salt and pepper

Cream butter, add other ingredients and beat together with a wooden spoon. Add a teaspoon of chopped olives, gherkin or horseradish sauce as required. Store in an airtight container in the refrigerator.

MOCK TURKEY SPREAD

knob of cheese the size of
  2 walnuts
1 small onion
1 slice stale bread

1 tomato, peeled
knob of butter the size
  of a walnut
sage and thyme

Grate cheese and onion and crumb bread. Chop tomato and cook all ingredients in a saucepan for 10 minutes, stirring often.

STEAK PASTE

500 g beef
1/2 cup (125 ml) water
1 blade mace
salt and pepper

1 tablespoon (20 g) butter
2 tablespoons (40 ml)
   anchovy sauce

Mince beef, put into saucepan with water, mace, salt and pepper, and simmer until meat is tender. Add butter and anchovy sauce. Blend all well together and put into jars. Will keep for several days in a tightly sealed container in the refrigerator.

FRITTERS, PANCAKES AND OMELETTES

INSTRUCTIONS FOR MAKING AND COOKING BATTER

1. Sift flour, and beat until smooth as liquid is added. A food processor or hand–held mixer will help with this.
2. Beat pancake or fritter batter well to make it light.
3. Allow batter to stand for some time before using. This softens the cellulose and makes a lighter batter.
4. Cook quickly and serve immediately.
5. Pancakes can be cooked, stacked between layers of plastic wrap and frozen for up to 3 months.
6. Cook fritters in hot oil for a light, crisp result. Test oil for temperature by dropping a small amount of batter into the oil. Oil should sizzle and batter should rise quickly to the surface.

BASIC FRITTER BATTER

1 cup (150 g) self-raising flour
1/4 teaspoon salt
1 tablespoon oil or melted butter

1/2 cup (125 ml) tepid water
1 egg white

Sift flour into bowl with salt, make a well in centre of flour. Pour in melted butter or oil. Stir into a batter, gradually adding tepid water. Beat well. Beat egg white stiffly and fold into batter just before using.

Use for:
- Sliced cooked meat.
- Fillets of raw fish, oysters, mussels or scallops.
- Sliced apple, pineapple rings or sliced bananas.

BLINIS
Makes 20–30 small savouries

2 eggs
3/4 cup (190 ml) milk
1/2 cup (75 g) buckwheat flour
1/2 cup (75 g) plain flour
1 teaspoon baking powder

25 g butter, melted
sour cream or cream cheese
smoked salmon

Lightly beat eggs and milk together. Sift flours and baking powder together and add egg and milk mixture. Beat well and stir in melted butter. Cook in spoonfuls in a hot greased frying pan and until blinis are golden brown on both sides. Serve topped with a little sour cream — or cream cheese — and smoked salmon.

CORN FRITTERS
Serves 4

1 x 310 g can sweet corn kernels
1/4 cup (60 ml) milk
2 eggs
1/2 cup (125 g) self-raising
   flour
1 tablespoon chopped chives

pinch of chilli flakes
vegetable oil for frying
yoghurt or sour cream
chopped chives

Process corn, milk and eggs until corn is coarsely chopped. Stir corn mixture into a bowl with flour, add chives and chilli. Heat oil in frying pan and drop spoonfuls of mixture into hot oil. Cook until brown on each side. Serve with a little yoghurt or sour cream and chopped chives.

CRÊPES
Serves 4

3/4 cup (110 g) plain flour
1 egg
1 cup (250 ml) milk

1 tablespoon melted butter
extra melted butter for cooking

Sift flour, make a well in the centre and add egg. Work in flour gradually and add milk, beating until mixture is smooth. Lastly add melted butter. Leave to stand before cooking. Use a 16.5 cm frying pan, put it over heat, swirl 1 teaspoon butter around pan, then wipe clean. Add a little extra butter, and heat again, taking care not to burn it. Pour in 3 tablespoons crepe mixture and tilt pan to spread the mixture. Cook until the surface of the crepe begins to dry out and base is golden brown. Turn and cook the other side. Repeat for remaining mixture.

OMELETTE
Serves 1

2 eggs
2 tablespoons water
salt and pepper
1 teaspoon butter

Beat eggs, water, salt and pepper together until combined. Melt butter in frying pan and pour in egg mixture, stir gently until mixture begins to thicken. Allow to cook until set and firm on top. Top with any of the following fillings, fold in half and serve immediately.

Fillings Choose from: freshly chopped mixed herbs, grated cheese, cooked asparagus, mushrooms, sliced tomato, bacon, finely chopped parsley.

SOUFFLÉ OMELETTE
Serves 1

2 eggs
2 tablespoons (40 ml) water
salt and pepper
1 teaspoon butter

Separate eggs and beat egg whites until stiff, gently fold egg yolks, water and seasoning into whites until well mixed. Heat a teaspoon of butter in frying pan. Pour in egg mixture and cook until base is set. Turn with egg lifter and brown the other side or brown top under griller. Top with any of the fillings suggested above for Omelette, and serve immediately.

PANCAKES
Serves 4

1 cup (150 g) plain flour	*1 tablespoon (20 g) butter*
1 egg	*caster sugar*
1 cup (250 ml) milk	*1 lemon*

Sift the flour, make a well in the centre and break the egg into it, gradually stirring in as much flour as the egg will take. Add half the milk by degrees and continue stirring until all the flour is absorbed. Continue beating until bubbles rise then stir in the rest of the milk gradually. Stand batter aside for at least half an hour. Take a small piece of butter and melt in a frying pan, then pour it out and wipe the pan out with kitchen paper towel. Put in another piece of butter and when it has melted pour in a little of the batter and cook until it is light brown. Turn with an egg lifter. When cooked on both sides, slip pancake on to a piece of paper, sprinkle with caster sugar and roll up. Continue in the same way until all the batter is used. Serve hot accompanied by lemon wedges.

PIKELETS OR DROP SCONES
Serves 4–6

2 cups (300 g) self-raising flour	*1 egg*
1/3 cup (80 g) sugar	*1 1/2 cups (375 ml) milk*

Sift flour, add sugar and make a well, drop unbeaten egg in the middle of the bowl and stir. Add enough milk to make a fairly thick batter and beat well. Have the griddle or frying pan well greased. Drop the mixture on to the griddle from the point of a tablespoon to make a good shape. Turn when bubbles appear, allow to brown on second side.

Variations
Apple Pikelets: Add 1 grated apple to the mixture before cooking.
Banana Pikelets: Add 1 mashed banana to the mixture before cooking.
Blueberry Pikelets: Add 1/2 cup fresh or frozen blueberries to the mixture before cooking.

TEMPURA
Serves 4

1 egg yolk
3/4 cup (190 ml) ice-cold
   water
1/2 cup (75 g) besan flour
1/2 cup (65 g) cornflour
oil for frying

vegetables for dipping — green beans topped and tailed, carrots sliced diagonally, zucchini sliced about 0.5 cm thick, onion rings, button mushroom caps — or seafood — prawns, calamari rings, scallops

Beat egg yolk and pour in ice water, add flours all at once and stir lightly until just combined. The batter should be still lumpy. Heat about 2 cups oil in a wok until hot. Dip vegetables or seafood in batter and deep fry until golden. Drain and serve with soy sauce for dipping. Serve as an entrée.

Note Besan flour is also known as chickpea flour and is available in the Asian section of the supermarket.

TUNA FRITTERS
Serves 4

1/2 cup (100 g) rice
1 x 180 g can tuna
1 onion, chopped
1/4 cup (60 ml) milk
2 tablespoons plain flour
1 teaspoon sugar
1 teaspoon vinegar
1 teaspoon chopped parsley
1/4 teaspoon salt
1/4 teaspoon pepper
2 eggs
oil for frying

Cook rice in boiling water for 12 minutes and drain. Combine cooked rice, drained tuna, chopped onion, milk, flour, sugar, vinegar, parsley, salt and pepper. Separate eggs and add the yolks to tuna mixture. Beat egg whites until soft peaks form. Then fold into mixture. Drop spoonfuls into hot oil and fry until golden.

WAFFLES
Serves 4–6

1¹/2 cups (225 g) self-raising flour 1 cup (250 ml) milk
1 egg   1 tablespoon melted butter

Sift flour, beat egg, add milk and butter. Make a well in the flour, pour in liquid, mix well, leave to stand for about an hour. Pour into a well-heated waffle iron. Cook until golden brown.

Desserts

Desserts often form the last course in a meal. They are now also quite popular served with afternoon tea instead of cake.

ᴄꜱ Steamed and Boiled ᴄꜱ Desserts

Important instructions

* Never let the water in which the pudding is being cooked go off the boil.
* If more water is needed, fill up with boiling water.
* If using a bowl, grease and allow room for swelling when covering pudding.
* Have pot in which pudding is to be steamed or boiled with enough boiling water to come halfway up bowl containing food.
* Do not let the water get into the pudding bowl.
* Stand baked custards in a dish of cold water in a cool oven.
* Sauce or ice-cream is usually served with boiled and steamed and some baked puddings.

Boiled Apple Pudding
Serves 6–8

8–9 apples (about 1 kg)　　2 tablespoons (30 g) moist
1 quantity (500 g) Suet Pastry　　brown sugar
(see p. 180)　　6 cloves

Peel, core and cut apples into thick slices. Make suet pastry. Cut off a quarter of the pastry and set aside for the lid. Roll out remainder and line a well-greased bowl. Put in half the fruit, then sugar and cloves and then the rest of the fruit and 3 tablespoons cold water. Roll out the rest of the pastry to fit the top of bowl, moisten the edges slightly with water, join them carefully to the edge of the pastry lining the bowl. Cover with lid, or with 2 folds of greased paper or greased foil. Place in pot of boiling water (water should come halfway up basin) and boil for 2½–3 hours.

Variations Plums, rhubarb or quinces may be used instead of apples.

CHOCOLATE PUDDING
Serves 4

2 tablespoons (40 g) butter
  or margarine
½ cup (125 g) sugar
1 egg, beaten
¾ cup (110 g) self-raising flour

1 tablespoon cocoa
¼ cup (60 ml) milk
¼ teaspoon bicarbonate of
  soda dissolved in ¼ cup
  (60 ml) boiling water

Cream butter and sugar together, add beaten egg and mix well. Add sifted flour and cocoa, alternately with milk. Lastly add bicarbonate of soda and water. Mix well. Steam for 1 hour.

CHRISTMAS PUDDING
Serves 6–8

2 cups (360 g) sultanas
1½ cups (270 g) raisins,
  chopped
1 cup (180 g) prunes, chopped
1 cup (180 g) mixed peel
rind of 1 lemon
rind of 1 orange
½ cup (60 g) chopped almonds
1 large carrot, grated

2 cups (120 g) fresh breadcrumbs
1 cup (150 g) plain flour
1 cup (250 g) sugar
½ teaspoon nutmeg
½ teaspoon mixed spice
2 cups (250 g) butter or suet
4 eggs
1 cup (250 ml) orange juice
¼ cup (60 ml) milk

Grease 3 medium or 2 large basins. Mix first 8 ingredients together, then mix crumbs, flour, sugar and spices in a large bowl. Rub butter into flour mixture, or mix in suet, then add fruit mixture. Mix eggs, juice and milk and combine with other ingredients. Transfer mixture to basins allowing space for pudding to swell. Place 2 thicknesses of foil on top of basins and tie securely or fold under rim (if preferred puddings may be cooked in prepared pudding cloth). Place puddings in boiling water in large pot and boil steadily for 5 hours for large or 3 hours for small. As water evaporates, replace with more boiling water. On the day the pudding is to be served, boil for 1 hour more (or microwave for 8–10 minutes depending on size). Serve with ice-cream or sauce.

EASY PLUM PUDDING
Serves 4

1 cup (250 ml) milk
1½ cups (270 g) mixed fruit
1 tablespoon butter or margarine
2 tablespoons (40 g) sugar

1 teaspoon bicarbonate of soda
1 cup (150 g) self-raising flour
1 teaspoon mixed spice
1 teaspoon cinnamon

Place milk, fruit, butter and sugar in a saucepan, bring to the boil then stir in bicarbonate of soda. Allow to cool. Sift in flour and spices and mix gently. Put in greased basin, cover and steam for 1½ hours.

FOUNDATION STEAMED PUDDING
Serves 4

¼ cup (60 g) butter or margarine
¼ cup (65 g) sugar
1 egg

1 cup (150 g) self-raising flour
2 tablespoons (40 ml) milk
½ teaspoon vanilla essence

Cream butter and sugar together, add egg and beat well. Add milk and vanilla essence, then sifted flour. Grease bowl, fill it two-thirds full with mixture, cover and steam for 1¼–1½ hours.

Variations
Chocolate Pudding: Replace 1 tablespoon flour with 1 tablespoon cocoa.
Coconut Pudding: Add 3 tablespoons desiccated coconut, 2 extra tablespoons milk and 4 drops almond essence.
Devon Pudding: Add 2 tablespoons sultanas to mixture.
Marguerite Pudding: Place 2 tablespoons jam in bottom of greased bowl.

GOLDEN SYRUP DUMPLINGS
Serves 4

1 cup (150 g) self-raising flour   1 cup (250 ml) water
2 tablespoons (40 g) butter   1 tablespoon golden syrup
   or margarine   *1/2* cup (125 g) sugar
milk   juice of 1 lemon

Rub butter into flour. Mix to a stiff dough with a little milk. Form into balls. Bring water, syrup, sugar and lemon juice to the boil. Drop dumplings into boiling syrup and cook for 20 minutes.

ᴄ✦ BAKED DESSERTS ✦ᴐ

APPLE NICHOLAS
Serves 3–4

4 cooking apples   2 tablespoons self-raising flour
1 tablespoon butter or margarine   1 cup (250 ml) cold water
   3/4 cup (185 g) sugar

Peel and core apples and slice crosswise. Place in lightly greased pie dish. Rub butter into flour and sprinkle on top of apples. Pour water and sugar over. Bake for 30 minutes in preheated moderate oven (180°C).

BAKED CHOCOLATE PUDDING
Serves 4

1 cup (150 g) self-raising flour   2 tablespoons (40 g) butter
2 teaspoons cocoa   *1/2* cup (125 ml) milk
3/4 cup (190 g) sugar   or margarine

SAUCE
1/2 cup (75 g) brown sugar   *1 3/4* cups (440 ml) boiling water
2 teaspoons cocoa

Sift flour with 2 teaspoons cocoa, add sugar. Melt butter and stir into flour mixture. Add milk and mix. Pour into pie dish. Combine brown sugar and 2 teaspoons cocoa. Sprinkle on top of mixture in dish and pour boiling water gently over this. Bake in a preheated moderate oven (180°C) for 45 minutes.

BAKED CUSTARD
Serves 4–6

3 eggs
2 tablespoons (40 g) sugar
2 cups (500 ml) milk

1/2 teaspoon vanilla essence
nutmeg
1/2 teaspoon butter

Beat eggs and sugar together lightly. Warm milk, add to egg mixture, add essence. Strain into pie dish, sprinkle with nutmeg, dot with butter. Stand pie dish in larger dish containing some water. Bake in moderate oven (180°C) for 45 minutes. To see if cooked, slip a knife in centre. If set, custard will show a cut when knife is removed.

BAKED PASSIONFRUIT CHEESECAKES
Serves 4

4 shortbread biscuits
1 cup (250 g) ricotta cheese
1 cup (250 g) cream cheese
2 eggs

1/2 cup (125 g) sugar
2 tablespoons (40 ml) lime juice
2/3 cup (170 ml) passionfruit
pulp

Preheat oven to 160°C. Put a biscuit in the base of 4 ramekins. Put the ricotta, cream cheese, eggs, sugar and lime juice in the food processor and process till smooth. Fold in the passionfruit pulp and spoon the mixture into each ramekin. Bake in oven for 15 minutes — when ready the topping should be firm. Serve warm or cold.

BAKED RICE
Serves 4

1/4 cup (50 g) rice
2 tablespoons (40 g) sugar

2 cups (500 ml) milk or 1 cup
(250 ml) each milk and water

Combine ingredients in a casserole. Bake in slow oven

(150°C) for 1½–2 hours. Stir occasionally. Serve with crushed pineapple.

Note *Baked Sago* can be made in the same way.

BREAD AND BUTTER PUDDING
Serves 4

2–3 thin slices white bread,
  buttered
2 tablespoons (30 g) sultanas
  or currants
2 eggs

1 tablespoon sugar
2 cups (500 ml) milk
½ teaspoon vanilla essence
a little grated nutmeg

Cut buttered bread into squares and lay them in a lightly greased pie dish with the sultanas. Beat eggs and sugar together, add milk and essence, and pour over bread. Grate a little nutmeg over the top. Allow the pudding to stand for 10 minutes for the bread to swell and absorb some of the milk. Bake in a preheated moderate oven (180°C) for 45 minutes.

Variation Try substituting fruit bread, brioches or panettone for white bread. Dried, chopped apricots can replace sultanas.

CARAMEL CUSTARD
Serves 4–6

½ cup (125 g) sugar
2 tablespoons (40 ml) water
3 eggs
1 tablespoon sugar

2 cups (500 ml) milk
½ teaspoon vanilla essence
½ teaspoon grated nutmeg
½ teaspoon butter

Put sugar and water in a small pan, and heat gently, stirring until sugar is dissolved. Increase heat without stirring until boiling and allow to boil until a pale amber colour. Pour quickly into pie dish, coating sides. Beat eggs and sugar together lightly. Warm milk, add to egg mixture, add essence. Strain into pie dish, sprinkle with nutmeg, dot with butter. Stand pie dish in larger dish containing some water. Bake in preheated moderate oven (180°C) for 45 minutes.

DUTCH APPLE TART
Serves 6–8

$^3/_4$ cup (190 g) butter or
   margarine
$^3/_4$ cup (190 g) sugar
2 cups (300 g) self-raising flour
2 eggs, beaten

8 apples (about 1 kg), peeled
   and sliced
1 tablespoon cinnamon
1 tablespoon caster sugar
1 cup (180 g) sultanas

Cream butter and sugar together, add the flour and most of the beaten eggs. Roll out and line a large round tin (base and sides) with four-fifths of the mixture. Spoon in the uncooked apple and sprinkle each layer with cinnamon, sugar and sultanas. Criss-cross remaining mixture over the apple and brush with egg. Cook in a preheated moderate oven (180°C) for 1 hour.

EVE'S PUDDING
Serves 4

6 apples (about 750 g),
   peeled and sliced
$^1/_4$ cup (60 g) sugar
2 tablespoons (40 ml) water
3 cloves

$^1/_4$ cup (60 g) caster sugar
$^1/_4$ cup (60 g) butter or margarine
1 egg
1 cup (150 g) self-raising flour
3 tablespoons (60 ml) milk

Put apples, sugar, water and cloves in saucepan and cook until tender. Place in greased pie dish. Cream butter and sugar, then beat in egg. Sift in flour and milk alternately and mix well. Cover apples with mixture and bake in preheated moderate oven (180°C) for 30–45 minutes.

FRUIT CRUMBLE
Serves 4

500 g fresh fruit e.g. rhubarb, apples or plums
$^1/_2$ cup (125 g) sugar $^1/_4$ cup (60 ml) water

TOPPING

$^1/_2$ cup (75 g) brown sugar
$^1/_2$ cup (75 g) plain flour
$^1/_2$ cup (45 g) desiccated
   coconut or muesli

1 teaspoon cinnamon
$^1/_4$ cup (60 g) butter or
   margarine, melted

Peel and slice fruit. Cook with water and sugar until soft. Place in a lightly greased pie dish. Mix topping ingredients together and cover fruit mixture. Bake in preheated moderate oven (180°C) for 30 minutes.

Note Other fruit, including canned, may be used.

LEMON DELICIOUS
Serves 4

1 tablespoon butter or margarine
1 cup (250 g) sugar
2 tablespoons self-raising flour
grated rind and juice of 1 lemon
1 cup (250 ml) milk
2 eggs, separated

Cream butter and sugar together, add flour, lemon rind and juice, milk and beaten yolks, and beat well. Beat the whites stiffly, fold into the mixture and pour into a lightly greased pie dish. Set dish in water bath and bake in moderately hot oven (190°C) for 45 minutes–1 hour, until set and golden brown.

PINEAPPLE UPSIDE DOWN CAKE
Serves 4–6

1 tablespoon butter or margarine
3 tablespoons (45 g) brown sugar
pineapple pieces (or other fruit)
1/4 cup (60 g) butter
1/4 cup (60 g) sugar
1 egg
2 tablespoons (40 ml) milk
1/4 teaspoon vanilla essence
1 cup (150 g) self-raising flour

Melt butter in 20 cm round cake tin, sprinkle with brown sugar. Arrange pieces of pineapple (or other fruit) in tin. Cream butter and sugar together, add egg and beat well. Add milk and vanilla, then sifted flour. Spoon mixture on top of fruit and bake in preheated moderate oven (180°C) for 45 minutes. Allow to stand in tin for 3–4 minutes before turning out onto a serving dish. Decorate with cherries or nuts and cream.

SPICED APPLE CAKE

Serves 4–6

1 cup (150 g) plain flour
1 teaspoon baking powder
1/2 cup (125 g) butter or margarine
1 teaspoon cinnamon
1 teaspoon mixed spice

1/2 teaspoon ground ginger
1/2 cup (75 g) brown sugar
1 egg, beaten
1 1/2 cups (375 g) stewed
    apple, cold

Sift flour and baking powder into bowl. Rub butter into flour, add spices and sugar. Add egg. Divide in two. Roll half into a round and place in greased sandwich cake tin. Spread with apple, then cover with remaining mixture. Bake in preheated moderate oven (180°C) for 45–60 minutes.

STICKY DATE PUDDING

Serves 6–8

1 cup (180 g) dates, chopped
1 small teaspoon bicarbonate
    of soda
300 ml boiling water
3 tablespoons (60 g) butter
    or margarine

3/4 cup (190 g) caster sugar
2 eggs, beaten
1 1/2 cups (225 g) self-raising
    flour
1/2 teaspoon vanilla essence

SAUCE

1/2 cup (125 g) unsalted butter
3/4 cup (190 ml) cream

3/4 cup (110 g) brown sugar

Put dates in a bowl. Add bicarbonate of soda and boiling water and mix together. Cream butter and sugar together until fluffy. Add eggs gradually, beating well. Fold in flour, then date mixture and vanilla. Pour mixture into a greased and lined 18 cm square tin and bake in a preheated 180°C oven for 35–40 minutes. Make sauce by putting ingredients into small saucepan, bringing to the boil and simmering for 5 minutes.

When ready to serve, turn pudding out into ovenproof dish, pour over some of the sauce, and put back in oven for 5 minutes. Cut into squares and serve with remaining sauce and cream or ice-cream.

Note Figs or apricots can be used instead of dates.

∽ COLD DESSERTS ∾

CHOCOLATE MOUSSE
Serves 4

125 g dark chocolate
2 teaspoons vanilla essence

4 eggs, separated
1 cup (250 ml) cream

GARNISH

chocolate curls

sliced strawberries

Chop chocolate roughly, put into top of double saucepan and stir over hot water until melted. Remove from heat, cool slightly, gradually add essence and egg yolks. Beat until mixture is smooth and thick. Whip cream in a separate bowl and fold into the chocolate mixture. Using clean beaters, whip egg whites until peaks form. Fold half the egg whites into the chocolate mixture. Gently fold the remaining whites through the mixture. Spoon into individual dishes or one large dish and chill until firm. Serve garnished with chocolate curls or sliced strawberries.

CHOCOLATE TIRAMISU (LOW-FAT VERSION)
Serves 4

150 g sponge or Madeira cake
1 tablespoon sugar
1/2 cup (125 ml) strong black
   coffee

2 teaspoons vanilla essence
3/4 cup (190 ml) low-fat vanilla
   yoghurt
chocolate shavings

Cut cake in 4 and put on serving plates. Dissolve sugar in coffee, and boil for 5 minutes. Cool coffee, add vanilla. Drizzle coffee mixture over cake. Allow to stand for at least 2 hours. Top with yoghurt and chocolate shavings just before serving.

CRÈME BRÛLÉE
Serves 4

2 cups (500 ml) cream
1 vanilla pod or a few drops
   vanilla essence

5 egg yolks
3 tablespoons (60 g) caster sugar
1/3 cup (80 g) sugar

Put cream and vanilla pod in saucepan over low heat. Allow cream to simmer for 3 minutes, and then stand for about 20 minutes to allow vanilla to flavour cream. Remove vanilla pod. Add egg yolks and caster sugar to cream, stirring over low heat until mixture coats the back of a wooden spoon. Pour mixture into 4 small ramekins. Place in a baking dish with sufficient water to come halfway up the sides and put baking dish in oven preheated to 180°C, cook for 20 minutes. Remove ramekins from baking dish and allow to cool in refrigerator. Sprinkle tops with sugar, place under hot grill for 1 minute until sugar melts and is golden brown, or use hand-held blowtorch to get same result.

Variation Wattle Seed Crème Brûlée is made with 2 teaspoons wattle seeds added to the cream.

LEMON CHEESECAKE
Serves 6–8

CRUST

2 cups (200 g) crushed
   biscuits

1/2 cup (125 g) butter or
   margarine

FILLING

1 cup (250 g) cream cheese
1 x 395 g can condensed milk

1/2 cup (125 ml) lemon juice

For crust, melt butter, add to crushed biscuits. Press into springform cake tin. Beat cream cheese, gradually add condensed milk, then lemon juice. Pour into crumb casing and refrigerate.

LEMON SAGO
Serves 4

2 cups (500 ml) water
³/4 cup (150 g) sago
¹/2 cup (125 ml) lemon juice

2 tablespoons (40 g) sugar
1 tablespoon honey

Bring water to the boil, add sago and stir until mixture boils, then simmer until cooked (15–20 minutes). Add lemon juice, sugar and honey and cook for 2 more minutes. Put into serving dish and allow to cool. Serve with cream or custard.

LEMON SNOW
Serves 4

2 tablespoons (20 g) cornflour
2 tablespoons (40 ml) cold water
2 cups (500 ml) water

1 cup (250 g) sugar
rind and juice of 1 lemon
2 egg whites, stiffly beaten

Blend cornflour with cold water. Put all ingredients except egg whites in pan. Heat, stirring, until mixture thickens. When cold, fold in stiffly beaten egg whites.

Note Custard can be made from the yolks.

LIME PARFAITS
Serves 4

1 x 85 g packet lime jelly crystals
1 cup (250 ml) boiling water
1 cup (250 g) cream cheese, softened
1 cup (250 g) sugar

1 tablespoon orange juice
1 tablespoon lemon juice
2 teaspoons grated lemon rind
1 cup (250 ml) whipped cream

Dissolve crystals in boiling water. Cool slightly. Beat cheese until smooth, then gradually add sugar, orange and lemon juice and rind, and the warm jelly mixture, mixing well. Chill until almost setting and fold in cream. Pour into parfait glasses and chill again.

Pavlova
Serves 6

4 egg whites
1 1/3 cups (335 g) caster sugar
1 tablespoon cornflour

2 teaspoons vinegar
few drops of vanilla essence

Grease an oven tray and dust with a little cornflour. Beat egg whites until stiff, add sugar gradually, beating all the time. Fold in cornflour, vinegar and essence. Pile mixture onto tray and cook in a slow oven (120–150°C) for 2 hours. When cold decorate with fruit and cream.

Pears Belle Hélène
Serves 5

1/2 cup (125 g) sugar
2 cups (500 ml) water

2 teaspoons vanilla essence
5 pears

Sauce

125 g dark chocolate
1 cup (250 ml) water

1/3 cup (80 ml) sugar

Dissolve sugar in water in a deep pan, stirring until dissolved. Add vanilla essence. Peel pears and carefully core. Place pears in pan and cook until tender. Cool in syrup, occasionally basting.

Make sauce: break up chocolate, add to water and simmer very gently until chocolate dissolves. Add sugar, simmer until sauce will coat back of spoon. Cool. To serve, drain pears and coat with sauce.

Pineapple Cream
Serves 4–6

1 x 440 g can crushed pineapple
1/2 cup (125 g) sugar
1 tablespoon butter or margarine

1 tablespoon cornflour
2 eggs, separated

Garnish

cream

chopped nuts

211

Drain pineapple, make juice up to 1 cup with water. Place juice, sugar and butter in pan, bring gently to the boil, stirring until sugar is dissolved. Remove from heat. Blend cornflour with a little cold water, add to mixture stirring rapidly. Return to heat. Cook for 2 minutes. Leave to cool slightly, add beaten egg yolks and mix well. Beat egg whites until stiff, fold into pineapple mixture. Decorate with cream and chopped nuts.

SUMMER PUDDING
Serves 4–6

1 cup (250 ml) water
1/4 cup (60 g) sugar
2 Granny Smith apples,
  peeled and sliced

2 cups berry fruits (see note)
butter or margarine
sliced white bread

BERRY SAUCE
reserved juice

cornflour

Boil water and sugar until sugar has dissolved. Add apples and berries, cook until pulpy. Strain fresh pulp, reserving juice. Add half the juice to pulp and reserve rest for sauce. Lightly grease a 1 L soufflé dish. Remove crusts and cut each bread slice in 3 sections; cover bottom and sides of dish with the bread. Spoon layer of pulp into dish, ensuring bread is well soaked. Continue layering bread and pulp, finishing with bread. Cover with greased plate of size to fit dish exactly. Press plate down with a heavy weight. Set overnight in refrigerator.

Make berry sauce: blend remaining cold juice with cornflour — 1 teaspoon cornflour per cup of juice — and boil for 1 minute until thickened. To serve, run knife round edge of soufflé dish and turn on to serving plate. Serve with berry sauce and cream.

Note Use fresh, frozen or canned raspberries, blackberries, boysenberries, but not strawberries.

TRIFLE
Serves 4–6

single layer sponge cake
2 tablespoons (60 g) raspberry
  or apricot jam
fruit juice

2¹/2 cups (625 ml) milk
2 tablespoons custard powder
2 teaspoons sugar

GARNISH

¹/2 cup (125 ml) cream
glacé cherries

chopped nuts

Spread jam on sponge and line a serving bowl with sponge cut into slices. Moisten slices with fruit juice. Make custard by blending powder with a little of the milk, heating remainder of milk in saucepan, adding blended powder, stirring all the time until boiling and cooking for 2 minutes, then mix in sugar. Pour into bowl, decorate with whipped cream, chopped nuts, glacé cherries or chopped jelly.

Hints

Swiss roll may be used instead of sponge cake, in which case omit jam.

Canned fruit may be placed on top of trifle.

Ready-made custard may be used if time is short.

∽ ICE-CREAMS ∾ AND FROZEN DESSERTS

ICE-CREAM MADE WITH POWDERED MILK
Serves 4–6

1 teaspoon gelatine
¹/4 cup (60 ml) boiling water
1 cup (250 ml) milk
2 tablespoons (40 g) sugar

4 tablespoons (40 g)
  powdered milk
1 teaspoon vanilla essence

Dissolve gelatine in boiling water. Place other ingredients in freezer-proof bowl. Add gelatine mixture and beat well with rotary or electric beater. Freeze to a mush, then beat again in chilled bowl until almost doubled in size. Freeze till firm.

Variations

Berry: Add 1/2 cup crushed chilled berries, e.g. strawberries or raspberries, at second beating.

Butterscotch: Brown 1 tablespoon butter with 3 tablespoons (40 g) brown sugar and allow to cool, add to chilled ice-cream at second beating.

Chocolate: Add 2 tablespoons (20 g) cocoa powder.

Coffee and Walnut: Omit vanilla, but add 2 teaspoons instant coffee dissolved in 1 tablespoon hot water and 1/2 cup chopped walnuts.

Pineapple: Add 1/2 cup crushed pineapple at second beating.

Plum Pudding: Add 1/2 cup fruit mince.

ORANGE AND LEMON SHERBET
Serves 4

1/2 cup (125 ml) orange juice
1/2 cup (125 ml) lemon juice
1 cup (250 g) sugar
1 cup (250 ml) milk
1 cup (250 ml) whipped cream

Combine orange and lemon juice and sugar. Add milk and freeze until firm. Remove from freezer and beat in whipped cream. Return to freezer for 2 hours.

PINEAPPLE SHERBET
Serves 4

1/2 cup (180 ml) maple or
*   golden syrup*
1/3 cup (80 g) sugar
2 cups (500 ml) milk
1 1/2 cups (375 ml) crushed pineapple
1 teaspoon grated lemon rind
1/4 cup (60 ml) lemon juice
2 egg whites

Mix ingredients except egg whites until sugar is dissolved. Freeze until firm. Return to bowl, beat until fluffy and then fold in stiffly beaten egg whites. Freeze again before serving.

Strawberry Gelati

Serves 4

2 cups (500 g) sugar
1¹/₂ cups (375 ml) water
4 cups (500 g) strawberries,
   mashed

juice of 1 lemon
2 egg whites
1 cup (250 ml) cream
   (optional)

Place sugar and water in saucepan and heat gently. Stir until all sugar dissolves. Increase heat to boiling and cook without stirring until the syrup will form into a soft ball when dropped into cold water. Pour over fruit, cool then add lemon juice. Freeze. Beat egg whites stiffly and fold into mixture, and fold in cream if using. Freeze again.

Note Other fruits may be used in place of strawberries.

Vanilla Ice-Cream

Serves 6

¹/₂ cup (125 g) sugar
1¹/₂ cups (375 ml) full cream
   or evaporated milk

2 eggs, separated
1 cup (250 ml) cream
1 teaspoon vanilla essence

Dissolve sugar in milk. Beat the egg whites till stiff. Beat yolks till thick and lemon coloured. Beat cream till thick but not stiff. Add vanilla. Combine all ingredients and mix well. Pour into tray and freeze, using coldest setting. Stir every 30 minutes until mixture holds its shape, then freeze till set.

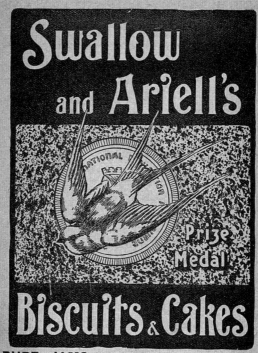

Cakes

Important instructions

1. When making cakes, all ingredients should be at hand before starting to mix. Also preheat oven, and prepare cake tins by lightly greasing, lining the base with paper or dusting with flour.
2. Flour and baking powder should always be sifted.
3. Butter and sugar should be beaten to a creamy consistency.
4. The whites of egg must be beaten stiffly enough to remain on the plate or in a bowl if turned upside down.
5. When baking fruit cakes the oven should be fairly hot for the first 15 minutes — this prevents the fruit sinking.
6. When baking large cakes, two thicknesses of brown paper and one of baking paper may be put in the tin to prevent uneven cooking.
7. When cakes are sufficiently brown, a piece of paper placed over the top prevents them getting any browner.
8. Sponge cakes require a moderate oven (180°C).
9. Flour, when added to sponge cakes, should be folded in as lightly as possible, as beating in flour makes the cakes tough and heavy.
10. To test if cakes are cooked, run skewer through the centre; if it comes out clean and dry the cake should be cooked.
11. Turn all cakes on to cake cooler — sponges should be turned out immediately after they are taken from the oven, but allow butter cakes to stand 5–10 minutes in tin before turning out.
12. For better results egg and milk should be at room temperature before use.
13. Margarine may be substituted for butter but avoid using 'light' margarine.

14. If using bicarbonate of soda, be very accurate when measuring it, as excess can give a cake a soapy taste.

BANANA CAKE

1/2 cup (125 g) butter
1/2 cup (125 g) caster sugar
2 eggs
2 small bananas, mashed

few drops of vanilla essence
1/2 teaspoon bicarbonate of soda
1 tablespoon milk
2 cups (300 g) self-raising flour

Cream butter and sugar together. Add eggs, one at a time, beating each in well. Then add bananas and vanilla. Dissolve bicarbonate of soda in milk and add to mixture. Lastly fold in flour. Bake in greased tin in preheated moderate oven (180°C) for 45 minutes. Can be iced with Lemon Icing (see p. 237).

BOILED FRUIT CAKE

150 g butter
1 1/2 cups (270 g) sultanas
1 1/2 cups (270 g) currants
1 cup (150 g) brown sugar
2 teaspoons mixed spice

1 teaspoon bicarbonate of soda
1 cup (250 ml) water
2 eggs
1 cup (150 g) plain flour
1 cup (150 g) self-raising flour

Boil together butter, fruit, sugar, spice, soda and water. Cool. Add well-beaten eggs and finally flour. Bake 65 minutes in preheated moderate oven (180°C) in prepared 20 cm round tin or 18 cm square tin.

BRACK

2 3/4 cups (500 g) mixed fruit
1 cup (150 g) brown sugar
1 cup (250 ml) cold black tea

2 cups (300 g) self-raising flour
1 egg, well beaten

Soak fruit and sugar overnight in tea. Add flour and egg. Bake in a prepared tin in preheated moderate oven (180°C) for about 1 1/2–1 3/4 hours or until cooked in the centre.

BRAN LOAF

1 cup (75 g) bran
1 cup (150 g) wholemeal flour
1/4 cup (40 g) brown sugar
1 teaspoon baking powder

1/2 teaspoon bicarbonate of soda
1 egg, beaten
3/4 cup (185 ml) milk soured
   with 1 teaspoon lemon juice

Mix all dry ingredients together. Add remaining ingredients. Place in oiled loaf tin. Bake in preheated moderate oven (180°C) for 45 minutes.

CARROT CAKE

3 eggs, well beaten
1 cup (250 ml) vegetable oil
2 cups (250 g) self-raising flour
1 cup (250 g) raw sugar
2 cups (200 g) grated carrot

1 teaspoon mixed spice
1 teaspoon cinnamon
1/2 cup (90 g) sultanas
1/2 cup (60 g) walnut pieces
1/2 cup (45 g) desiccated coconut

Mix beaten egg and oil together. Combine the other ingredients, mix well then add egg mixture and beat well. Grease and line an 18 x 11 cm loaf pan, add mixture and bake for 1 1/2 hours in a preheated moderate oven (180°C). Cool on wire rack, removing paper, then ice with Cream Cheese Frosting.

CREAM CHEESE FROSTING

1 1/2 tablespoons (30 g) butter
3 tablespoons (60 g) cream cheese
1 1/2 cups (270 g) icing sugar

1 teaspoon grated lemon rind
1 tablespoon lemon juice
1/2 cup (45 g) desiccated coconut

Beat butter and cream cheese until creamy. Add remaining ingredients except coconut, beating well. Spread on cake and sprinkle with coconut.

🐜 🐜 🐜
Black Cake

Ingredients — 1½ lb brown sugar, 1¼ lb butter, 1¼ lb flour (after it is browned, as it loses weight in browning), 1½ doz. eggs, 2 lb currants, 1 lb citron peel, 2 lb raisins, cinnamon, nutmeg, allspice to taste, an even tablespoon of carbonate of soda, 1 teacup molasses or golden syrup.

Mode — Beat the butter to a cream. To it add the sugar, then the eggs, one by one, beating well between each one. Then add the fruit and the flour alternately, sifting the flour in. Then add the molasses, and the soda last.

🐜 🐜 🐜

CHOCOLATE CAKE

3 eggs, separated
1 cup (250 g) caster sugar
1/3 cup (45 g) cocoa
1/2 cup (125 ml) water

1 tablespoon butter
1 cup (150 g) flour
1 teaspoon cream of tartar
1/2 teaspoon bicarbonate of soda

Beat egg whites until stiff then gradually add sugar and egg yolks. In a saucepan blend cocoa with water, add butter and bring to the boil. Sift the flour, cream of tartar and bicarbonate of soda and add to the egg mixture. Finally fold in hot chocolate mixture. Place in lightly greased sandwich tins and cook 20 minutes in preheated moderately hot oven (190°C).

CHOCOLATE MUD CAKE

1 cup (250 g) chopped butter
150 g dark chocolate, chopped
2 cups (500 g) sugar
1 cup (250 ml) hot water
1½ cups (225 g) flour

1/4 cup (65 g) self-raising flour
1/4 cup (40 g) cocoa
2 eggs, lightly beaten
icing sugar

Grease a 23 cm square pan, line with paper and grease again. Combine butter, chocolate, sugar and water in double saucepan or in heatproof bowl over hot water. Stir until melted and mixture is smooth; cool till lukewarm. Transfer mixture to large bowl, stir in sifted flours and cocoa, then egg. Pour into prepared pan. Bake in preheated moderately slow oven (160°C) for about 1¼ hours. Stand for 10 minutes before turning on to wire rack to cool. Serve dusted with sifted icing sugar. Cake keeps and also freezes well.

CHOCOLATE ROLL

3 eggs, separated
½ cup (125 g) sugar
1 tablespoon golden syrup
½ cup (65 g) cornflour
½ cup (75 g) self-raising flour

1 tablespoon cocoa
caster sugar
1 cup (250 ml) whipped cream
  or Chocolate Butter
  Icing (see p. 237)

Beat egg whites until stiff. Gradually add sugar and beat until dissolved. Add yolks one at a time, beating well. Beat in syrup. Sift cornflour, flour and cocoa three times and fold in. Put into a greased and lined slice or Swiss roll tin. Bake in a preheated moderate oven (180°C) for about 12 minutes. Turn on to paper sprinkled with caster sugar. Trim edges and roll up cake with paper. When cool, unroll and spread with whipped cream or Chocolate Butter Icing and re-roll.

CHOCOLATE WALNUT CAKE

5 tablespoons (100 g) butter
¾ cup (190 g) caster sugar
3 eggs
⅓ cup (80 ml) milk
1½ cups (225 g) self-raising
  flour

1 tablespoon cocoa
1 teaspoon mixed spice
½ cup (60 g) walnut pieces
Chocolate Butter Icing
  or Chocolate Glacé Icing
  (see p. 237)

Beat butter and sugar to a cream. Add the eggs, one at a time, beating each in well. Add the milk alternately with the sifted flour, cocoa and spice, and lastly the walnuts. Place mixture in two well-greased sandwich tins and bake in preheated moderate oven (180°C) 15–20 minutes. When cold fill with whipped cream or filling and ice with either Chocolate Butter Icing or Chocolate Glacé Icing.

CHRISTMAS CAKE (RICH)

2³/4 cups (500 g) raisins
2³/4 cups (500 g) sultanas
2³/4 cups (500 g) currants
²/3 cup (125 g) mixed peel
²/3 cup (125 g) glacé cherries
²/3 cup (125 g) chopped dates
1 cup (125 g) almonds
¹/4 cup (60 ml) orange juice
1 teaspoon almond essence
1 teaspoon lemon essence

1 teaspoon vanilla essence
3 cups (450 g) plain flour
175 g self-raising flour
1 teaspoon ground nutmeg
2 teaspoons mixed spice
2 teaspoons cinnamon
8 eggs
2 cups (500 g) butter
2³/4 cups (410 g) brown sugar
2 tablespoons (60 g) marmalade

Prepare fruit and almonds, cutting into small, even pieces, mix well together. Mix orange juice and essences together and pour over fruit. Leave overnight. Line a tin — 25 cm square or 28 cm round tin or 2 x 20 cm cake tins — with 2–4 layers of baking paper. Sift dry ingredients together. Beat eggs well. Cream butter and sugar, add beaten eggs gradually, then marmalade, and flour and fruits alternately. Put in oven preheated to 160°C for 1 hour then reduce to 150°C and bake for another 3–3¹/2 hours. Test with skewer: cake is ready when skewer put into centre comes out clean.

Note Extra glacé pineapple, apricots, etc., may be added to make a richer cake.

CHRISTMAS CAKE (EASY AND ECONOMICAL)

2 cups (360 g) raisins
1¹/2 cups (270 g) sultanas
1¹/2 cups (270 g) currants
¹/2 cup (90 g) mixed peel
¹/2 cup (90 g) glacé cherries
¹/4 cup (60 ml) orange juice
1 teaspoon vanilla essence
1 teaspoon lemon essence
1 teaspoon almond essence

1¹/2 cups (225 g) plain flour
²/3 cup (100 g) self-raising flour
¹/2 teaspoon ground nutmeg
1 teaspoon mixed spice
1 teaspoon cinnamon
1²/3 cups (250 g) brown sugar
1 cup (250 g) butter
¹/2 cup (125 ml) milk
4 eggs, well beaten

Prepare fruit, mix orange juice and essences and pour over fruit. Leave for 2 hours. Line a 25 cm square tin or 28 cm round tin well with baking paper. Sift dry ingredients together. Melt butter, sugar and milk together. Let cool then pour over fruit, add flour and spices and mix well, lastly add beaten eggs and mix well. Bake for 3 hours at 150°C.

Note 1 kg mixed fruit may be used instead of the dried fruit, peel and cherries.

DATE LOAF

1 tablespoon butter
1 cup (250 g) sugar
1 cup (250 ml) water
1¹/2 cups (270 g) chopped
   dates

¹/2 cup (60 g) walnut pieces
1 teaspoon bicarbonate of soda
1 egg, beaten
2 cups (300 g) self-raising flour

Put butter, sugar, water, dates and walnuts in saucepan and bring slowly to the boil. Remove from heat, add bicarbonate of soda and allow to cool. Add egg and fold in flour and place in 2 prepared log tins. Cook in preheated moderate oven (180°C) for 45 minutes.

DATE, ORANGE AND BANANA HEALTH LOAF

¹/3 cup (80 g) butter
2 teaspoons grated orange rind
1 cup (150 g) brown sugar
2 eggs
3 very ripe bananas, mashed

³/4 cup (135 g) chopped dates
2 cups (300 g) wholemeal
   self-raising flour
¹/2 cup (125 ml) orange juice

Lightly grease a 14 x 21 cm loaf tin and line base with baking paper. Cream butter, rind and sugar together with an electric mixer until light and fluffy. Beat in eggs one at a time, add banana and beat until combined. Stir in dates, then half the flour and orange juice. Stir in the remaining flour and juice. Spread the mixture in tin and bake in a preheated moderate oven (180°C) for about 1 hour. Leave for 5 minutes in tin before turning on to rack to cool. Keeps well for 3 days.

EGGLESS CHOCOLATE CAKE

1/2 cup (125 g) butter
1/2 cup (125 g) sugar
2 tablespoons (60 g) golden syrup
1 teaspoon vanilla essence
1 cup (120 g) walnuts, chopped

2 cups (300 g) self-raising flour
4 tablespoons cocoa
1/2 teaspoon bicarbonate of soda
1 1/2 cups (375 ml) milk

Cream butter and sugar together until light and fluffy. Beat in syrup and vanilla. Stir in walnuts. Sift together flour, cocoa and bicarbonate of soda and add to butter mixture alternately with milk, mixing until smooth. Can divide mixture into 2 well-greased tins or 1 larger one. Bake in preheated moderate oven (180°C) for 30 minutes for smaller tins or for 35–40 minutes for large tin.

Hint This cake is best left for a day before use.

EGGLESS MICROWAVE CAKE

1 cup (250 g) sugar
1 cup (250 ml) milk
1 tablespoon butter

1/2 teaspoon bicarbonate of soda
1 1/2 cups (225 g) self-raising
  flour
2 tablespoons cocoa

Put sugar, milk and butter in glass dish and melt on HIGH in microwave for 2 minutes. Sift dry ingredients and mix into butter mixture using a beater. Transfer to microwave cake tin or casserole dish with a small glass in middle. Cook on HIGH for 4 minutes. If mixture is still partly uncooked, cook for a further 30 seconds.

FESTIVAL CAKE

1 1/2 cups whole Brazil nuts
1 1/2 cups (180 g) walnut
  halves
2 cups (360 g) pitted dates
2/3 cup (120 g) candied peel,
  chopped
1/2 cup (90 g) glacé green cherries

1/2 cup (90 g) glacé red cherries
1/2 cup (90 g) seeded raisins
3 eggs
3/4 cup (110 g) light brown sugar
3/4 cup (115 g) plain flour
1/2 teaspoon baking powder

Leave nuts and fruit whole. Mix well, and place in medium-sized tin that has been greased and lined with baking paper or foil. Beat eggs until frothy and add sugar, then fold in sifted flour and baking powder. Pour over the fruit in tin, and bake in a very slow oven (120°C) for 2 1/2 hours.

Variations
250 g glazed pineapple, apricots and ginger can be added to the cake.

Different nuts, such as hazelnuts instead of walnuts, can be used.

FRENCH COFFEE CAKE

1/2 cup (125 g) butter
flour
1/2 cup (125 g) sugar
2 eggs

1 1/2 cups (225 g) self-raising
1 tablespoon instant coffee
2 tablespoons (40 ml) milk

ICING
2 teaspoons butter
3 tablespoons (45 g) icing sugar
1 teaspoon instant coffee
1 teaspoon water

Beat butter and sugar together to a cream, beat eggs well and add, then add the flour and instant coffee. When all are well blended together, add the milk. Bake in a prepared flat tin for 30 minutes in a preheated moderate oven (180°C). Make the icing by warming butter slightly, beat in the icing sugar and coffee until a smooth paste. Add water and pour over the cake when it is cold.

Fruit Cake

This cake is great for diabetics and people with high cholesterol.

1 kg mixed dried fruit *2 cups (500 ml) fruit juice*
2 cups (300 g) self-raising flour

Mix all together. Line a 20 cm square tin and add mixture. Cook in preheated oven at 180°C for 1¹/2 hours. Turn heat off and leave cake in oven for an extra 30 minutes.

Hint If diet conscious, use a fruit juice with no added sugar.

Genoa Cake

1 cup (250 g) butter *¹/4 cup (45 g) mixed peel*
1 cup (250 g) sugar *¹/2 cup chopped almonds*
2¹/2 cups (375 g) plain flour *grated rind of 1 lemon*
1 teaspoon baking powder *4 eggs*
1¹/2 cups (270 g) sultanas

Cream butter and sugar together. Sift baking powder into flour. Mix fruit, peel, nuts and rind. Beat eggs until light, then add a little of the egg and a little of the flour alternately to the butter and sugar, stirring well each time until the mixture is perfectly blended. When flour and egg are all mixed in, add the fruit. Bake in a very slow oven (120°C) for 1¹/2–2 hours.

Note ³/4 cup (135 g) sultanas and ³/4 cup (135 g) currants can be substituted for the sultanas.

Ginger or Cocoa Fluff Sandwich

1 teaspoon golden syrup *1 teaspoon ground ginger or cocoa*
3 eggs, separated *2 teaspoons flour*
¹/2 cup (125 g) sugar *¹/2 teaspoon bicarbonate of soda*
³/4 cup (100 g) cornflour *¹/2 teaspoon cream of tartar*

Warm the syrup. Separate eggs, beat whites until thick then add sugar to them gradually. Beat a little longer, then add dry ingredients, sifted twice. Fold in beaten yolks, then add warm golden syrup, folding in gradually. Pour into two prepared sandwich tins, bake 12–15 minutes in preheated moderate oven (180°C). Sandwich together with 150 ml double cream, whipped, Butter Icing (see p. 237) or Mock Cream (see p. 240).

HEALTH LOAF

1/2 cup (125 g) butter
3/4 cup (135 g) raw sugar
1 egg
2 bananas, mashed
1/4 cup (60 ml) yoghurt

1 cup (150 g) wholemeal
  plain flour
1/2 cup (75 g) wholemeal
  self-raising flour

Cream butter and sugar together. Add egg and beat well. Mix in bananas and yoghurt. Stir in flours. Place in oiled loaf tin. Bake in a preheated moderate oven (180°C) for 50 minutes.

KENTISH CAKE

1 cup (125 g) butter
3/4 cup (190 g) caster sugar
2 eggs
1 tablespoon milk
2 tablespoons desiccated coconut
1 cup (150 g) self-raising flour

1 1/2 tablespoons cocoa
1/2 cup (70 g) blanched almonds
Chocolate Glacé Icing (see p. 237)
extra desiccated coconut and
  blanched almonds

Beat butter and sugar to a cream and beat in the eggs one by one. Add milk, coconut, flour, cocoa and finely chopped almonds. Put in a greased tin and bake in a preheated moderate oven (180°C) for 30–45 minutes. Ice with Chocolate Glacé Icing, and sprinkle with more coconut and almonds.

LAMINGTON CAKES

1 cup (250 g) butter, melted
4 eggs, well beaten
1¹/₂ cups (375 g) caster sugar
3 cups (450 g) self-raising flour
1 cup (250 ml) milk

1 teaspoon vanilla essence
Chocolate Icing (see below)
1¹/₂ cups (135 g) desiccated
 coconut

Allow butter to cool a little in large bowl, add beaten egg then sugar, flour, milk and vanilla essence. Beat with an electric mixer for 3 minutes. Bake in greased lamington tin (or Swiss roll tin) for approximately 30 minutes (test with skewer) in a preheated moderate (180°C) oven. When cool cut into lamington-size squares. Ice with chocolate icing and coat with coconut.

Hint Sponge is less crumbly if cold before cutting; it is best to leave in refrigerator overnight before cutting and icing.

CHOCOLATE ICING FOR LAMINGTONS

2¹/₂ tablespoons (50 ml)
 boiling water
3 tablespoons (60 g) butter

2 cups (360 g) icing sugar
3 teaspoons cocoa
¹/₂ teaspoon vanilla essence

Pour water over butter. When butter has melted mix with the combined icing sugar and cocoa, add vanilla. Beat well and use to cover sponge squares. If icing becomes too stiff stand container over hot water for a few minutes.

Hint While icing, hold the cake squares with a fork and dip the knife for spreading frequently in hot water.

LEMON LOAVES

¹/₂ cup (125 g) butter
1¹/₂ cups (225 g) self-raising
 flour
1 cup (250 g) caster sugar

grated rind of 1 lemon
2 eggs, lightly beaten
¹/₂ cup (125 ml) milk

Melt butter. Sift flour, add sugar and lemon rind to it. Stir in melted butter, eggs and milk; beat well for 5 minutes. Put mixture into 2 well-greased log tins. Bake in preheated moderate oven (180°C) for approximately 30 minutes. Cakes can be left plain or topped with Lemon Icing (see p. 237).

LIGHT AND FLUFFY SPONGE CAKE

4 eggs, separated
3/4 cup (185 g) caster sugar
1 teaspoon cream of tartar

1/2 teaspoon bicarbonate of soda
1 cup (130 g) cornflour

Beat egg whites until peaks form, add caster sugar and beat until sugar is dissolved, add yolks. Lightly fold in mixed dry ingredients. Place in a greased 23 cm springform tin and cook for 40 minutes in a preheated moderate oven (180°C). Turn out immediately on to cooling tray. Spread top with Passionfruit Glacé Icing (see p. 238).

LOCH KATRINE CAKE

BASE

1/2 cup (125 g)
  self-raising flour
3 tablespoons (60 g) butter

1 tablespoon sugar
milk

TOPPING

raspberry jam
currants
3 tablespoons (60 g) butter
1 cup (250 g) caster sugar

2 eggs
1 cup (150 g) self-raising flour
milk

Make base: combine flour and butter with fingertips, then mix in sugar and add enough milk to make a shortcrust pastry. Roll out and line a greased shallow baking dish 25 x 18 cm with pastry.

For topping, spread with raspberry jam and sprinkle a few currants on top. Cream butter and sugar, add eggs one at a time and beat well. Fold in sifted flour and add enough milk to make good consistency. Pour over base and jam and bake for 30 minutes in preheated hot oven (200°C). When cold, ice with Lemon Icing (see p. 237).

Madeira Cake

3/4 cup (185 g) butter
2/3 cup (120 g) caster sugar
grated rind of 1 lemon
3 eggs, beaten

2 cups (300 g) self-raising flour
2 tablespoons (40 ml) milk
candied peel

Cream butter and sugar until light and fluffy, add lemon rind, mix well, and then add egg gradually, beating well after each addition. Add flour and milk alternately to the mixture. Put mixture into a greased 20 cm square tin and sprinkle the top with candied peel. Bake in a moderate oven (180°C) for approximately 1 hour.

Orange Cake

1/2 cup (125 g) butter
1 1/2 cups (225 g) self-raising flour
1 cup (250 g) sugar
3 eggs

1/4 cup (60 ml) milk
2 tablespoons orange juice
2 teaspoons grated orange rind

Preheat oven to 200°C. Grease 20 cm cake tin. Melt butter and allow to cool. Put flour, sugar, egg, milk, juice and rind in bowl and add butter. Combine well and beat with an electric mixer for 3 minutes on medium speed. Pour mixture in prepared tin and place in oven. Reduce heat to 175°C and cook for 30 minutes then reduce heat again to 160°C and cook for further 20–25 minutes.

Orange and Almond Cake
(gluten-free)

2 medium oranges
4 eggs
3/4 cup (190 g) caster sugar
2 cups (200 g) almond meal

2 tablespoons gluten-free baking powder
pure icing sugar

Put oranges in saucepan. Cover them with cold water, bring to boil and cook for 1 hour or until soft. Pour off water. Cut oranges open and remove pips. Crack eggs into a bowl and set aside. Mix sugar, almond meal and baking powder in a large bowl. Place oranges in food processor and purée well before mixing in the egg. Pour orange mixture on to the dry ingredients and combine until smooth. Pour into an 18 cm round cake tin that is lightly greased and lined on the base with paper. Bake in a preheated moderate oven (180°C) for 1 hour until golden brown. Dust with pure icing sugar.

ORANGE MACAROON CAKE

2 tablespoons (40 g) butter
1/2 cup (125 g) caster sugar
1 teaspoon grated orange rind

2 egg yolks
5 tablespoons (100 ml) milk
1 cup (150 g) self-raising flour

TOPPING

2 egg whites
1/2 cup (125 g) caster sugar

1/2 cup (45 g) desiccated coconut
1/2 teaspoon vanilla essence

Beat butter and sugar together until creamed, add orange rind then egg yolks. Stir in milk with flour alternately. Place in prepared deep cake tin.

For topping, beat egg whites until stiff. Gradually add sugar and beat until thick, then stir in coconut and vanilla. Spread on top of uncooked cake. Bake in preheated moderate oven (180°C) for about 45 minutes.

PLAIN CAKE

1/2 cup (125 g) butter, melted
3/4 cup (190 g) sugar
1/4 cup (60 ml) milk

2 eggs
1 cup (150 g) self-raising flour
2 tablespoons cornflour

Place cooled, melted butter in small bowl, then add remaining ingredients. Combine and then beat with electric mixer for 5 minutes on medium speed. Bake in a greased 20 cm cake tin for 50 minutes in a preheated moderate oven (180°C).

POTATO LOAF

1 cup (250 g) cold mashed potato   1 cup (250 g) caster sugar
2¹/₂ cups (375 g) self-raising flour   1 cup (180 g) currants
1 cup (250 ml) milk

Mix all ingredients together. Divide into two prepared
24 cm loaf tins and bake in a preheated moderate oven
(180°C) for 30 minutes.

PUMPKIN FRUIT CAKE

³/₄ cup (190 g) butter   1 cup (250 g) mashed pumpkin
2 tablespoons (60 g) golden syrup 1 cup (150 g) self-raising flour
2 tablespoons (40 g) sugar   1 cup (150 g) plain flour
2²/₃ cups (480 g) mixed fruit   1 teaspoon mixed spice
2 eggs, well beaten   1 teaspoon nutmeg

Melt butter, add golden syrup, sugar and mixed fruit. Stir
until sugar is dissolved. Remove from heat, add eggs and
mashed pumpkin. When cool add flours and spices, place in
prepared 20 cm square cake tin and bake in preheated moderate oven (180°C) for 1¹/₂ hours.

RAINBOW CAKE

4 cups (600 g) self-raising flour   1 teaspoon lemon essence
4 eggs   1 tablespoon cocoa
1 cup (250 g) butter   1 teaspoon vanilla essence
1¹/₂ cups (375 g) caster sugar   enough carmine or cochineal to
³/₄ cup (190 ml) milk   give colour

Grease 3 x 20 cm sandwich tins, sift flour, beat eggs well, and
beat butter and sugar together to a cream. Add the egg gradually to the butter and sugar, beat in, then pour in the milk
slowly and mix in the flour, stirring well. Divide the mixture into three. Add lemon essence to one, cocoa to the
second, vanilla and carmine to the third. Put into tins and
bake in preheated moderate oven (180°C) for 20–30

minutes. When cold, fill and ice with Soft Icing (see p. 238) and decorate with crystallised fruits or sprinkle with desiccated coconut.

Note 2 tablespoons grated chocolate can be substituted for cocoa.

SIMPLICITY CHOCOLATE CAKE

4 tablespoons (40 g) cocoa   *1 cup (250 ml) milk*
2 cups (300 g) self-raising flour   *3 eggs*
1 cup (250 g) caster sugar   *1 teaspoon vanilla essence*
3/4 cup (190 g) butter

Sift dry ingredients together into a bowl. Add softened butter, milk, eggs and vanilla. Beat hard for 3 minutes. Bake for 50 minutes in a greased 20 cm round tin in a preheated moderate oven (180°C).

SPONGE CAKE

4 eggs, separated   *1 tablespoon boiling water*
1 cup (250 g) caster sugar   *whipped cream*
1 cup (150 g) self-raising flour   *pure icing sugar*

Preheat oven to 180°C. Lightly grease two 18 cm sponge cake tins and dust with flour. Separate eggs and beat whites until thick and creamy. Add sugar and beat until dissolved. Beat in egg yolks. Fold in sifted flour, lastly boiling water. Put into prepared sandwich tins and bake for 30 minutes. When cool join with whipped cream and dredge top with icing sugar.

SPONGE GINGERBREAD

3/4 cup (190 g) butter   *1 egg*
1 cup (250 g) caster sugar   *2 cups (300 g) flour*
3/4 cup (270 g) golden syrup,   *1 tablespoon ground ginger*
* warmed*   *2 teaspoons cinnamon*

1 cup (250 ml) milk   Lemon Butter (see p. 239) or
1 teaspoon bicarbonate of soda   Lemon Filling (see p. 240)

Lightly grease two 18 cm sponge cake tins and line bases
with baking paper. Cream butter and sugar together, add
warm golden syrup and beat well, then beat in egg. Sift in
flour, ginger and spice and when thoroughly blended add
the milk in which the soda has been dissolved. Bake for
about an hour in a moderate oven (180°C). When cool
sandwich together with Lemon Butter or Lemon Filling.

SULTANA CAKE

2³/4 cups (500 g) sultanas   2 eggs
1 cup (250 ml) water   2 cups (300 g) flour
1 cup (250 g) butter   1/2 cup (75 g) self-raising flour
1 cup (250 g) caster sugar

Soak the sultanas overnight in the water. Cream the butter
and sugar together, add the eggs, beating well. Sift flours and
add alternately with sultanas and water. Mix well and place
in greased and lined 20 x 7 cm round or square cake tin.
Bake in moderate oven (180°C) for 1¹/2–2 hours or until
skewer placed in centre of cake comes out clean.

SWISS ROLL

2 eggs   1/2 cup (75 g) self-raising flour
1/2 cup (125 g) sugar   caster sugar
1 tablespoon milk   jam
1 tablespoon water

Beat eggs, add sugar gradually, beating well with each addition. Add milk and water, then sift in flour. Bake in a greased
and lined shallow tin (Swiss roll) in a preheated hot oven
(200°C) for about 10 minutes. Sprinkle caster sugar on a
damp cloth, turn cake out on to cloth and roll up cake in it
quickly, unroll, trim off crisp edges. Spread with jam and roll
again. Serve cold.

TEA CAKE

2 tablespoons (40 g) butter
2 tablespoons (40 g) caster sugar
1 egg
1½ cups (225 g) self-raising flour

½ cup (125 ml) milk
cinnamon
extra sugar

Beat butter and sugar to a cream, add egg and beat well, then beat in the flour and milk until batter is moderately stiff. Bake in greased 20 cm sandwich tin for about 15 minutes in preheated moderate oven (180°C). Sprinkle with cinnamon and sugar.

Variation *Apple Tea Cake*: Cover top with slices of apple. Sprinkle with ¼ cup (60 g) caster sugar and 2 teaspoons cinnamon before baking.

THREE MINUTE SPONGE CAKE

1 cup (150 g) self-raising flour
¾ cup (190 g) caster sugar
3 eggs
3 tablespoons (60 ml) milk

1 tablespoon melted butter
raspberry or strawberry jam,
or whipped cream

Put all the ingredients into a basin and beat together for 3 minutes. Bake in 2 x 18 cm greased and lined sandwich tins for about 20–25 minutes in moderate oven (180°C). Join together with jam or whipped cream

VICTORIA SANDWICH

3 eggs
½ cup (125 g) caster sugar

1 cup (150 g) self-raising flour
2 tablespoons (60 g) butter

Beat egg and sugar together until quite thick and spongy, sift flour and fold in lightly. Melt butter and add to the mixture. Bake in two greased and lined sandwich tins for 15 minutes in a preheated hot oven (200°C). When cool add filling and topping of your choice (see pp. 236–40).

WALNUT CAKE

1/2 cup (125 g) caster sugar
1/2 cup (125 g) butter
1/2 cup (180 g) golden syrup,
  warmed
2 eggs, beaten

1/2 cup (125 ml) milk
2 1/2 cups (375 g) self-raising
  flour
2 teaspoons mixed spice
1 cup (125 g) walnut pieces

Beat butter and sugar to a cream, add warm golden syrup and beat well. Add the beaten eggs. Stir in milk. Sift in the flour and spices and add the walnuts. Put into a greased 22 cm round or 20 cm square tin, and bake in a preheated moderate oven (180°C) for about an hour.

✌ CAKE TOPPINGS ✍

CHOCOLATE NUT TOPPING

1/2 cup (65 g) nuts, finely chopped   *1 cup grated chocolate*

Combine ingredients and sprinkle thickly over the top of a butter cake before baking.

CRUMBLY CINNAMON TOPPING

2 tablespoons (40 g) butter,
  melted
2 tablespoons brown sugar
1/4 cup (40 g) flour

1/4 cup (30 g) biscuit crumbs
  or desiccated coconut
1 teaspoon cinnamon

Combine butter and sugar and mix with other ingredients. Sprinkle over the top of a butter cake before placing in oven.

Hint This topping may be used on stewed fruit, such as stewed pears or apple purée, to make a Fruit Crumble.

✂ ICINGS ✄

BUTTER OR VIENNA ICING

3/4 cup (135 g) icing sugar
2 tablespoons (40 g) butter

few drops of vanilla essence
2 teaspoons boiling water

Sift icing sugar, cream butter, add icing sugar gradually to butter, then add essence and a little water. Add more water if softer icing is desired.

Variations
Chocolate: Blend 1/2 tablespoon cocoa in 1 tablespoon boiling water and add to creamed mixture.
Coffee: Add 1 teaspoon powdered instant coffee to creamed mixture.
Lemon or Orange: Add 2 teaspoons grated rind and 2 teaspoons juice to the creamed mixture.

CHOCOLATE GLACÉ ICING

1 cup (180 g) icing sugar
2 tablespoons grated chocolate
*   or 1 tablespoon cocoa*

1 1/2 tablespoons water

Sift sugar and put in a saucepan with chocolate or cocoa. Add the water and stir until warm. Pour over the cake.

ORANGE OR LEMON ICING

1 1/2 cups (270 g) icing sugar
grated rind and juice of
*   1 orange or lemon*

2 teaspoons butter, melted

Put sugar, rind and juice in a bowl, stir until all lumps are removed and a thick cream is formed, stir in butter and pour over cake.

Passionfruit Glacé Icing

2/3 cup (120 g) icing mixture   *1 tablespoon passionfruit pulp*

Mix sugar and fruit pulp together and spread over cake (add a teaspoon or two of water if too thick).

Royal Icing

1 egg white   *few drops of lemon juice*
1 1/2 cups (270 g) pure icing
  sugar

Place a little egg white in a basin, add sugar gradually, working well with a wooden spoon until the desired consistency is achieved. When free from lumps add the lemon juice and mix well.

Note It is important to use pure icing sugar in this recipe; icing mixture is not suitable.

Soft Icing

2 1/2 cups (450 g) icing sugar   *flavouring*
2 1/2 tablespoons (50 ml) hot water   *colouring*

Put sugar in saucepan, add water gradually and stir until smooth like treacle. Place over heat and stir until thin enough to spread evenly. Add colouring and flavouring as desired.

∽ Cake Fillings ∾

Apple Filling

2 large apples, peeled   *1/2 cup (125 g) sugar*
grated rind of 1 lemon

Grate the apples into a saucepan, add the grated lemon rind and sugar. Cook for 5 minutes, stirring constantly. When cold, spread on cake.

COFFEE BUTTER CREAM

½ cup (125 ml) strong coffee
1 cup (250 g) sugar

1 cup (250 g) butter
vanilla essence (optional)

Boil coffee and sugar to a thick syrup. Set aside to cool. Work butter to a cream, add syrup gradually, and mix well. Add vanilla if desired.

CHOCOLATE AND HONEY FILLING

2 tablespoons (60 g) honey
2 tablespoons (40 g) butter
1 cup (180 g) icing sugar

2 tablespoons cocoa
3 teaspoons boiling water

Melt honey and butter over hot water, stir in sifted icing sugar and cocoa. Add boiling water and mix until smooth.

DATE FILLING

1 cup (180 g) stoneless dates,
    chopped
1 tablespoon water

juice of 1 lemon

Put dates in saucepan with water. Simmer until mixture is the consistency of marmalade. Remove from the heat and stir in the lemon juice. Use when cold.

LEMON BUTTER

4 eggs
½ cup (125 g) butter
2 cups (500 g) sugar

grated rind of 2 lemons
juice of 4 lemons

Beat the eggs, put butter and sugar into a double saucepan and stir until both are melted, then add eggs, lemon juice and rind and stir until the mixture is honey thick. Put in jars and keep in a cool, dry place.

Hint If you do not have a double saucepan, put a bowl over a saucepan partly filled with water.

Lemon Filling

1 cup (250 g) sugar
1 cup (250 ml) water
grated rind and juice of 2 lemons

4 tablespoons (40 g) cornflour
1 tablespoon butter

Dissolve sugar in water. Add lemon rind and juice and when nearly boiling add cornflour blended in a little cold water. Cook for 1 minute then add butter.

Mock Cream

1 tablespoon cornflour
1 cup (250 ml) milk
1 tablespoon butter

1 tablespoon caster or
   icing sugar
flavouring

Blend cornflour with a little cold milk. Heat remainder of milk and add blended cornflour. Stir until boiling and cook 2 minutes. Cool. Cream butter and sugar, and gradually add the cornflour mixture, beating well. Flavour as required.

Vanilla Filling

2 tablespoons (40 g) butter
1 cup (180 g) icing sugar

2 teaspoons vanilla essence

Blend well, and spread on cake.

SMALL CAKES

APPLE AND CINNAMON MUFFINS
Makes 18

1¹/₂ cups (225 g) plain flour
¹/₂ cup (75 g) self-raising flour
³/₄ cup (135 g) brown sugar
1–2 teaspoons cinnamon
2 medium golden delicious,
   apples, peeled and finely
   chopped or grated

¹/₂ cup (90 g) raisins (optional)
1 egg, lightly beaten
³/₄ cup (190 ml) buttermilk
   or milk
¹/₂ cup (125 ml) light
   vegetable oil

Preheat oven to 180°C. Grease a ¹/₃ cup capacity muffin pan. Sift the flours, sugar and cinnamon into a large bowl. Add the apples and raisins and stir until combined. Beat egg lightly in a small bowl, add the milk then the oil. Add liquid ingredients to flour mixture, and stir with a spoon until just combined. Spoon mixture into muffin pan. Bake for 15–20 minutes until golden and cooked through. Remove from the oven and turn out on to a wire rack.

APPLE CAKES
Makes 12–15

3 cups (450 g) self-raising flour
1 cup (250 g) caster sugar
1 cup (250 g) butter
2 eggs

¹/₄ cup (60 ml) milk
2 cups (400 g) stewed apple
icing sugar

Sift flour, add sugar and rub in butter. Beat eggs well, add the milk, pour on to the dry ingredients and knead all together to make a pastry. Cut pastry into rounds and line greased patty pans, put a spoonful of stewed apple on each round. Moisten the edge of the lower round and top with another round of pastry. Bake in a preheated moderate oven (180°C) for 10–15 minutes. When cold, dust with icing sugar.

BLUEBERRY MUFFINS
Makes 12 large muffins

1½ cups (225 g) self-raising
 flour
½ cup (75 g) plain flour
½ cup (125 g) caster sugar
1 egg
¾–1 cup (190–250 ml)
 buttermilk or milk

¾ cup (190 ml) light vegetable
 oil
1 cup (200 g) blueberries
½ cup (60 g) chopped pecans
 (optional)
1 teaspoon vanilla essence
icing sugar

Preheat oven to 200°C. Grease a set of muffin tins of ⅓ cup capacity, or line with muffin papers. Sift flours into a mixing bowl, stir in sugar, then make a well in the middle. In a small bowl beat the egg, add milk, vanilla and oil, then pour into the flour and sugar mixture. Add the blueberries and nuts, and stir gently only until the flour is completely moistened — do not beat. Divide the mixture evenly between the muffin tins. Bake for 15–20 minutes, until golden brown. Allow the muffins to stand for a few minutes then carefully remove from the tin. Serve warm or cold with a sprinkling of icing sugar on top.

CHOC-ORANGE MUFFINS
Makes 12

1½ cups (225 g) self-raising
 flour
½ cup (65 g) cocoa
1 cup (250 g) caster sugar
¾ cup (190 ml) buttermilk
 or milk

1 egg, lightly beaten
½ cup (125 g) butter, melted
2 teaspoons grated orange rind
2 tablespoons orange juice

Preheat oven to 200°C. Grease 12-hole muffin pan or line with muffin papers. Sift flour and cocoa into a large bowl. Add sugar. Mix buttermilk with egg and butter, rind and juice. Then add liquids to dry ingredients and mix until just combined. Spoon mixture into muffin pans and bake for about 20 minutes. Turn out onto cake rack.

Variation To make *Orange Poppy Seed Muffins*, substitute
$1/3$ cup (30 g) almond meal for cocoa, only use $1/2$ cup
caster sugar and add $1/3$ cup poppy seeds.

NEENISH TARTS
Makes 20

20 Sweet Pastry tart cases (see
  p. 180) or bought cases (see note)
2 tablespoons (40 g) butter
2 tablespoons (30 g) icing sugar
2 tablespoons condensed milk

2 teaspoons lemon juice
Soft Icing (see p. 238)
1 teaspoon cocoa
a few drops pink food colouring
  (optional)

Blind bake pastry cases if necessary. Cream butter and gradually add icing sugar. Beat until fluffy, slowly add condensed
milk and lastly lemon juice. Fill cases. Flavour half the icing
mixture with cocoa, leave the other half white or colour
with pink food colouring. Ice tarts with half chocolate and
half white or pink icing.

Note Make pastry cases using Sweet Pastry to line patty
pans or purchase ready-cooked or pre-cut frozen cases.

PATTY CAKES
Makes 12

$1/2$ cup (125 g) butter
$3/4$ cup (190 g) caster sugar
$1/2$ teaspoon vanilla essence
2 eggs

$1^{1}/2$ cups (225 g) self-raising
  flour
6 tablespoons (120 ml) milk

Cream butter and sugar together and add vanilla. Lightly
beat eggs and gradually add to butter and sugar mixture. Add
milk and sifted flour alternately. Spoon into greased patty
pan tins or paper cases and bake for 10–15 minutes in a preheated moderate oven (180°C).

Variations
Chocolate Cakes: Add 1 tablespoon cocoa blended with 1
tablespoon water.
Cinnamon or Spice Cakes: Add 1 teaspoon cinnamon or
mixed spice to flour.

Coffee Cakes: Add 2 teaspoons instant coffee to milk.
Orange Cakes: Add grated rind of 1 orange and substitute 2 tablespoons orange juice for milk in the recipe.
Queen Cakes: Add 1/4 – 1/2 cup sultanas or currants.

RASPBERRY FRIANDS
Makes 12 friands

1/2 cup (125 g) butter, melted
1 cup (100 g) almond meal
1 1/2 cups (270 g) icing sugar
1/2 cup (75 g) plain flour
  mixture

6 egg whites, lightly beaten
1/2 cup (50 g) raspberries
icing sugar

Preheat oven to moderately hot (190°C). Grease a 12-hole friand or muffin tray. Gently fold butter, almond meal, icing sugar and flour into egg whites. Stir until just combined. Fold raspberries through mixture. Place mixture in tray and bake for 25 minutes. Remove from oven and allow to stand in the tray for 5 minutes. Turn on to a wire rack to cool. Serve dusted with a little extra icing sugar.

Notes
Either frozen or fresh raspberries may be used in this recipe. Substitute other berries if desired.

Friand trays feature 6 or 12 oval-sized cups that each has a 1/3 cup capacity. Muffin trays may be used instead.

Biscuits

Hints for biscuit baking

- Baking trays stay cleaner and biscuits are less likely to stick if baking trays are lined with non-stick baking paper.
- Space biscuits well apart on the baking tray to allow for spreading as they bake.
- Hot biscuits with a high sugar content are soft to touch when removed from the oven. Allow to cool a little and firm up before removing from the tray.
- Biscuits keep best in an airtight container away from direct sunlight.
- When directed to roll out biscuit dough for cutting, roll between 2 sheets of non-stick baking paper to avoid dough sticking.

Ada's Biscuits

1 cup (250 g) butter
1 cup (250 g) caster sugar
1 egg

2 cups (300 g) self-raising flour
almond halves (optional)

Preheat oven to moderate (180°C). Cream butter and sugar together, gradually beat in egg and mix in flour. Place in tea-spoonfuls on a greased baking tray. Bake 10–12 minutes. May be decorated with almond halves.

Afghans

³/4 cup (190 g) butter
¹/3 cup (60 g) brown sugar
1¹/4 cups (190 g) self-raising
 flour

2 tablespoons cocoa
1³/4 cups (50 g) cornflakes
Chocolate Glacé Icing (see p. 237)
walnut halves

Preheat oven to moderate (180°C). Cream butter and sugar. Add flour and sifted cocoa, and then work in the cornflakes gradually. Drop in teaspoonfuls on a greased tray and bake for 12–15 minutes. When cold, ice with Chocolate Glacé Icing and top with half a walnut.

ALMOND BREAD

4 egg whites
2/3 cup (170 g) caster sugar

1 cup (150 g) plain flour
1 cup (100 g) almonds (not blanched)

Preheat oven to moderate (180°C). Beat egg whites stiffly. Gradually add sugar and continue beating until the mixture is stiff. Fold in the flour and almonds. Place in a prepared loaf tin and bake for 1 hour. Cool on a cake cooler, wrap in a clean tea towel and allow to stand for a week. Slice very thinly, place on an oven tray and dry slices in a slow oven (150°C) for about 30 minutes, until crisp.

ALMOND FINGERS

1/2 cup (125 g) butter
1/4 cup (60 g) caster sugar
1 egg, separated
1 1/2 cups (225 g) self-raising flour

1/2 cup (75 g) plain flour
3/4 cup (135 g) icing sugar
1/2 cup (60 g) almonds, chopped

Preheat oven to moderate (180°C). Rub butter into sugar and add yolk of egg. Sift in the flours and mix into a soft dough. Roll out very thinly and cut into fingers 4 x 8 cm. Put in lined biscuit tray. Beat the egg white stiffly, add the icing sugar and almonds, and beat together. Spread over the biscuits, and bake until light brown (about 15 minutes).

Note Walnuts, hazelnuts or coconut may be substituted for almonds.

ANZAC BISCUITS

1 cup (100 g) rolled oats
1 cup (150 g) flour
3/4 cup (70 g) desiccated coconut
3/4 cup (190 g) sugar
1/2 teaspoon bicarbonate of soda

2 tablespoons boiling water
1/2 cup (125 g) butter, melted
2 tablespoons (60 g) golden
    syrup

Preheat oven to moderately slow (160°C). Combine oats, flour, coconut and sugar. Dissolve the soda in the boiling water and add to melted butter and golden syrup. Pour into the dry ingredients and mix well. Place in teaspoonfuls on a greased baking tray. Bake for 15 minutes or until golden brown.

Variation Muesli Biscuits: Omit rolled oats and add 1 cup natural untoasted muesli.

BISCOTTI

1 cup (250 g) caster sugar
2 eggs
1/2 teaspoon finely grated
    orange rind
1 1/3 cups (200 g) plain flour

1/3 cup (50 g) self-raising
    flour
2/3 cup (65 g) almond meal
1 cup (200 g) chocolate chips
1/2 cup (100 g) glacé cherries

Preheat oven to moderate (180°C). Whisk sugar, eggs and orange rind in a medium bowl. Add sifted flours and almond meal, chocolate chips and cherries. Mix to a sticky dough, divide in half and roll into logs 20 cm long. Place on greased oven trays and bake for 35 minutes or until lightly browned. Cool. Using a sharp knife, slice logs diagonally into 1 cm thick slices. Place on an oven tray and bake in a slow oven (150°C) until dry and crisp.

Bran Biscuits

3 tablespoons (60 g) butter
1/2 cup (125 g) caster sugar
1 egg

1 cup (150 g) plain flour
1 teaspoon baking powder
1 cup (90 g) bran

Preheat oven to moderate (180°C). Cream butter and sugar together. Add the egg, flour sifted with baking powder and bran. Roll thinly, cut into strips or squares and bake until golden brown, for 10–15 minutes. Serve spread with butter.

Note Self-raising flour may be used in place of plain flour and baking powder.

Brandy Snaps

1/3 cup (90 g) golden syrup
90 g butter
1/2 cup (90 g) sugar

9 tablespoons (90 g) plain
  flour
2 teaspoons ground ginger

Preheat oven to moderate (180°C). Place syrup, butter and sugar in a saucepan and melt and combine over low heat. Remove from heat and add sifted flour and ginger. Stir until thoroughly mixed. Place on a greased tray in pieces the size of a walnut. Bake for 10 minutes. Remove from the oven and roll quickly round the greased handle of a wooden spoon. When cold fill with whipped cream.

Burnt Butter Biscuits

almonds (optional)
1/2 cup (125 g) butter
1/2 cup (125 g) sugar
1 egg

few drops of vanilla essence
1 1/2 cups (225 g) self-raising
  flour

Preheat oven to moderate (180°C). Blanch and halve almonds. Heat butter in saucepan until light brown. Cool but do not allow to set. Add sugar and combine. Beat the egg and add gradually. Add vanilla and sifted flour, mix well. Roll into small balls, flatten and press 1/2 almond on each. Bake for 15 minutes, or until golden brown.

CHEESE BISCUITS

1 cup (120 g) grated tasty
  cheese
1/2 cup (125 g) butter
1/4 teaspoon cayenne pepper

6 tablespoons (60 g) self-raising
  flour
pinch of salt
desiccated coconut, for rolling

Preheat oven to moderate (180°C). Mix grated cheese, butter, pepper, flour and salt together until blended. Chill. Roll into small balls and toss in coconut. Place on a greased oven tray and press flat with a fork. Bake for 15 minutes.

CHEESE STRAWS

90 g plain flour
pinch of salt
pinch of cayenne pepper
1/4 cup (60 g) butter

1/2 cup (60 g) grated tasty
  cheese
1 egg yolk
1 teaspoon lemon juice

Preheat oven to moderately hot (190°C). Sift flour, salt and cayenne together, rub butter into flour, add cheese and mix in egg yolk and lemon juice. Roll out thinly and cut into thin strips and circles. Place on tray and bake for 6 minutes, until a light golden brown. When serving, thread about 4 strips through a circle.

CHERRY DROPS

1 1/2 cups (135 g) desiccated
  coconut
1/2 cup (90 g) cherries, chopped
1/2 cup (60 g) walnuts, chopped

1/2 cup (90 g) chocolate bits
1/2 x 395 g can condensed
  milk
1/2 teaspoon baking powder

Preheat oven to moderate (180°C). Combine all ingredients with condensed milk and mix well. Place teaspoonfuls on a greased tray. Bake for 10 minutes. Remove from the tray while still warm.

CHOCOLATE CHIP BISCUITS

1/2 cup (125 g) butter
1/2 cup (125 g) caster sugar
1/2 cup (90 g) brown sugar
1/2 teaspoon vanilla essence

1 egg, lightly beaten
1³/4 cups (260 g) self-raising flour
pinch of salt
1 cup (180 g) chocolate chips

Preheat oven to moderate (180°C). Cream butter, sugars, and vanilla together, and gradually add lightly beaten egg. Mix in sifted flour and salt. Stir in chocolate chips and mix well. Shape spoonfuls of the mixture into small balls and place on lightly greased oven trays. Bake for 10–12 minutes.

COCONUT TARTLETS

PASTRY

2 cups (300 g) plain flour
1 teaspoon baking powder
1 tablespoon sugar

1/2 cup (125 g) butter
1 egg yolk
milk

FILLING

5 tablespoons (100 g) raspberry or apricot jam
3 egg whites

1 cup (250 g) caster sugar
1/2 cup (45 g) desiccated coconut
almonds, blanched

Preheat oven to moderate (180°C). Sift flour, baking powder and sugar into a bowl. Rub in butter, mix to firm dough with beaten egg yolk, adding a little milk if necessary. Roll out, cut into circles and line greased patty tins. Place 1 teaspoon jam in each one. Beat egg whites until stiff, and add sugar gradually, beating well. Add coconut. Place 1 teaspoon mixture in tart cases and top with an almond. Bake for 15 minutes.

CORNIES

1/2 cup (125 g) butter
3/4 cup (190 g) sugar
1 egg

1 cup (180 g) raisins
1 cup (150 g) self-raising flour
cornflakes for rolling

Preheat oven to moderate (180°C). Cream butter and sugar, add egg and beat well. Add raisins then flour to the mixture. Roll mixture into balls, toss in cornflakes and place on lightly greased tray. Bake until crisp.

FLORENTINES

75 g butter
100 g sugar
1 tablespoon glacé cherries
1 tablespoon mixed peel

50 g sultanas
1 cup (100 g) flaked almonds
1 tablespoon cream
400 g chocolate

Preheat oven to moderately hot (190°C). Melt butter in a small saucepan, add sugar and bring to the boil. Remove from the heat. Finely chop cherries and mixed peel. Add fruit and almonds, mix well. Add cream. Place mixture in small heaps on a baking tray lined with baking paper. Flatten mixture and bake until light golden brown in colour, about 8–10 minutes. While still hot, ease in the edges with a circular biscuit cutter. When biscuits are cool, melt chocolate in a double boiler over gentle heat and cover the bases with melted chocolate.

GINGER NUTS

$1/2$ cup (125 g) butter
1 cup (250 g) sugar
2 teaspoons golden syrup
1 egg, beaten

2 cups (300 g) self-raising flour
$1/2$ teaspoon bicarbonate of
    soda
3 teaspoons ground ginger

Preheat oven to moderate (180°C). Melt butter, sugar and syrup together over a low heat. Remove from heat and add beaten egg. Add sifted dry ingredients and mix well. Refrigerate and, when hardened, roll into small balls. Place on greased trays, leaving room for spreading. Bake for 10–15 minutes. Remove from trays immediately.

GINGERBREAD MEN

$1/2$ cup (125 g) butter
2 tablespoons (60 g) golden
    syrup
$3/4$ cup (185 g) sugar
1 egg, beaten

315 g self-raising flour
pinch of salt
2 teaspoons ground ginger
currants
glacé cherries

Preheat oven to cool (150°C). Melt butter and golden syrup in a saucepan over gentle heat. Remove from the heat and add sugar and egg. Then add the sifted flour, salt and ginger. Mix well. Turn onto a floured board, knead lightly and roll out thinly. Use a cutter to shape gingerbread men, place on a greased tray. Mark features with currants and cherries. Bake until golden brown, about 10–12 minutes.

INDIAN BISCUITS

1/2 cup (125 g) sugar
1/2 cup (125 g) butter
1 tablespoon coffee essence
1 teaspoon vanilla essence

1 egg, beaten
2 cups (300 g) self-raising flour
almonds
preserved ginger

Preheat oven to moderate (180°C). Cream the butter and sugar, add the coffee essence, vanilla and half the egg. Mix well, then sift in the flour. Roll out and cut into thick biscuits. Brush over the top with the remainder of the egg and sprinkle with pieces of roughly chopped almonds and ginger. Bake 12–15 minutes, until golden brown.

JAM DROPS

1/2 cup (125 g) butter
3/4 cup (190 g) sugar
2 eggs

2 cups (300 g) plain flour
2 teaspoons baking powder
jam

Preheat oven to moderate (180°C). Cream butter and sugar together, add eggs one at a time, beating well. Add sifted flour and baking powder. Mix well. Roll into small balls, place on a greased tray, press hole in centre and place a little jam in the hole. Bake for 15 minutes.

MERINGUES

To each egg white, allow 2 rounded tablespoons sugar. Preheat oven to very slow (120°C). Beat whites until very stiff, add the sugar a little at a time, beating well until the mixture stands up in peaks. Add flavouring and drop dessertspoons of mixture on greased paper on a cold tray. Cook for 1–1¹/₂ hours or until dried out but not brown. Lower oven temperature during cooking if necessary.

NUTTIES

¹/₂ cup (125 g) butter
1 cup (250 g) caster sugar
1 egg
1¹/₂ cups (225 g) plain flour
1 teaspoon cinnamon

1 cup (160 g) dates
¹/₂ cup (60 g) walnuts or almonds
1 teaspoon bicarbonate of soda
1 cup (250 ml) warm milk

Preheat oven to moderate (180°C). Cream butter and sugar until light and fluffy, gradually beat in the egg. Sift flour and cinnamon, add the dates and nuts and lastly the soda dissolved in the warm milk. Drop teaspoonfuls on to a greased baking tray and bake for 12–15 minutes.

OAT CAKES

¹/₂ cup (125 g) butter
1 tablespoon sugar
1 cup (150 g) plain flour
1 teaspoon bicarbonate of soda

1 teaspoon cream of tartar
1 cup (100 g) oatmeal
warm water

Preheat oven to moderate (180°C). Rub butter into sugar, sift flour, soda and cream of tartar and add to butter and sugar. Mix in the oatmeal and enough warm water to mix to stiff dough. Roll out thinly and cut into rectangles. Bake for 10–12 minutes, until golden brown.

ONE EGG WHITE MERINGUE

1 egg white
1 cup (250 g) caster sugar
1 teaspoon vinegar

1 teaspoon baking powder
1 teaspoon vanilla essence
2 tablespoons boiling water

Place egg white in basin; add sugar, vinegar, baking powder, vanilla, water. Beat until stiff and glossy. Drop in teaspoons on greased paper on an oven tray. Bake in a slow oven (150°C) for 1 hour.

Note Meringues stored in an airtight container will keep well.

PEANUT DROPS

1/2 cup (125 g) butter   *1 cup (150 g) self-raising flour*
1/2 cup (125 g) sugar   *1 cup (120 g) chopped peanuts*
1 egg   *or 1/2 cup crunchy peanut butter*

Preheat oven to moderate (180°C). Cream butter and sugar, gradually beat in the egg, then mix in other ingredients. Drop in teaspoons on to a greased baking tray. Bake for 15–17 minutes.

REFRIGERATOR BISCUITS

1/2 cup (125 g) butter   *1 3/4 cups (260 g) self-raising*
3/4 cup (190 g) caster sugar   *flour*
1 egg   *pinch of salt*
1 teaspoon vanilla essence

Cream butter and sugar in a mixing bowl, add egg and vanilla, and beat well. Sift and add flour and salt. Divide into half and roll into logs, wrap in plastic wrap and chill until firm. Preheat oven to moderate (180°C). Slice logs into 6 mm thick slices, place on a greased baking tray and bake for 10–15 minutes.

Variations
Chocolate: Sift 1 tablespoon cocoa into the mixture with the flour.
Coffee: Dissolve 1 tablespoon instant coffee in a little hot water and add to the mixture with the vanilla; top biscuits with an almond.
Lemon: Replace vanilla essence with lemon essence and the grated rind of 1 lemon.

Note The uncooked mixture will keep well for months in the freezer if wrapped securely in plastic wrap.

ROCK CAKES

3 tablespoons (60 g) butter	1/2 teaspoon mixed spice
1/2 cup (125 g) sugar	1/2 teaspoon cinnamon
1 egg	1/2 cup (75 g) mixed peel
2 cups (300 g) self raising flour	3/4 cup (135 g) sultanas
1 teaspoon ground ginger	about 1/2 cup (125 ml) milk

Preheat oven to moderately hot (190°C). Cream butter and sugar together, add the egg and beat well. Sift in the flour and spices and add fruit. Add sufficient milk to make a very stiff dough. Place spoonfuls on a greased baking tray. Bake for 10–15 minutes.

SAVOURY SOUR CREAM BISCUITS

2 cups (300 g) plain flour	2 egg yolks, beaten
pinch of salt	2 tablespoons onion flakes
30 g butter	1/3 cup (85 g) freshly grated
1/2 cup (125 ml) sour cream	Parmesan cheese
1/4 cup chopped spring onions	
about 1/4 cup (60 ml) water	

Sift flour and salt into a bowl, rub in butter. Stir in sour cream, spring onions and enough water to make dough. Knead until smooth, cover and refrigerate for 30 minutes.

Preheat oven to moderately hot (190°C). Divide mixture in half and roll each piece thinly. Brush with a little of the egg yolk. Sprinkle with onion flakes and cheese. Cut into squares and place on a greased oven tray. Bake for about 10 minutes, or until lightly browned. Serve with dips or soups.

Shortbread

3 cups (450 g) plain flour
1/2 cup (65 g) rice flour
1/4 teaspoon salt

1 cup (250 g) butter
1/2 cup (125 g) caster sugar

Preheat oven to slow (150°C). Sift flour, rice flour and salt.
Cream butter and sugar together, add dry ingredients and
mix to a firm dough. Turn onto a floured board and knead
well. Divide mixture into four portions. Shape each portion
into a round about 1.5 cm thick. Pinch edges and cut each
round diagonally into eight wedges. Place on a greased oven
tray and bake until shortbread just begins to colour, about
20–30 minutes. Allow to become quite cold before storing
in airtight containers.

Swiss Tarts

1/2 cup (125 g) butter
2/3 cup (120 g) icing sugar
1 1/2 cups (225 g) plain flour

glacé cherries for decoration
icing sugar

Preheat oven to moderate (180°C). Cream butter and sugar
together, add sifted flour and mix well. Pipe in rosettes onto
a baking tray, decorate with a small piece of cherry, and bake
for 15 minutes. When cool dust with icing sugar.

Yo-Yos

3/4 cups (190 g) butter
1/3 cup (60 g) icing sugar
1 cup (130 g) custard powder

1 cup (150 g) plain flour
1/2 teaspoon vanilla essence

Preheat oven to moderate (180°C). Cream butter and sugar
together. Add remaining ingredients and mix well. Roll
pieces of mixture into balls, place on oven tray and flatten
with a fork. Bake for 15–20 minutes. Two biscuits may be
joined together with Soft Icing (see p. 238) flavoured with a
little vanilla or jam.

SLICES

∽ UNBAKED SLICES ∾

ALMOND SLICE

125 g Marie biscuits
1/2 cup (125 g) sugar
1 1/2 cups (135 g) desiccated
  coconut

1/2 cup (60 g) flaked almonds
1/2 cup (125 g) butter
1 teaspoon almond essence

Crush biscuits finely, add sugar, coconut and almonds. Melt butter and pour over dry ingredients together with almond essence. Press into a log tin, refrigerate and cut into fingers.

APRICOT MARSHMALLOW

1 cup (120 g) crushed biscuits
1 cup (180 g) dried apricots
125 g marshmallows

1 cup (250 ml) condensed milk
1 tablespoon chopped nuts
1/2 cup (45 g) desiccated coconut

Crush biscuits finely and chop apricots and marshmallows. Mix together biscuits, apricots, marshmallows and nuts with condensed milk and make into rolls. Roll in coconut and refrigerate. Slice thinly when needed.

APRICOT TRUFFLES

1 1/3 cups (250 g) dried apricots
1/2 cup (45 g) desiccated coconut
1/2 x 395 g can sweetened
  condensed milk

1/2 cup (90 g) brown sugar
1 teaspoon lemon juice
extra coconut for rolling

Mince apricots, combine with other ingredients and blend well. Roll teaspoonfuls of mixture into balls and toss in extra coconut. Store in a container in refrigerator.

Note This recipe is gluten free.

CHERYL'S PEANUT SLICE

90 g butter
1 tablespoon golden syrup
1/2 x 395 g can condensed milk
1 packet malt biscuits, crushed

3/4 cup (75 g) peanuts
1/2 cup (90 g) sultanas
Chocolate Glacé Icing (see p. 237)
desiccated coconut

Melt butter, golden syrup and condensed milk together. Add crushed biscuits, nuts and sultanas. Mix well and spread in a greased slice tin 28 x 18 cm. Set in fridge, ice with chocolate icing and sprinkle with coconut. Cut into small fingers.

CHOCOLATE NUT SLICE

250 g chocolate
1/2 x 395 g can condensed
   milk

1/2 cup (60 g) roast hazelnuts
1/2 cup (60 g) pecan nuts
1/2 cup (60 g) blanched almonds

Place roughly chopped chocolate in top of double saucepan and heat gently. When melted, stir in condensed milk then nuts. Line the bottom and sides of a 25 x 8 cm loaf tin with aluminium foil. Spread mixture evenly in tin and refrigerate until firmly set. Remove from tin and cut into wafer-thin slices. Store in refrigerator. Keeps well for 1 month.

Hint Any combination of nuts may be used.

DATE SLICE

1 cup (160 g) dates
1/2 cup (90 g) brown sugar
juice of 1/2 orange
1 egg, well beaten

250 g sweet biscuits, finely
   crushed
desiccated coconut for topping

Place dates, sugar, butter and orange juice in a pan. Stir over heat until dates are soft. Cool. Add egg and fold in biscuits. Mix well. Press into scone tray. Top with coconut. Refrigerate. Cut into fingers to serve.

GINGER SLICE

1/2 cup (125 g) butter
3/4 cup (135 g) brown sugar
1/2 x 395 g can condensed milk
125 g preserved ginger

1/2 teaspoon ground ginger
250 g malt biscuits, crushed
Lemon Icing (see p. 237)
desiccated coconut

Melt butter, sugar and condensed milk together and stir well until sugar is dissolved, then add preserved ginger, ginger and biscuits. Mix well and press evenly into greased 30 x 20 cm tin. Ice with lemon icing and sprinkle with coconut.

HEDGEHOG

1/2 cup (125 g) butter
150 g caster sugar
2 tablespoons cocoa
2 tablespoons desiccated
  coconut
1 egg, beaten

1/2 cup (60 g) chopped
  walnuts
1/4 cup (45 g) glacé cherries
1/2 teaspoon vanilla essence
2 cups (220 g) crushed sweet
  biscuits

Melt butter and sugar together, add cocoa and mix well. Remove from heat and stir in coconut and egg. Add walnuts, cherries and vanilla. Stir in biscuit crumbs and mix well. Press into a greased 20 cm square pan and chill. Cut into squares. May be iced with Chocolate Glacé Icing (see p. 237).

JELLY SLICE

BASE

250 g Marie biscuits, crushed   3/4 cup (180 g) butter, melted

LEMON LAYER

1 x 395 g can condensed milk
juice of 2 lemons (about
  1/2 cup)

2 teaspoons gelatine
3/4 cup (190 ml) boiling
  water

TOPPING

1 packet strawberry jelly crystals   2 cups (500 ml) boiling water
1 teaspoon gelatine

For base, mix butter and biscuits well together. Press evenly into a greased 28 x 18 cm lamington tin. Chill well.

Make lemon layer: blend condensed milk with lemon juice, add gelatine dissolved in boiling water. Mix well and spread over base. Chill until set.

Make topping by dissolving gelatine and jelly in boiling water. Cool and when the consistency of egg white, pour over slice. Chill until firmly set. Cut into squares to serve.

LEMON OR ORANGE SLICE

1/2 cup (125 g) butter
250 g sweet biscuits, crushed
1/2 x 395 g can condensed milk
1 cup (90 g) desiccated coconut

grated rind of 1 lemon
or orange
Lemon or Orange Icing
(see p. 237)
extra coconut

Melt butter and add rest of ingredients. Spread evenly in a greased 28 x 18 cm slice tin. When set, ice with Lemon or Orange Icing and sprinkle with coconut. Cut into fingers.

MARS BAR SLICE

100 g butter
3 Mars Bars
3 cups rice bubbles

Chocolate Glacé Icing (see
p. 237) or melted chocolate

Melt Mars Bars and butter together in double saucepan, and then add to rice bubbles. Mix well and spread in greased 28 x 18 cm slice tin. Ice with chocolate icing or melted chocolate. Cut into fingers.

PEPPERMINT SLICE

BASE

1/2 cup (125 g) butter
250 g Marie biscuits, crushed

3/4 cup (70 g) desiccated
coconut

$^1/_2$ x 395 g can condensed
    milk

1 tablespoon cocoa

1 cup (180 g) icing sugar
2 tablespoons (40g) butter,
    softened
1 tablespoon cream

1 teaspoon peppermint
    essence
few drops of green colouring

90 g dark chocolate
30 g butter

few drops of cochineal

To make base, melt butter, mix all ingredients well. Press into greased 30 x 20 cm slice tin and chill in refrigerator to set. Mix all filling ingredients well together and spread on base. For topping, melt chocolate and butter together, add cochineal, spread on top of slice. When set cut into small fingers.

TRUFFLES

250 g Marie biscuits
1 x 395 g can condensed milk
1 tablespoon cocoa

1 cup (90 g) desiccated coconut
1 tablespoon lemon juice
extra coconut

Crush biscuits finely. Mix biscuits with condensed milk, cocoa, 1 cup coconut and lemon juice, then roll into balls and toss in extra coconut.

∾ BAKED SLICES ∾

BROWNIES

150 g butter
1 cup (250 g) sugar
$^1/_2$ teaspoon vanilla essence
2 eggs
$^1/_2$ cup (75 g) plain flour

75 g cocoa
$^1/_2$ cup (50 g) walnuts, chopped
$^1/_4$ cup chocolate chips
icing sugar

Preheat the oven to 150°C. Spray a 20 cm square pan with oil spray and line with paper. Soften butter and cream it with sugar and vanilla until light and fluffy. Beat eggs in gradually. Sift flour and cocoa and fold into the butter mixture. Stir in chopped walnuts and chocolate chips. Spoon batter into the baking tin and cook for 45 minutes until risen and just firm to touch. Cut into squares. Serve dusted with icing sugar.

CANADIAN COCONUT SLICE

1/2 cup (125 g) butter
1 cup (90 g) desiccated coconut
1 cup (150 g) self-raising flour
1 cup (30 g) cornflakes, crushed

1/2 cup (125 g) sugar
1 tablespoon cocoa
Chocolate Glacé Icing (see
p. 237)

Preheat oven to moderate (180°C). Melt butter and mix well with dry ingredients. Press into shallow tin. Bake 20–25 minutes. While hot, spread with Chocolate Glacé Icing, cut into squares and leave until cold.

CARAMEL FINGERS

1/2 cup (125 g) butter
2/3 cup (120 g) brown sugar
1 egg, beaten

few drops of vanilla essence
1 cup (150 g) self-raising flour
3/4 cup (100 g) dates
3/4 cup (75 g) walnuts

Preheat oven to moderate (180°C). Heat butter and sugar, stir until dissolved. Take off heat, mix in egg, vanilla, flour, dates and nuts. Put into greased tin and bake 20 minutes. Leave until cold, cut into fingers.

CHOCOLATE CARAMEL SLICE
BASE

1/2 cup (125 g) butter
1 cup (150 g) self-raising flour
1 large cup (40 g) cornflakes

1/2 cup (45 g) desiccated
coconut
3/4 cup (180 g) sugar

CARAMEL FILLING

1 x 395 g can condensed milk
2 tablespoons (60 g) golden
  syrup

2 tablespoons (40 g) butter
1 tablespoon sugar

CHOCOLATE TOPPING

3 tablespoons (60 g) Copha

$^1/_2$ cup drinking chocolate

For base, melt butter, pour over dry ingredients and mix well. Press into an 18 x 28 cm slice tin and bake 10 minutes in a moderate oven (180°C). For caramel filling, put all ingredients in a saucepan and boil for 10 minutes, stirring all the time. Pour over base. For icing, melt Copha and mix with chocolate. Pour over caramel. Cut into squares when set.

CHOCOLATE MARSHMALLOW SLICE

BASE

1 cup (150 g) self-raising
  flour
1 cup (90 g) desiccated
  coconut
1 cup (30 g) cornflakes

2 tablespoons cocoa
$^1/_2$ cup (125 g) sugar
pinch of salt
$^1/_2$ teaspoon vanilla essence
$^1/_2$ cup (125 g) butter, melted

MARSHMALLOW

1$^1/_2$ tablespoons gelatine
1$^1/_2$ cups (375 ml) hot water

3 cups (750 g) sugar
squeeze of lemon juice

TOPPING

3 tablespoons (60 g) Copha
$^1/_2$ cup (90 g) icing sugar

2 tablespoons cocoa

Preheat oven to moderate (180°C). For base, combine dry ingredients and vanilla then add melted butter and mix well. Press into 2 greased slice tins and bake for 15 minutes. Prepare marshmallow by placing all ingredients except lemon juice in saucepan. Bring to boil stirring constantly, add lemon juice and allow to cool. Beat until thick, pour over base. Place in refrigerator until set. Prepare topping by melting Copha over gentle heat. Stir in sieved dry, ingredients. Pour over the marshmallow and allow to set. Cut into squares.

Ginger Crunch

Base

1/2 cup (125 g) butter	1 cup (150 g) self-raising flour
1/4 cup (60 g) sugar	1 teaspoon ground ginger

Topping

4 tablespoons (60 g) icing sugar	1 teaspoon ground ginger
2 tablespoons (40 g) butter	3 teaspoons golden syrup

For base, cream butter and sugar together, add sifted flour and ginger. Mix well and press into greased slab tin. Bake in preheated moderate oven (180°C) for 15–20 minutes. Make topping: put all ingredients in a saucepan, stir over gentle heat until butter is melted and all ingredients are well mixed. Pour over biscuit while both are still warm. Cut into slices when cool.

Raisin Slice

1/2 cup (125 g) butter	1 cup (150 g) self-raising flour
3/4 cup (180 g) sugar	1 teaspoon cinnamon
1 egg	1 teaspoon vanilla essence
1 cup (180 g) raisins	chopped nuts

Preheat oven to moderate (180°C). Melt butter and sugar, simmer for 2 minutes, then cool slightly. Add egg and beat well. Add raisins then flour, cinnamon and vanilla. Spread into a greased 20 x 25 cm slice tin, sprinkle with nuts and bake for 20–25 minutes. Cut into squares when cold.

Raspberry Shortbread

1/2 cup (125 g) butter	1/2 cup (75 g) plain flour
1/4 cup (60 g) butter	2 tablespoons raspberry jam
2 eggs, separated	1/2 cup (125 g) caster sugar
1 cup (150 g) self-raising flour	1 cup (90 g) desiccated coconut

Preheat oven to moderate (180°C). Beat sugar and butter together to a cream, add egg yolks then the sifted flours. Mix

to a soft dough. Roll out on oven slide, spread with raspberry jam, then beat the egg whites until stiff, add sugar and
coconut and spread over jam. Bake for 20 minutes and cut
in slices when cold.

THREE LAYER CHOC-MINT SLICE

BASE

1¹/2 cups (225 g) self-raising flour   ¹/2 cup (90 g) brown sugar
1 cup (90 g) desiccated coconut   ³/4 cup (180 g) butter

FILLING

1¹/4 cups (225 g) icing sugar   1 tablespoon Copha, melted
1¹/2 tablespoons (30 ml) milk   1 teaspoon peppermint essence

TOPPING

100 g cooking chocolate   1 tablespoon Copha

For base, mix dry ingredients, stir in melted butter. Press
into greased tin. Bake in a preheated moderate oven
(180°C) for 15–20 minutes. Mix all filling ingredients
together and pour over the base while still warm. Allow to
set. For topping, melt chocolate and Copha in a heatproof
bowl over boiling water. Spread over the filling and allow to
cool. Cut into finger lengths.

Yeast Breads and Buns, Scones

Yeast cooking is a fascinating and worthwhile task. Yeast is a living organism and needs warmth, moisture and food in order to grow. If any one of these conditions is not present, the yeast may take hours to work. Cold retards its growth and heat will kill it. It is the carbon dioxide that is released as yeast grows that causes bread to rise.

Types of yeast most commonly used

Instant dried yeast, including vacuum-packed, is available in most stores. Keep in a cool dry place. Once opened reseal any remaining and store in an airtight glass container in the refrigerator or freezer.

Compressed yeast is putty coloured and breaks sharply. Keeps in an airtight container in the refrigerator for 1–2 weeks or for a longer time in the freezer. Compressed yeast can be bought in most health stores.

To measure yeast

Dried yeast: 1 tablespoon weighs 10 g; some packets contain sachets, e.g. 12 sachets, containing 7 g per sachet.
Compressed yeast: Should be pressed well into the bowl of the spoon. 1 tablespoon weighs 20 g.

Note 7 g dry yeast = 15 g compressed yeast

Flour

Most flour is made from wheat but it can be made from a variety of cereals, so there are a number of different types of flour available — your choice depends on diet and preference. Once you become proficient in making your own bread it is great fun to experiment with different flours and other ingredients. The heavier flours, such as multigrain or wholemeal, may require the addition of a little extra liquid and a little extra yeast. Flour rich in gluten is best for bread. It is also possible to buy gluten flour, which can be added to other flour to improve its breadmaking qualities — add 2 tablespoons (30 g) to 1 kg flour.

IMPORTANT INSTRUCTIONS

- Utensils and ingredients should be warm.
- Very thorough kneading is essential.
- Dough must be covered during proving.
- A hot oven is essential in the initial cooking of yeast mixtures.
- A loaf or bun is cooked when tapping on the crust produces a hollow sound and the loaf has shrunk slightly from the sides of tin.
- Bread machines are popular; there are a number of brands from which to choose.

PROVING BREAD

To prove bread, place the dough in a warm container and cover with plastic wrap. Keep in a warm place until dough has doubled in bulk.

BREAD GLAZE

Mix 1 egg white with 1 tablespoon water and brush over loaves or rolls before baking is completed.

SWEET BUN GLAZE

1/2 cup (125 g) sugar   *1 teaspoon gelatine*
1/4 cup (65 ml) water

Mix together in a saucepan and heat gently until sugar and gelatine have dissolved. Glaze buns after they are cooked.

Buns

Makes 16 buns

5 cups (750 g) plain flour
3 tablespoons (60 g) butter
  or margarine
1 teaspoon mixed spice
1¹/2 cups (270 g) mixed
  fruit

¹/2 cup (125 g) sugar
2 teaspoons powdered milk
1¹/2 cups (375 ml) tepid
  water
30 g compressed yeast or 3
  teaspoons dried yeast

Sift flour into warm basin. Rub in butter using fingertips, add spice and fruit. Mix sugar and powdered milk into half of tepid water. Crumble yeast into remainder of water. Stir milk liquid into flour, add yeast to make a soft dough. Knead until elastic (about 10 minutes) then return to bowl and cover with plastic wrap. Leave in warm place to double its size. Turn on to a floured board and knead again. Divide into 16 parts, form small buns. Place on lightly greased tray and leave in warm place until doubled in size again. Bake in a preheated hot oven (200°C) for 25 minutes.

Hot Cross Buns

1 quantity Bun mixture (see above)

Piping batter

¹/4 cup self-raising flour
1 tablespoon caster sugar

2 tablespoons water

Mix flour, water and sugar until smooth. Pipe on to buns after buns have doubled in bulk and bake.

Coffee Scrolls

Makes 20–24

2 teaspoons dried yeast
¹/4 cup (60 g) sugar
1¹/2 cups (375 ml) warm milk
2 tablespoons (40 g) butter
4 cups (600 g) plain flour
1 egg, beaten

2 tablespoons (40 g) butter
1 tablespoon cinnamon
1 tablespoon caster sugar
1¹/2 tablespoons (30 g) sultanas
3 tablespoons (30 g) chopped
  walnut pieces

Cream yeast with a little of the sugar, moisten with a little of the milk, set in a warm place for 10 minutes. Rub butter into flour and add the beaten egg. Add the yeast mixture and rest of the milk and work into a dough. Knead well, return to basin, cover and prove until it doubles in size. Turn out and knead again. Roll into an oblong shape, put butter on in small pieces and fold in three. Roll out again, and fold in three, repeat once more. Roll out, fold the sides to centre, and then fold the dough over again from the side. Roll into a long oblong, sprinkle with cinnamon, sugar, sultanas and walnuts. Wet the edges and roll up. Cut in slices. Set on greased tray and put in warm place to prove. Bake in a pre-heated very hot oven (220°C) for 12–15 minutes. Brush with Sweet Bun Glaze (see p. 267).

CRUMPETS
Makes 24

4 cups (600 g) plain flour
2 teaspoons sugar
2 teaspoons dried yeast
2 cups (500 ml) milk

1/4 teaspoon bicarbonate of
    soda
1/2 teaspoon salt
1 tablespoon warm water

In large bowl mix 2 cups flour, sugar and yeast. Heat milk to lukewarm, gradually add to ingredients in bowl and mix well. Add remainder of flour and beat for 5 minutes. Cover and stand for 1 hour until doubled in size. Dissolve soda and salt in warm water. Stir into mixture, cover, and allow to prove again for 1 hour. Heat heavy-based frying pan or electric pan to moderate heat (180°C). Oil egg ring and base of pan. Pour in enough batter to nearly fill ring. Allow to cook until top has set, about 5 minutes. Remove ring, turn crumpet and cook for a few seconds. Turn again and allow to dry thoroughly on the underside. Cool on wire rack. Toast and serve with butter.

Danish Pastry

1 quantity Sally Lunn mixture
  (see opposite)
2 tablespoons butter or
  margarine

apricot jam
finely chopped nuts
Soft Icing (see p. 238)

Prove the dough for 1 hour. After kneading, roll out. Spread butter over dough, and fold in three, as for Rough Puff Pastry (see p. 179). Roll out and fold again. Roll out and spread with a very thin layer of jam, and sprinkle with nuts. Roll up, put in a well-greased tin and allow to rise. Bake in a preheated moderate oven (180°C) for about 30 minutes, or until golden brown and cooked. Put a little Soft Icing on top, and sprinkle with chopped nuts.

Note This dough can be made into individual Danish pastries.

Pocket Bread
Makes 16 pocket breads

5 cups (750 g) plain flour
2 x 7 g sachets dried yeast
¼ cup (60 ml) oil

2 cups (500 ml) warm water
1 tablespoon sugar
1 teaspoon salt

Stir together flour and yeast. Warm oil, water, sugar and salt together to blood heat and add to flour mixture. Beat until smooth, about 3 minutes. Stir in extra flour, if necessary, to make a moderately soft dough. Turn on to floured surface, knead until smooth and elastic, about 5–10 minutes. Cover dough and allow it to rest 30 minutes. Roll into a 40 cm log, cut into 16 equal pieces and shape them into balls. Roll out to 12 cm circles and place on greased trays. Let rise in warm place for 30–45 minutes or until puffy. Bake in a preheated hot oven (200°C) for 8–10 minutes or until lightly browned. Remove from baking tray, immediately wrap in foil to cool. Cut pocket in bread and add filling.

SALLY LUNN

30 g compressed yeast or 2
   teaspoons dried yeast
1/4 cup (60 g) sugar
1 cup (250 ml) milk

2 tablespoons (40 g) butter
4 cups (600 g) plain flour
1 egg, beaten

Cream yeast with a little of the sugar and mix in the warm milk. Set in a warm place for 10 minutes. Rub butter into flour, add remaining sugar. Make a well in the centre, pour in yeast mixture and egg. Work the whole into a soft dough. Divide the dough into two, knead well and press into greased tins. Prove till dough reaches top of tin. Bake 20 minutes in a preheated hot oven (200°C), and glaze.

WHITE BREAD
Makes 2 loaves

1 tablespoon dried yeast
1 tablespoon sugar
2 1/2 cups (625 ml) warm water

1 kg plain flour
1 teaspoon salt

Combine yeast, sugar and 1/2 cup warm water and stand in a warm place until bubbles form. Mix flour and salt and add yeast mixture. Work flour in and gradually add remaining 2 cups warm water until all the flour is taken up. Turn on to clean board and knead for 10 minutes. Place in lightly oiled bowl and stand in a warm place until the mixture has doubled in size. Turn on to board and knead again for 10 minutes. Form into 2 loaves, place in oiled tins and again leave in warm place until doubled. Bake in a preheated very hot oven (220°C) for 15 minutes, reduce heat to moderate (180°C) and cook for a further 25 minutes.

Note *White Bread Rolls*: Follow recipe for White Bread. After kneading for the second time shape half of the dough into 15 rolls, place on greased oven tray and put in a warm place until rolls double their size (10–15 minutes). Bake in preheated hot oven (200°C) for 15–20 minutes.

WHOLEMEAL BREAD
Makes 2 loaves

4 cups (600 g) plain flour
4 cups (600 g) wholemeal flour
4 cups (600 g) stone ground flour
1 teaspoon salt
4 cups (1 L) warm water

2 teaspoons honey
1 tablespoon dried yeast
milk
1 tablespoon sesame seeds

Sieve flours and salt together, place in warm place in a warm bowl. Mix 1 cup warm water with honey and add yeast. Leave 10–15 minutes until mixture froths. Mix yeast mixture with warm flour and add remainder of warm water. Turn on to a floured board and knead well for about 10 minutes. Return to bowl. Cover with plastic wrap and leave in a warm place until dough doubles its bulk (30–40 minutes). Knead again, halve and shape into 2 loaves. Place in oiled loaf tins. Cover and leave in warm place until mixture comes to the top of the tins. Glaze with milk and sprinkle with sesame seeds. Bake in a preheated very hot oven (220°C) for 10 minutes then reduce heat to moderate (180°C) and cook for a further 30–40 minutes.

∿ SCONES ∿

PLAIN SCONES
Makes 12

2 cups (300 g) self-raising flour
1 teaspoon sugar

1 tablespoon butter or
margarine
3/4 cup (190 ml) milk

Sift flour, add sugar and rub butter in using fingertips. Pour in milk almost all at once, working lightly into a soft dough. Turn on to a lightly floured board, knead as lightly as possible, roll out to about 1.5 cm thick, and cut out with scone cutter. Place on lightly oiled or lightly floured baking tray. Glaze tops with yolk of egg or milk and bake in a preheated very hot oven (220°C) for 12 minutes.

Variations

Cheese Scones: Add 2 tablespoons (20 g) grated cheese, 1/4 teaspoon mustard, 1/4 teaspoon cayenne pepper.

Date Scones: Add 1/2 cup (90 g) chopped dates.

Fruit Scones: Add 2 tablespoons (30 g) currants or sultanas.

PUMPKIN SCONES
Makes 12

2 cups (300 g) self-raising
  flour
1 tablespoon butter or
  margarine

1 tablespoon sugar
1 egg, beaten
1 cup (250 g) cooked and
  mashed pumpkin

Sift flour, rub butter into flour using fingertips, and add sugar, pumpkin and egg, mixing to a soft dough. Knead lightly on floured board. Roll out to about 1.5 cm thick, cut with scone cutter and bake in a preheated very hot oven (220°C) for 10–12 minutes.

SAVOURY SCONES
Makes 12

2 cups (300 g) self-raising flour
2 tablespoons grated onion
1 tablespoon chopped celery
  (optional)
1 tablespoon grated carrot
2 tablespoons (20 g) grated
  cheese

1 tablespoon powdered milk
  (optional)
1/4 teaspoon salt
3 tablespoons (60 g) butter
  or margarine
milk

Mix flour with next 6 ingredients, and rub in butter. Add enough milk (about 1/2 – 2/3 cup) to form a soft dough. Bake as for Plain Scones (see previous page).

SAVOURY SCONE RING

3 cups (450 g) self-raising flour
1/2 teaspoon salt
4 tablespoons (80 g) butter
  or margarine
1 1/2 cups (375 ml) milk
extra 1 tablespoon butter,
  melted

1 onion, chopped
1 cup (125 g) grated
  cheddar cheese
1 bacon rasher, chopped
1 egg, beaten
poppy seeds

Sift flour and salt together. Rub butter into flour, add milk and mix into a soft dough. Turn on to floured board and knead lightly. Roll thinly into oblong shape, brush with melted butter. Sprinkle with onion, cheese and bacon. Roll up lengthwise and form into a ring. Snip with scissors at intervals halfway through ring. Brush with egg and sprinkle with poppy seeds. Bake in a preheated hot oven (200°C) for 15–20 minutes.

Note A *Fruit Ring* can be made similarly by substituting 4–5 tablespoons dried fruit, 1 tablespoon sugar and a teaspoon of mixed spice for the savoury filling.

WHOLEMEAL SCONES
Makes 16–20

2 tablespoons (40 g) butter
  or margarine
3 cups (450 g) wholemeal
  self-raising flour

1 tablespoon golden syrup
1 cup (250 ml) milk

Rub butter into flour. Warm golden syrup, combine with milk. Add to flour mixture to form an elastic dough. Knead lightly, roll out to about 1.5 cm thick, cut with scone cutter and bake in a preheated very hot oven (220°C) for 10–15 minutes.

Preserves

Important instructions

1. Fruits with a high pectin content are the easiest to make into jams and jellies, e.g. apples, citrus fruits, cranberries, plums, quinces. Fruits with a medium amount are apricots, blackberries, loganberries and raspberries, and those with a low content are cherries, figs, grapes, peaches, pears, pineapples, rhubarb and strawberries. It is advisable to mix fruits with low pectin with those with a high content, or to use commercially prepared pectin (jam setting mixture). For jams to set well, fruits with low pectin will need extra acid, which helps to extract pectin from fruit.

2. Use good quality fruit that is firm, sound but not over-ripe. Over-ripe fruit is low in pectin (substance that makes jams and jellies set).

3. Use a wooden spoon and a good flat, large pan.

4. Carefully follow directions as to length of time for cooking; preserves are spoiled by too much cooking as well as by too little.

5. Skim carefully any scum that rises.

6. Watch carefully that preserves do not burn.

7. Test jams and marmalades for setting point (see 'How to tell if jam or marmalade is ready', below) before putting into warmed, sterilised jars.

8. Cover jam immediately to exclude air and store in a cool, dry place.

9. If making jam in microwave oven, use much smaller amounts of ingredients and a very large bowl.

How to tell if jam or marmalade is ready

There are three tests:

- Place a teaspoon of jam on a cold saucer, and allow to

cool (e.g. in refrigerator). Touch cold jam with a finger and if it wrinkles and forms a skin it has reached a good set.

- Dip a wooden spoon into jam. Wait a few seconds, then tilt the spoon and let jam drip off. If it forms a heavy clot as it falls off, it is ready.
- Dip a sugar thermometer in hot water and then in jam mixture, but do NOT touch the bottom of pan. If jam has reached 108°C it is ready.

∾ Jams ∾

Apricot or Peach Jam

1.5 kg fruit *6 cups (1.5 kg) sugar*
1¼ cups (310 ml) water *½ teaspoon tartaric acid*

Peel and stone fruit and cut in quarters or halves and put in large pan. Add water and cook over a low heat until soft. Add sugar and cook over a low heat, stirring constantly until dissolved. Bring to boil and boil until setting point is reached (about 15 minutes). Add tartaric acid 10 minutes before removing from heat. Pour into warmed, sterilised jars and seal.

Note A 50 g packet of jam setting mixture may be used in lieu of tartaric acid.

Black Currant or Blackberry Jam

1 kg black currants *3 cups (750 g) sugar*
2 cups (500 ml) water

Boil fruit in water for 30 minutes or until soft. Dissolve sugar in fruit, and boil until jam will jell, approximately 30 minutes — cooking time varies with the amount of fruit being cooked. Pour into warmed, sterilised jars and seal.

```
┌─────────────────────────────────────────────────┐
│ ╔═══════════════════════════════════════════════╗ │
│ ║              🐦 🐦 🐦                          ║ │
│ ║            Quince Honey                        ║ │
│ ║                                                ║ │
│ ║  Ingredients — 5 large quinces, 1 pint water, 5 lb sugar. ║ │
│ ║  Mode — Boil sugar and water well, then add the quinces, which ║ │
│ ║  have been grated. Boil 15 minutes.            ║ │
│ ║              🐦 🐦 🐦                          ║ │
│ ╚═══════════════════════════════════════════════╝ │
└─────────────────────────────────────────────────┘
```

FEIJOA JAM

1 kg feijoas
¹/2 cup (125 ml) water

juice and rind of 1 lemon
4 cups (1 kg) sugar

Peel and slice feijoas and place in large pan with water, lemon rind and juice. Boil until fruit is soft. Add sugar, stir until dissolved, and then boil rapidly without stirring until mixture jells when tested (approximately 20 minutes). Allow to cool for 5 minutes, put in warmed, sterilised jars and seal.

FIG JAM

3.5 kg figs
12 cups (3 kg) sugar
2 lemons

1¹/3 cups (240 g) preserved
ginger
4 cups (1 L) water

Wipe figs, cut off ends, then cut in small pieces, cover with half of sugar and stand overnight. Next day peel lemons and cut up rind in small strips, squeeze juice and cut ginger finely; add rest of sugar, water, ginger, lemon juice and rind to figs and boil until thick and clear and jelling well (about 30 minutes–1 hour). Allow to cool for 5 minutes, put in warmed, sterilised jars and seal.

PEACH AND PINEAPPLE JAM

3.5 kg yellow peaches
1 pineapple

12 cups (3 kg) sugar
juice of 3 lemons

Peel and stone peaches, cracking half the stones and blanching the kernels. Pare and slice pineapple. Cut fruit and put in the preserving pan, with just enough water to keep the fruit at the bottom from catching. Heat slowly to a simmering boil, and cook gently for 30 minutes. Add sugar gradually, so as not to reduce the temperature below simmering point, then add the juice of lemons and the peach kernels. Boil gently for 20 minutes. Pour into warmed, sterilised jars and seal.

PEAR JAM

4 cups (1 L) water
6 cups (1.5 kg) sugar
10–12 pears (about 2 kg)

juice and grated rind of 3 lemons
1^1/$_3$ cups (240 g) preserved
    ginger, chopped

Make a syrup of water and sugar. Peel, core and cut up pears. Add pears, lemon rind, juice and ginger to the syrup and simmer until setting point is reached. Pour into warmed, sterilised jars and seal.

PLUM JAM

3 kg plums
3 cups (750 ml) water

12 cups (3 kg) sugar

Boil plums with water until soft, add sugar and boil fast until jam sets. Pour into warmed, sterilised jars and seal.

RASPBERRY OR LOGANBERRY JAM

3 kg raspberries or loganberries   12 cups (3 kg) sugar

Cover fruit with sugar and stand overnight. Next day put into preserving pan and bring slowly to the boil, making sure all the sugar is dissolved before it comes to the boil. Boil fast for 8–10 minutes or until setting point is reached. Pour into warmed, sterilised jars and seal.

Rhubarb and Pineapple Jam

1 large bunch (600 g prepared)   1 x 825 g can pineapple
    rhubarb   6 cups (1.5 kg) sugar

Cut rhubarb stems into short pieces. Cut up pineapple
finely and add to rhubarb along with juice; boil together for
10 minutes. Add sugar and boil till setting point is reached
(about 10 minutes). Pour into warmed, sterilised jars and
seal.

Strawberry Jam

3 kg strawberries   12 cups (3 kg) sugar
juice of 2 lemons

Hull strawberries, put fruit and juice in pan and heat gently.
Add sugar, stir until setting point is reached. Remove scum
and allow jam to cool until a skin forms on the surface; stir
and pour into warmed, sterilised jars.

Strawberry Jam (Microwave)
Makes 2 cups

2 punnets (500 g) strawberries   2 cups (500 g) sugar
1/4 cup (60 ml) lemon juice

Wash and hull strawberries, place in large bowl with lemon
juice, cook on HIGH for 4 minutes. Stir in sugar, cook on
HIGH for 20 minutes or until jam jells, stirring occasionally
during cooking. Stand for 5 minutes before pouring into
warmed, sterilised jars, seal while hot.

Note Any berries can be substituted for strawberries, vary
cooking time if necessary.

∾ Fruit Jelly Making ∾

Fruit for jelly should be fully matured, but not over-ripe. Put fruit in the pan with enough water to come to the level of the fruit, but not to cover it. Boil fast until fruit is soft. Strain through a clean cloth or jelly bag, and allow liquid to run through, but do not press it through as this makes the jelly cloudy. Measure the liquid and to each cup allow 1 cup (250 g) of sugar; put liquid and sugar into a pan and boil until it jells when tested on a cold plate. Gooseberry, black and red currants, blackberry and loquat jelly may be made in this way. Apples, crab apples and quinces should be roughly cut up before being boiled. The flavour of apple jelly is improved if juice of 1 lemon is allowed to every 2.5 kg of apples. For guava jelly very little water should be used.

Quince Jelly

7 quinces, washed, cored and
    chopped
juice of 3 lemons

sugar
water

Just cover the quinces with water in a large saucepan and boil until soft. Strain out the liquid, reserving the pulp for Quince Paste. Return the liquid to the saucepan, and add lemon juice and 2 cups (500 g) sugar for every 600 ml liquid. Reduce the liquid, stirring frequently, until the mixture jells. Pour into warmed, sterilised jars in the usual manner.

Quince Paste

Weigh and purée the pulp reserved from the jelly. Place the pulp and the same weight of sugar in a heavy-based saucepan. Simmer slowly for up to 3 hours, stirring every few minutes, until the paste changes to a dark rose colour and is quite thick. (It is suggested to wait until you can see the bottom of the pan in the trail of the spoon). Tip out the mixture into oiled flat trays so that you get a slab about

2 cm thick. Let it cool overnight. Paste should then be solid but still sticky. Turn each slab on to a sheet of muslin and wrap the muslin over the slab of paste to enclose it. Place the muslin-wrapped slabs on wire racks and put them in a cool dark place. After a month or so the surface will have dried out and the paste is ready to eat. Divide the slabs into small segments and store in icing sugar in a sealed container.

Serve quince paste thinly sliced with cheese, particularly the stronger flavoured cheeses; with thinly sliced apple or pear as a nibble; and with coffee, cut into cubes and dusted with icing sugar. Paste is also good stirred into gravy for chicken or lamb.

∾ Marmalades ∾

Cumquat Marmalade

1 kg cumquats
1¹/2 cups (375 ml) boiling
  water

6 cups (1.5 kg) sugar
juice of 2 lemons

Wash cumquats. Slice thinly, retaining seeds. Place seeds in muslin bag, tie and add to fruit. Add water. Cook gently until fruit is tender. Add sugar, stir until dissolved, and add juice of lemons. Cook rapidly until set. Leave to stand to let fruit settle. Put in warmed, sterilised jars, seal and label.

Grapefruit Marmalade

2 kg grapefruit
9 cups (2 L) water

8 cups (2 kg) sugar

Cut fruit into quarters, remove seeds and white centres, and slice fruit finely. Put seeds and centres into a small bowl with a little of the water. Cover the grapefruit with the rest of the water and set aside for 24 hours. Pour water off the seeds and add to the fruit. Pour into pan and boil for 1 hour. Add sugar and boil until it jells. Allow to cool slightly, and pour into warmed, sterilised jars.

LEMON MARMALADE

6 lemons   6 cups (1.5 kg) sugar
7 cups (1.75 L) boiling water

Slice lemons thinly and cover with water, let stand overnight. Next day, cook gently until rinds are soft, approximately 20–30 minutes. Add sugar, stir until dissolved and quickly boil for 25–45 minutes or until fruit will jell. Allow to cool slightly, and pour into warmed, sterilised jars.

ORANGE MARMALADE

1 kg oranges   5 cups (1.25 kg) sugar
6–8 cups (1.5–2 L) water   juice and peel of 1 lemon

Shred oranges finely, removing pips. Cover fruit with water and leave for 24 hours. Put pips in a separate basin with water. Next day strain this off and add liquid to the fruit. Put oranges in large pan. Add lemon juice and peel to pan. Boil until fruit begins to fall to the bottom of pan (about 1 hour). Add sugar, and boil until it jells (about 1–1^1/2 hours). Remove lemon peel, cool slightly and pour into warmed, sterilised jars.

PROCESSOR LEMON MARMALADE

Any citrus fruit or combination of citrus fruits can be substituted for lemons. The cooking time depends on type of fruit. Limes need much longer cooking than other citrus fruit.

3 large lemons   3 cups (750 g) sugar
1 cup (375 ml) water

Quarter lemons, discard seeds. Chop lemons finely in processor or blender. Place in deep dish with water, cook on HIGH in microwave for 10 minutes or until fruit is tender. Stir in sugar, cook on HIGH for 18 minutes or until it jells when tested, stir occasionally during cooking. Stand for

5 minutes, then pour into warmed, sterilised jars and seal.

THREE FRUIT MARMALADE

1 sweet orange
1 grapefruit
2 lemons

6 cups (1.5 L) water
6 cups (1.5 kg) sugar

Shred rinds thinly, cut up rest of fruit, cover with water and stand overnight. Next day simmer until fruit is soft, add sugar, stirring until dissolved. Then boil rapidly until fruit jells when tested. Cool, place in warmed, sterilised jars and seal.

CHUTNEYS, PICKLES AND SAUCES

∾ CHUTNEYS ∾

APPLE CHUTNEY

12 apples (about 2 kg)
4 large onions
2²/3 cups (480 g) preserved
  ginger
2 tablespoons cloves

1 tablespoon allspice
6 cups (1.5 L) vinegar
³/4 teaspoon cayenne pepper
2 teaspoons salt
¹/4 teaspoon white pepper

Peel, core and dice apples, slice onions finely, dice ginger, and put cloves into muslin bag. Put apples, onions and vinegar into a pan and boil for a few minutes, then add remaining ingredients and clove bag and simmer for 2 hours. Remove bag of cloves, and bottle chutney in warmed, sterilised jars.

APRICOT OR PLUM CHUTNEY

1.5 kg stoned and sliced apricots
  or plums
2 cups (500 g) sugar
¹/4 teaspoon cayenne pepper
1 cup (180 g) sultanas
3 cups (750 ml) vinegar

1 clove garlic, crushed
¹/2 teaspoon pepper
2 cm fresh ginger, scraped and
  bruised
2 teaspoons salt
4 large onions, sliced

Place all ingredients in pan, simmer for 1¹/2 hours or until of a good consistency. Remove ginger root. Bottle in warmed, sterilised jars and seal.

```
╔══════════════════════════════════════════════╗
║                                                ║
║              ≥♣  ≥♣  ≥♣                         ║
║              Aspic Jelly                       ║
║                                                ║
║  Ingredients — 1¹/₂ pints water, ¹/₄ pint of these vinegars mixed ║
║  — tarragon, malt, and chili (most of malt, and only a little chili), ║
║  juice of 2 lemons, 1 carrot, 1 turnip, 1 onion, 1 stick celery, ║
║  ¹/₂ teaspoon salt, a small bunch of tarragon, chervil, and ║
║  parsley, the rind of 1 lemon, 2 oz of French gelatine, whites and ║
║  shells of 2 eggs, 10 white peppercorns. ║
║                                                ║
║  Mode — Put all the ingredients into a stewpan together, and ║
║  whisk over the fire until it boils. Then draw it to the side of the fire ║
║  for a few minutes, and strain through a clean cloth (scalded). ║
║              ≥♣  ≥♣  ≥♣                         ║
╚══════════════════════════════════════════════╝
```

PAW PAW CHUTNEY

1 kg paw paw   2 cups (500 g) sugar
2 cups (500 ml) vinegar   1 cup (180 g) mixed dried fruit
2 teaspoons salt   1 teaspoon allspice
a few cloves

Boil together until soft and thick. Bottle in warmed,
sterilised jars and seal.

TOMATO CHUTNEY

6 apples (about 1 kg)   4 cups (1 kg) sugar
10 onions   2 tablespoons (40 g) salt
3 kg ripe tomatoes   1 tablespoon ground
1 tablespoon cloves   ginger
1 tablespoon peppercorns   1²/₃ cup (240 g) sultanas
1 tablespoon pimentos   3 tablespoons (30 g) cornflour
5 cups (1.25 L) vinegar

Peel, core and chop apples, peel and chop onions and tomatoes. Place cloves, peppercorns and pimentos in a muslin
bag. Put apples, onions, tomatoes, vinegar, sugar, salt and
spice bag in pan. Cook for 1 hour then add ground ginger
and sultanas and cook for a further 30 minutes. Remove

spice bag, add cornflour blended with a little cold water and cook for 3–5 minutes. Bottle chutney while hot in warmed, sterilised jars, seal when cold.

ᗝ SAUCES ᗝ

PLUM SAUCE

3 kg dark plums
3 cups (750 ml) vinegar
1 teaspoon white pepper
1 tablespoon cloves

6 cups (1.5 kg) sugar
1½ tablespoons (30 g) salt
¾ teaspoon cayenne pepper
25 g knob of fresh ginger

Put all ingredients in pan together and boil until fruit is soft. Strain through a colander, pour into warmed, sterilised, wide-necked bottles and seal. If sauce is too thick, add a little more vinegar before removing from heat.

WORCESTER SAUCE

7 cups (1.25 L) brown vinegar
30 g knob of fresh ginger
3 cups (1 kg) treacle
¾ teaspoon cayenne pepper

30 g cloves
1½ tablespoons (30 g) salt
30 g chopped garlic

Boil all ingredients together for 30 minutes. Strain and put in warmed, sterilised bottles.

ᗝ PICKLES AND RELISHES ᗝ

IMPORTANT INFORMATION

- Most vegetables can be pickled.
- Use lined or stainless steel pans, glazed stoneware vessels, or glass jars when preparing, boiling and storing pickles. Both brine and vinegar corrode other metals so avoid their use.
- Use a plastic rather than a metal colander, and use a wooden spoon.

- Use cellophane or plastic jar covers and not metal ones.
- Choose a good vinegar.
- Use coarse or rock salt in preference to table salt, which contains additives that can affect a pickle's flavour.

BRINE

Boil 1 cup (250 g) salt and 4 cups (1 L) water. Allow to cool before using.

PICKLE FOR VEGETABLES

4 cups (1 L) vinegar
1 teaspoon allspice berries
1 blade mace
1¹/2 teaspoons salt

2 teaspoons peppercorns
knob of fresh ginger, bruised
¹/2 teaspoon cayenne pepper

Boil all ingredients in pan for 5–10 minutes. Strain before using. Use this liquid hot where vegetables need to be softened, and cold when wishing to keep vegetables crisp. Sufficient for pickling 8 cups (2 L) prepared vegetables (1 kg vegetables make approximately 4 cups/1 L when prepared).

CUCUMBER RELISH

1 tablespoon chillies, sliced
3–4 large cucumbers (about
   1.5 kg), peeled
4 green apples, diced
2 tablespoons (40 g) salt
2 tablespoons (40 g) sugar

4 onions, sliced
¹/4 teaspoon cayenne pepper
2 cups (500 ml) vinegar
1 tablespoon flour
1 tablespoon turmeric
a little water

Boil first 7 ingredients with vinegar for 20 minutes. Stir in flour and turmeric blended with water. Boil gently for 2 minutes, stirring all the time. Bottle in warmed, sterilised jars and seal.

Green Tomato Pickles

3 kg green tomatoes
3 tablespoons (40 g) salt
4 cups (1 L) vinegar
1 1/2 teaspoons ground cloves
2 teaspoons peppercorns

1 teaspoon ground ginger
1 teaspoon cayenne pepper
1 cup (250 g) sugar
3 medium onions
1/2 cup (90 g) raisins

Slice tomatoes into earthenware dish, sprinkle each layer with salt, leave overnight. Boil vinegar, spices and sugar, then strain. Slice onions, add to vinegar mixture with drained tomatoes and raisins. Simmer until tender, bottle in warmed, sterilised jars when cold.

Pickled Green Olives

2 kg green olives
2 lemons, sliced
4 fennel sprigs
4 hot chillies

1 1/2 cups (375 g) salt
6 cups (1.5 L) water
2 tablespoons (40 ml) olive oil

Using a mallet gently hit 1 or 2 olives at a time to split them but leaving stone intact. Halve lemons lengthwise and slice crosswise. Place olives in glass jar interspersed with lemon, fennel and chillies. Fill with brine made from salt dissolved in water. Cover and set aside for 1 week, then add oil. Store in a cool place for at least 3 weeks before use.

Pickled Onions

2 cups (500 g) salt
8 cups (2 L) water
2 kg small pickling onions
6 cups (1.5 L) vinegar

1 cup (250 g) sugar
1 tablespoon pimento
1 tablespoon peppercorns
1 tablespoon cloves

Make brine by dissolving salt in water. Peel onions and put in brine 2–3 days, turning occasionally with a wooden spoon. Put other ingredients into a pan and bring to the boil. Rinse onions well and add to pan. Bring back to boiling point and remove from heat. Cool, put in sterilised jars and cover. Leave for 6 weeks before using.

PICKLED WALNUTS

green walnuts
6 cups (1.5 L) water
1½ cups (375 g) salt
4 cups (1 L) vinegar

1 tablespoon peppercorns
1 tablespoon allspice
1 teaspoon salt

Prick the walnuts well, put them into an earthenware vessel and cover with strong cold brine. Stir walnuts 2–3 times daily for 6 days, then drain and cover with fresh brine made from same amounts of salt and water. After 3 more days, drain again, spread walnuts on large dishes, place in the sun and leave till quite black. Fill sterilised wide-necked bottles three-quarters full with walnuts. Boil sufficient vinegar to cover them, adding peppercorns, allspice and 1 teaspoon salt, and boil for 15 minutes. Pour over walnuts, close bottles securely, and store in dry, cool place for 6 weeks before using.

SUGAR-FREE PICKLED VEGETABLES

1 kg cauliflower, chopped
2 teaspoons coarse salt
2–3 small cucumbers, chopped
1 green capsicum, chopped
1 red capsicum, chopped

2 cups (500 ml) white vinegar
2 teaspoons coarse salt
8 peppercorns
bay leaf

Place cauliflower in colander, sprinkle with 1 teaspoon salt, cover and leave overnight. Next day, add cucumber and remaining salt, stand 1 hour, rinse under cold tap, drain. Add all vegetables to pan of boiling water, boil for 5 minutes. Rinse vegetables under cold tap, drain and cool. Boil vinegar, salt, peppercorns and bay leaf in pan for 5 minutes, strain and cool. Pack vegetables into large sterilised jar, cover with spiced vinegar and seal.

Tomato Relish

2 kg large ripe tomatoes
4 large onions
1 tablespoon salt
2 cups (500 g) sugar
vinegar

1 tablespoon curry powder
$1/2$ tablespoon mustard
5 chillies
cayenne pepper to taste

Cut tomatoes and onions to size of walnuts, sprinkle with salt and stand overnight. In the morning, drain off the liquid, put tomato and vegetables in a pan and boil for 5 minutes with sugar and sufficient vinegar to cover. Add other ingredients and boil for 1 hour. Bottle when cool and seal in sterilised jars.

Vegetable Mustard Pickle

2 kg mixed vegetables, e.g. cauliflower, green tomatoes, onions, beans, celery, cucumber

Brine
6 cups (1.5 L) water $1^1/2$ cups (375 g) salt

Vinegar solution
1 cup (250 ml) vinegar   4 cups (1 L) water

Mustard mixture
4 cups (1 L) vinegar
2 cups (500 g) sugar
2 teaspoons turmeric

2 tablespoons (20 g) mustard
4 tablespoons (40 g) flour

Soak vegetables in brine overnight. Drain. Steep in vinegar solution for 20 minutes, then bring to boil. Boil until vegetables are a little tender but not soft. Drain. In separate saucepan prepare the mustard mixture: bring vinegar to boil and add dry ingredients. Now boil the vegetables in this mixture a few minutes. Pour into warmed, sterilised jars and seal.

CONFECTIONERY

COOKING SUGAR IN CONFECTIONERY

- In order to avoid crystals forming, always make sure that sugar is fully dissolved in water before raising the cooking temperature to boiling point and do not stir the mixture once it is boiling.
- Brush down the sides of the saucepan with a wet pastry brush from time to time to avoid crystals forming.
- A sugar or candy thermometer can be used to test the temperature of the cooking syrup, but it is not essential. To test that boiling sugar has reached the correct temperature, drop a teaspoonful of the mixture into a glass of cold water:
  - ★ if a soft ball of sugar syrup is formed, then the temperature of the sugar is 115°C, suitable for fondant
  - ★ if a hard ball is formed, then the temperature of the sugar is 118°C, suitable for fudge and marshmallow
  - ★ if the syrup crackles as it drops into the water, then the temperature is 135–150°C, suitable for toffees.

CANDIED PEEL

Take the peel from 2 or 3 oranges, wash well and slice into strips. Place in saucepan, cover with cold water and bring to the boil. Pour off the water. Repeat this process 3 times. Then weigh the peel and measure an equal quantity of sugar. Place peel and sugar in a saucepan with just sufficient water to dissolve the sugar. Bring to boil slowly and then boil quickly until the liquid has evaporated, taking care not to overcook. Toss the peel in more sugar and spread out on greaseproof paper until dry. Peel can be packed in airtight tins and used as required.

CHOCOLATE TRUFFLES
Makes 25 truffles

200 g dark chocolate
1/4 cup (60 ml) thickened cream
1 cup (100 g) almonds or
    walnuts

2 teaspoons vanilla essence
flaked almonds, finely chopped
    walnuts or sifted cocoa

Chop chocolate coarsely and place with the cream in the top of a double boiler or a heatproof bowl over a saucepan of boiling water (water should not touch the bottom of the bowl). Stir until melted and blended together. Remove from the heat and stir in nuts and vanilla essence. Allow the chocolate mixture to cool until firm enough to handle. Roll into balls, and toss in chopped nuts or sifted cocoa to coat each truffle.

COCONUT ICE

1 cup (250 ml) milk
4 cups (1 kg) sugar

1 1/2 cups (135 g) desiccated
    coconut

Put sugar and milk in saucepan, dissolve sugar slowly on low heat. Bring to the boil for 10 minutes. Remove, stir in coconut and, when thoroughly mixed, turn onto a buttered plate.

COCONUT ICE — UNCOOKED

2 cups (150 g) pure icing sugar
1/4 teaspoon cream of tartar
1 x 395 ml can condensed milk

3 1/2 cups (315 g) desiccated
    coconut
pink food colouring

Sift icing sugar and cream of tartar, add coconut and mix condensed milk through until combined. Divide the mixture in two and press half into the base of a greased, lined lamington tin. Tint the remaining mixture pale pink and spread over the top. Refrigerate overnight, or until set. Cut into squares.

EVERTON TOFFEE

2 cups (500 g) sugar
2 tablespoons vinegar

4 tablespoons water
1 tablespoon butter

Combine ingredients. Dissolve over low heat, stirring continuously. Boil without further stirring until mixture changes colour to pale gold. Test by dropping a teaspoonful into cold water: the mixture should crackle (135°C). Remove from heat immediately and pour into patty papers or on to a greased tray.

FONDANT

2 cups (500 g) sugar
1 teaspoon liquid glucose

1 cup (250 ml) water
1/4 teaspoon cream of tartar

Place all ingredients in a pan, stir until dissolved. Bring to the boil and cook until a soft ball forms when tested in water. Cool, pour into a bowl and beat until thick.

Note Liquid glucose can be purchased at chemists.

FUDGE

1/2 cup (125 g) milk
2 1/2 cups (625 g) sugar
1/2 cup (125 g) butter

1 tablespoon cocoa
1 teaspoon vanilla essence
chopped nuts (optional)

Boil milk and sugar until sugar dissolves. Add butter and cocoa and boil for about 20 minutes or until a firm ball forms when tested in cold water. Add vanilla and nuts, if using, remove from heat, and beat until quite thick. Pour on to buttered plates or a foil-lined lamington tin, and when set, cut into squares.

GINGER CREAM

2 cups (500 g) sugar
1/2 cup (100 g) preserved ginger

1/2 cup (125 ml) milk

Bring ingredients to the boil and cook for 5–6 minutes, stirring all the time. Remove from heat and beat until creamy. Pour into a buttered dish and cut into squares when firm.

HONEYCOMB TOFFEE

2 tablespoons (60 g) golden
  syrup
2 tablespoons sugar

1 teaspoon bicarbonate
  of soda

Boil syrup and sugar for about 10 minutes until mixture begins to change colour, remove from heat and stir in soda quickly. While still bubbling, pour on to a greased baking dish. Break into pieces when cool.

HONEY HEALTH CANDY

$3/4$ cup (180 g) dried apricots,
  chopped
$1/2$ cup (125 ml) water
1 cup (100 g) skim milk powder
$1/2$ cup (125 g) honey
$1/2$ cup (90 g) sultanas
$1/2$ cup (45 g) desiccated coconut

$1/3$ cup (40 g) almonds, finely
  chopped
1 tablespoon wheat germ
1 teaspoon lemon rind
1 teaspoon lemon juice
1 teaspoon orange juice
extra coconut for rolling

Combine apricots and water and bring to the boil. Simmer until tender. Remove from heat, add the remainder of ingredients except extra coconut. Divide into four, wet hands and form into rolls. Roll in the extra coconut. Put into refrigerator for several hours or overnight. Rolls can be cut into slices as required.

HONEY TOFFEE

4 cups (1 kg) sugar
$1/4$ cup (60 g) honey
$1^1/2$ cups (325 ml) water

$1/2$ cup (40 g) blanched
  almonds or walnuts

Place sugar, honey and water in saucepan. Bring slowly to boil, stirring constantly, then do not stir after it has begun to boil. Test by dropping a teaspoonful into cold water: the mixture should crackle. Add nuts and pour into patty papers or on to a buttered tray.

JELLY SUNBEAMS

4 cups (1 kg) sugar
60 g gelatine
1/4 cup (60 ml) cold water
1 cup (250 ml) boiling water

1 1/2 tablespoons (30 ml)
lemon juice
flavouring

Soak gelatine in cold water for 10 minutes, then add boiling water. Stir until gelatine is dissolved. Place dissolved gelatine and sugar in a pan and boil for 20 minutes. Add flavouring and lemon juice. Pour into a flat dish and chill. When set, cut into small squares and roll in sugar.

MARSHMALLOW

1 cup (250 g) sugar
1 cup (250 g) water
1 tablespoon gelatine
2 teaspoons lemon juice

1 teaspoon vanilla essence
colouring (optional)
toasted desiccated coconut

Place sugar, water and gelatine in saucepan, stir until dissolved over low heat. Bring to boil and boil without stirring for 10 minutes. Allow to cool. Add lemon juice and vanilla and beat until thick, fluffy and white. Colouring may now be added. Pour into a greased tin. When set, cut into squares and toss in toasted coconut.

POPCORN

2 tablespoons popping corn
1 teaspoon vegetable oil

Heat an electric frying pan. Place oil in pan and allow to spread over surface. Add corn and quickly replace the lid. Allow lid to remain in position until all corn has popped. Sprinkle with salt and serve.

TURKISH DELIGHT

2 cups (500 g) sugar
1 cup (250 ml) water
3 tablespoons gelatine
$^1/_2$ teaspoon citric acid

$^1/_2$ teaspoon vanilla essence
   or rosewater
icing sugar

Place sugar, water and gelatine in pan. Stir over low heat until dissolved. Boil without stirring for 20 minutes, then add citric acid and flavouring. Pour into a lightly greased rectangular tray or dish. Refrigerate until set. Cut into squares and roll in icing sugar.

WHITE CHRISTMAS

250 g Copha
1 cup (30 g) rice bubbles
1 cup (150 g) icing sugar
1 cup (100 g) milk powder

1 cup (175 g) mixed dried and
   glacé fruit
1 cup (90 g) desiccated coconut

Melt Copha over gentle heat. Combine remaining ingredients. Pour Copha over the mixture and stir together well. Press into a greased tray and chill until firm. Cut into squares.

Beverages

Cocoa

Allow 1 teaspoon cocoa, $1/2$ cup milk and $1/2$ cup water per serving, sugar to taste. Mix cocoa smoothly with a little cold water, boil the remainder of the water and milk, pour on cocoa, add sugar and stir well. If preferred the liquid can be added to the blended cocoa and heated in the microwave.

Coffee

Coffee was discovered in Ethiopia as early as 800 BC and grew in popularity in Europe from the fifteenth century onwards. There are two main types of coffee beans, robusta and arabica. Robusta is grown in a wide variety of equatorial climates and has a bolder taste. Arabica is of higher quality and is more sensitive to climate and altitude.

Plunger coffee should be a medium coarse grind, drip filter coffee a medium grind and domestic espresso machines need a relatively fine grind.

Lebanese, Turkish and Greek coffee is made in a long-handled coffee pot and usually served in small handleless cups. Put into pot 1 heaped teaspoon pulverised coffee for each cup of water, stir well and cook until foam rises to top of pot. The pot is removed from heat and base tapped on a flat surface to reduce foaming. Heat twice more with taps in between. Pour immediately into cups.

Coffee beans or ground coffee are best stored in an airtight container in a cool, dark and dry place but never in the freezer. The sooner the coffee is used after roasting, the better.

DRINKING CHOCOLATE

Heat milk or half milk and half water in cup or mug. Add 1–2 heaped teaspoons chocolate powder and stir. Top with 2 marshmallows if desired.

🍵 🍵 🍵
Barley Water

Ingredients — 2 oz pearl barley, 1 quart water, flavour with lemon to taste.

Mode — Boil 20 minutes. Strain. Flavour with lemon. Can be used to dilute milk.

🍵 🍵 🍵

TEA

China introduced tea to the world and today, China, India and Sri Lanka still produce much of the world's teas.

There are five main types of tea — black, oolong, blended, green and herbal. Popular types of black tea include Darjeeling, Ceylon and lapsang souchong. Oolong teas are milder than black teas and are often scented with jasmine, gardenia or rose petals. Blended teas are a combination of 15–20 leaves from different areas. Well-known blended varieties include English Breakfast and Earl Grey. Green tea is very popular in Asia and is believed to aid digestion. Green tea is always made weak and milk and sugar are never added. Herbal teas have the benefit of minimal caffeine and added health properties of the individual herbs. Herbs with healing properties include mint, echinacea, lemongrass, ginger, dandelion, chamomile, ginseng, lavender and thyme.

To make the perfect cup of tea, bring cold water to the boil rapidly. Add 1 heaped teaspoon of tea for each cup and 'one for the pot' to a china or earthenware teapot that has been preheated by swirling hot water in it. Add the water to the teapot when it is still boiling as this helps agitate the leaves and release the full flavour. Put the lid on the teapot and infuse for 5 minutes. If using milk, add to the cup before the tea.

To make herbal tea, pour boiling water over fresh or dried herbs and allow the tea to infuse.

Fruit Punch
Makes 7 litres

3 cups (750 ml) orange cordial
2 cups (500 ml) passionfruit juice
3 cups (750 ml) pineapple juice
3 cups (750 ml) cold black tea
10 cups (2.5 L) water
juice of 1 lemon
fresh fruit slices
3 x 1.25 L bottles ginger ale

Blend together orange cordial, passionfruit juice, pineapple juice, cold tea, water and lemon juice. Pour over sliced fresh fruit and ice cubes. Before serving add ginger ale.

Ginger Beer

2 lemons
2¹/2 cups (625 g) sugar
25 g fresh ginger, bruised
1 teaspoon cream of tartar
24 cups (6 L) boiling water
1 tablespoon (30 g) brewer's yeast

Pare lemons as thinly as possible, strip off every particle of white pith, cut lemons into thin slices, removing pips. Put sliced lemon into earthenware bowl with sugar, ginger and cream of tartar, and pour in boiling water. Allow to stand till lukewarm, then stir in yeast and leave in warm place for 24 hours. Skim yeast off top, strain liquid carefully, bottle, tie corks down securely, and in 2 days it will be ready for use.

Lemon Cordial

8 cups (2 kg) sugar
1 tablespoon tartaric acid
1 tablespoon Epsom salts
2 tablespoons (20 g) citric acid
rind and juice of 6 lemons
6 cups (1.5 L) boiling water

Put all dry ingredients in a large heatproof jug, add lemon juice and water, mix and dissolve, strain and bottle.

LEMON SYRUP

1 lemon
2 cups (500 g) sugar

2 tablespoons (20 g) tartaric
   acid
2 cups (500 ml) boiling water

Pare lemon finely and put rind in a heatproof jug. Remove all pith, slice lemon thinly, and put in jug with sugar and tartaric acid. Pour on water and stir till sugar is dissolved. When quite cold, strain into a bottle and cork lightly. Use 1 part syrup to 6 parts water.

ORANGEADE

1½ cups (375 g) sugar
2 cups (500 ml) water

rind of 2 oranges
juice of 1 orange

Put sugar and water in pan and heat to dissolve sugar. Pour over rind. Allow to cool, strain and add orange juice. For a child's drink, dilute orangeade to water 1:2 or 1:3. Add 1 bottle ginger ale to this quantity for teenagers or adults.

Note To make Lemonade, substitute lemons for oranges.

PASSIONFRUIT SYRUP

4 passionfruit
1 cup (250 g) sugar

1 cup (250 ml) water
1 teaspoon citric acid

Remove pulp from passionfruit. Bring sugar and water to boil, pour over fruit and add citric acid. Allow to cool. Dilute with water to taste. May be used with other fruit juices.

Variation To colour passionfruit syrup pink, place passionfruit skins in saucepan, cover with water; simmer 5–10 minutes, strain and add to syrup.

Tomato Juice

8 medium tomatoes
4 cups (1 L) water
2 teaspoons sugar

salt and pepper to taste
lemon juice
Worcester sauce (optional)

Place tomato, water and sugar in a saucepan, bring to boil and simmer 10 minutes or until pulped. Strain and chill, season to taste. Serve in small glasses with a squeeze of lemon juice to each glass. A little Worcester sauce may be added.

USED BY ALL LEADING LAUNDRIES.

THE

"SILVER STAR"

THE BEST IN THE WORLD

WON'T STICK TO THE IRON

RICE

STARCH

ROBERT HARPER & Cº.

BEWARE OF INFERIOR BRANDS!!!

HOUSEHOLD HINTS

COUGH MIXTURE

Equal parts of olive oil, glycerine, lemon juice and honey. Make up in small quantities and use as required.

Hint A teaspoon each of butter, lemon juice and honey mixed together also makes an effective remedy.

PLAY DOUGH

¹/₂ cup (125 g) salt	1 cup (250 ml) water
1 cup (150 g) flour	1 tablespoon vegetable oil
2 tablespoons cream of tartar	food colouring

Mix dry ingredients, blend to smooth paste with water, add oil and colouring. Cook on medium heat 3–5 minutes. Will keep well in a plastic container with a well-fitting lid.

POT POURRI

2 cups lavender flowers and leaves	1 teaspoon ground cloves powder
4 cups rose petals	1 teaspoon rose geranium oil
2 cups scented geranium leaves	1 tablespoon (10 g) cinnamon
1 cup verbena leaves	1 teaspoon lavender oil
2 tablespoons (20 g) orris root	12 cloves
	2–4 cinnamon sticks

Dry flowers and leaves. Take a wide-topped jar or earthenware crock. Put all flowers and leaves in, mix well. Blend orris root, ground cloves and powdered cinnamon together in a bowl, add oils and mix well into powders. Add the mixture to the dried flowers and mix gently and thoroughly. Add cinnamon sticks and whole cloves. Cover crock well and leave for 1 month.

Sugar Stiffening for Lace or Crochet

Stir 1 cup sugar into 1/2 cup water over gentle heat until sugar dissolves then let boil gently for one or two minutes. Dip lace in syrup and shape over form.

TO REMOVE CHEWING GUM

Method 1: Wrap ice cube in cloth. Apply to chewing gum until chilled. Gum will then lift off.

Method 2: Apply eucalyptus oil and scrape off any remaining gum.

Wicks

To prevent new lamp wicks from smoking, soak them thoroughly in vinegar before using, and let them dry before being put into the lamp.

TO REMOVE STAINS FROM WASHABLE FABRICS

1 tablespoon borax   *2 cups (500 ml) water*

Mix borax with water. For obstinate stains a paste may be applied. Soak for 1 hour, then wash in normal way. This solution is effective with tea, coffee, beetroot, pickle, chutney, tomato sauce, orange and other fruit stains.

Blood Stains: Soak in cold salt solution, then wash in normal way.

Grass Stains: 2 parts methylated spirits, 1 part ammonia and 3 parts water. Soak soiled part, then wash in normal way.

WINDOW CLEANER

1 cup (250 ml) methylated spirits   *1 cup (250 ml) ammonia*
1 cup (250 ml) kerosene   *1 cup (250 ml) water*

Combine all ingredients in large bottle. Always shake well before using. Apply to windows, then polish with clean cloth.

WOOLLY WASH

1 cup (250 ml) methylated spirits   *4 cups soap flakes*
3 tablespoons (60 ml) eucalyptus oil

Mix well together. Use only 1 tablespoon mixture per bowl of washing water. Woollies do not require rinsing after washing in this way.

The Caring
Outreach of the
Churches

∽ Ministries of the ∽
Presbyterian Church of
Victoria

Presbyterian Women's Missionary
Union of Victoria

Serving the Church at home and abroad

PWMU began in Melbourne in 1890. Today PWMU gives
prayerful and practical support to missionaries who have
gone to carry the name of Christ and his message of reconciliation and redemption cross-culturally to Australia and
overseas. The PWMU general office is on the first floor of
the Assembly Hall, 156 Collins Street, Melbourne; tel.
(03) 9655 1405. There is a missionary lending library.
PWMU produces a monthly newsletter, a quarterly children's magazine called *Dayspring* (named after a boat that
was used in the nineteenth century by missionaries in the
New Hebrides) and *Mission Challenge*, an annual children's
missionary competition. Funds from this cookery book provide bursaries for overseas students to increase their
usefulness to their indigenous churches by receiving theological training at the Presbyterian Theological College.

Australian Presbyterian World
Mission

Taking the gospel cross-culturally

APWM is involved in recruitment and training for the
mission field and organises prayer and financial support for
missionaries and ministries.

CHRISTIAN EDUCATION AND NURTURE

Teaching the world in the Way

This is done by providing suitable material for churches to use in the practice of faith and worship. Leadership is provided in the training of Presbyterian youth.

CHURCH AND NATION

Setting out the biblical and Christian position on social and ethical issues

This provides appropriate information to the church, through several publications and other means, as well as contacting state and national bodies about issues of concern.

CHAPLAINCIES

Reaching people for Christ

Trained chaplains work in many fields:

Presbyterian Campus Ministries: Reaching future leaders in universities and TAFE colleges.

Defence Forces Chaplaincies: Land, sea and air.

Health and Community Chaplaincy: Ministering in hospitals, aged care facilities and prisons, and to police, to ministers and their families.

HOME MISSIONS

Taking the Gospel into the Australian community

Home Missions spread the gospel by means of evangelism, church planting and the nurture of small congregations, ethnic congregations and home mission stations. Home Mission work within the state is also supported by PWMU.

Presbyterian Youth of Victoria: *Uniting youth in Victoria in fellowship and service of the Kingdom of God* through youth groups and a vigorous camping program.

Home Mission Workers Association: *Giving support to students for the ministry and to home mission stations.*

Scots and Presbyterian Joint Mission

Ministering to the needy multi-cultural population of Melbourne
This works through its base in Flemington.

Social Services

Providing quality aged care facilities

Theological Education

Entrusting the Gospel to reliable people who will also be qualified to teach others
The Presbyterian Theological College trains men for the ordained ministry and also men and women from various denominations as workers and missionaries for service in the church in Australia and overseas.

Interdenominational Enterprises

Working together for the common cause of Christ
Christian Television Association of Victoria
Council for Christian Education in Schools
Council for Chaplaincies in Tertiary Institutions
Inter Church Chaplaincy Committee Vic. Inc.
Displan — sudden disaster response

The work of mission today is continued in the same spirit as that which inspired those responsible for the publication, a hundred years ago, of the first cookbook, all done in the spirit of our Lord and Master, Jesus Christ, who said: *Go into all the world and preach the Gospel to every creature.*

∾ THE UNITING CHURCH ∾ IN AUSTRALIA (SYNOD OF VICTORIA)

Formed in 1977, the Uniting Church brought together the outreach of the former Congregational, Methodist and some Presbyterian churches. The Church's name was a deliberate choice. While it grew out of decades of intense ecumenical feeling, those who shaped the Church were keen to see it as a step in a continuing process of inter-church co-operation and union. Hence it is a uniting church rather than a united church. Some of the outreach programs are mentioned below.

UNITING CHURCH ADULT FELLOWSHIPS (UCAF)

UCAF represents groups of members who meet in practical and prayerful ways and are involved in their local churches and the community. Sales proceeds of this book are used for a 'Pastoral Theology Prize' to a final-year student. One of UCAF's activities is to raise funds through the sale of used postage stamps, providing funding for various outreach works throughout Australia and overseas. General enquiries can be directed to the office at 130 Little Collins Street, Melbourne; tel. (03) 9251 5200.

FRONTIER SERVICES

This covers 85 per cent of Australia's land mass, employs 400 staff, has 99 vehicles and thousands of volunteers. This *Christianity with sleeves rolled up* is focused on patrol ministry, early childhood and family services, medical clinics and respite care.

JUSTICE AND INTERNATIONAL MISSION UNIT

The unit works to assist, encourage, and empower members of the wider community to be active on issues of social justice and human rights.

Outreach Ministries

These co-ordinate the strategic placing of chaplains, community ministers and deacons to work in schools, hospitals and other organisations with people who are outside the community of faith in the Church.

Covenanting

The understanding of reconciliation, through listening, respecting culture and history, and building understanding and relationships.

United Aboriginal Islander Christian Congress

Aboriginal people in the church assisting towards self-determination and building communities of fellowship. Congress gives priority to holistic evangelism — meeting people in their needs: physical, social, cultural and spiritual.

Uniting*Care*

The umbrella for all community services in Australia. In Victoria, it includes 160 separate agencies. These provide emergency relief, crisis and financial counselling, services for children and families, young people and the elderly. This large network of care embraces more than 350,000 people in need each year.

The SHARE Community Appeal

Raises funds to distribute through Uniting*Care* agencies and community groups, to people in need. This also includes distribution of food vouchers to more than 70 Community CARE programs across the state.

UCA Funds Management

Provides ethical investment funds for churches, charities and individuals. Individuals can invest in the Development and Funeral Funds — for more information tel. (03) 9251 5230.

Congregations consist of … many faces … many places … many forms … There are older people and young, families and single people, people of one culture or many — forty different languages are used in worship in the Uniting Church each week.

Index of Recipes